A STUDENT'S INTRODUCTION TO GEOGRAPHICAL THOUGHT

PAULINE COUPER

A STUDENT'S INTRODUCTION TO

GEOGRAPHICAL THOUGHT

THEORIES, PHILOSOPHIES, METHODOLOGIES

Los Angeles | London | New Delhi
Singapore | Washington DC

Los Angeles | London | New Delhi
Singapore | Washington DC

SAGE Publications Ltd
1 Oliver's Yard
55 City Road
London EC1Y 1SP

SAGE Publications Inc.
2455 Teller Road
Thousand Oaks, California 91320

SAGE Publications India Pvt Ltd
B 1/I 1 Mohan Cooperative Industrial Area
Mathura Road
New Delhi 110 044

SAGE Publications Asia-Pacific Pte Ltd
3 Church Street
#10-04 Samsung Hub
Singapore 049483

Editor: Robert Rojek
Assistant editor: Keri Dickens
Production editor: Katherine Haw
Copyeditor: Catja Pafort
Marketing manager: Michael Ainsley
Cover design: Francis Kenney
Typeset by: C&M Digitals (P) Ltd, Chennai, India

Library of Congress Control Number: 2014937948

British Library Cataloguing in Publication data

A catalogue record for this book is available from
the British Library

ISBN 978-1-4462-8295-3
ISBN 978-1-4462-8296-0 (pbk)

At SAGE we take sustainability seriously. Most of our products are printed in the UK using FSC papers and boards.
When we print overseas we ensure sustainable papers are used as measured by the Egmont grading system.
We undertake an annual audit to monitor our sustainability.

Contents

List of Figures, Tables and Boxes

List of Tables

List of Boxes

About the Author

Pauline Couper is Head of Programme for Geography at York St John University. Prior to this she was Senior Lecturer and Research Coordinator at the University of St Mark & St John (Marjon) in Plymouth, where she taught research methods and guided undergraduates through research projects for over a decade and supported staff research within the University from 2004 to 2014. In 2014 she was awarded the Marjon Students' Union 'Student-Led Teaching Award' for 'Outstanding Supervisor'. Also winner of the RGS-Blackwell *Area* prize (2005), Pauline has a PhD in fluvial geomorphology and professional experience in geo-conservation, and has always maintained enthusiasm for the breadth of the discipline. Her research interests now lie predominantly in philosophy of geography and human/environment relations, particularly in terms of how geographical and environmental knowledges are developed and performed.

Preface

Appropriately for a geography book, the existence and form of this one have undoubtedly been influenced by place. When I first moved to Plymouth (UK) I had no inkling that I would ever own a boat but, after several years in the city, it seemed a perfectly reasonable idea. There are boats for almost every budget, which was quite a revelation for someone who grew up with a notion that boats were solely the preserve of the rich and glamorous. Owning an old boat means winters were spent in the boatyard for maintenance and restoration. Many jobs benefit from two pairs of hands, but space inside a boat can be somewhat restrictive. So it was that I found myself standing out of the way at the back of the boat, enjoying the sunshine of a crisp early spring morning on the bank of the river, with time for my mind to wander. 'I wish there was a book that…' was followed by a 'Maybe…' kind of thought. I found a scrap of paper in my pocket with various boat dimensions written on one side, turned it over and scribbled a list of half a dozen chapters I thought might be needed in such a book. Later that summer, and with Robert Rojek's encouragement, I was developing that initial list into a full proposal. The boat was now in the water, and half way across Plymouth Sound one Sunday afternoon it occurred to me that the question, 'What is a beach?' could provide a way in to different philosophical perspectives. So this book is very much a product of the place in which it was written.

Specifically, my wish was for a book that provides clear explanations of the various '-isms' that have influenced geography, in terms of what they are, where they came from, and what they mean for geographical research. This, then, has been my guiding aim, and it is an aim that implies making the connections between abstract philosophy or theory and the practices of research methodology.

Chapter 1 uses the question, 'What is a beach?' to introduce some basic philosophical concepts, drawing out some of the different ways that geographers might answer that question. The beach provides a convenient site for thinking across the breadth of the discipline and, I hope, an accessible introduction to what can be difficult ideas.

In Chapters 2 to 8, I have tried to make the philosophy-theory-methodology connections explicit by:

1. Providing an account of recent published research (at least one journal article, and in some chapters more than one) to illustrate how those abstract assumptions or ideas translate into research practices. In most cases the examples used are from 2010 or later.

2. Developing an exercise for each chapter that requires students to read a selected
    journal article (available via the companion website) and answer questions about
    it, making the connections between philosophy or theory and methodology
    for themselves. Again, the papers used are from 2010 or later. Knowing the
    frustration of exercises without the possibility of feedback, the companion web-
    site provides some answers or commentary responses to the questions, enabling
    students to obtain some form of 'feedback' on their own thinking if they are
    working independently.

3. Speculating about the kind of research that could be conducted at the beach
    using the perspective(s) discussed in the chapter. These speculations are intended
    as starting points, initial ideas or sketches, for the purpose of illustrating the
    (often tentative) moves between philosophy, theory and methodology as a
    potential research project begins to take shape. These 'at the beach' discussions
    form relatively minor components of Chapters 2 to 8, but enable further com-
    parison of geography's different '-isms' in Chapter 10.

For Chapters 2 to 8, in particular, there is potential to make the book and its companion website more interactive. At the end of Chapter 1 I invite readers to send
me (via Twitter) details of any recent journal article that provides a good example
for one of the chapters, for listing on the companion website. I would ask academics to encourage students in this; if the invitation is taken up the website has potential to build into a more substantial resource for everyone.

Finally, this was always going to be a book that addressed the breadth of the discipline, at least to the extent that my own education, interests, experience and time
to read allow. I have always felt vaguely disappointed to pick up a text that claims
to be about 'geography' and find half of the discipline neglected. This is not to claim
that there is nothing missing here, and the approach taken certainly risks losing the
coherence of chronological narrative that others (such as Unwin, 1992 or Holt-
Jensen, 2009) have offered, but I have endeavoured to keep the whole of geography
in mind. My reasons for doing so are evident in the concluding discussion of the
book as well.

Those, then, were the aims I set out with. The degree to which I have achieved
them must be left for others to judge. I have certainly learnt a lot from writing this,
and I hope that others find something of value in it too.

Acknowledgements

My understanding of geographical research was shaped by the Worcester geographers of the 1990s. In no particular order, this means: Brian Adlam, Les Morris, Rex Hall, Ian Maddock, Dave Storey, Heather Barratt, Richard Yarwood (now at Plymouth University), Bill Kelly, Nick Evans, John Fagg, Cheryl Jones, Paul Larcombe, Des McDougall, Tim Hall (now at the University of Winchester), David Sudlow, Paul Larcombe, Patch Hopcroft and a few others. Some are still at the University of Worcester, some have moved on, and some are sadly no longer with us. The degree they provided undoubtedly laid the foundations for the work presented here. I needed no encouragement to stay on for a doctorate, supervised by Ian. Thanks also to Ruth Thornhill, for many geographical discussions and happy field days together.

Since leaving Worcester, working for over a decade in small institutions has brought the benefit of many conversations both across the discipline and between disciplines. The former geography staff and students at (what is now) the University of St Mark & St John were central to this, and I am also grateful for the collegiality of the outdoor adventure education staff there. Particular thanks go to geographers Wendy Gill for answering questions about beach biodiversity, and Tony Atkin for the use of his photograph of the Lyd Valley (Figure 6.1).

I am indebted to philosopher Paul Grosch (University of St Mark & St John, retired) for his endless willingness to answer questions and share his knowledge of his own discipline. We have had countless discussions over the years, interspersed with musical interludes, and life is the richer for both. I am particularly grateful to Paul for reading drafts of some of the chapters here and providing feedback on the philosophical content. I am also grateful to the six anonymous reviewers of the original proposal for this book, and to the two anonymous chapter reviewers, for their constructive comments. One of these reviewers gave the time and effort to provide feedback on the majority of the chapters, and this pushed me to refine my thinking about what I was doing, as well as improve the content. It goes without saying that errors and omissions remain my own.

Thanks to Robert Rojek at SAGE, for listening to an idea, working with and contributing to it, answering questions, and generally being at the other end of email when I have needed it. Thanks also to Keri Dickens, Katherine Haw and the others at SAGE.

A big thanks to my parents, Sue and Glynn Davies, for a life lived with books. They, my sister Lizzy Glyn-Jones, and the rest of the family have been constant in their interest and support, even though there were times they heard little from me because of the book.

Finally, the biggest thanks must go to my husband Kevin Couper: for sharing the ups and downs; for not complaining about the endless succession of evenings and weekends that I was working on this; for generously letting me use so many photographs, and – even better – being interested enough to take some especially for the book. Most of all, thanks for always believing in me, and for always being there.

Reproduction of copyright material

The author would like to thank the following for permission to reproduce copyright material:

Kevin Couper for the photographs reproduced as Figures 1.1, 1.2, 1.4, 7.2b, 8.1, 8.3b, 8.4 and 8.6a.

Taylor & Francis for Figure 2.2, from O'Loughlin, J. and Witmer, F.D. (2011) 'The localized geographies of violence in the North Caucasus of Russia, 1999–2007'. *Annals of the Association of American Geographers* 101 (1): 178–201.

Sage for Figure 4.1, from Yeung, H.W. (1997) 'Critical realism and realist research in human geography: a method or a philosophy in search of a method?' *Progress in Human Geography* 21 (1): 51–74.

Wiley for Figure 5.2, from Couper, P.R. and Ansell, L. (2012) 'Researching the outdoors: exploring the unsettled frontier between science and adventure', *Area* 44 (1): 14–21; for Figure 8.2, from Inkpen, R. (2007) 'Interpretation of erosion rates on rock surfaces', *Area* 39 (1): 31–42.

Tony Atkin for the photograph reproduced as Figure 6.1.

About the Companion Website

A Student's Introduction to Geographical Thought's companion website **https://study. sagepub.com/couper** contains a variety of resources to help you get the most out of the book. These are arranged by chapter for convenience, and consist of:

- Materials to support the exercises in each chapter, including:
  - Full-text access to journal articles used in the exercises;
  - Answers or commentary responses to the exercises, so that students working independently can assess their own understanding.
- Full-text access to collections of papers from *Progress in Human Geography* and *Progress in Physical Geography*, enabling students to follow up on the ideas introduced in each chapter and develop their understanding further.
- Supplementary materials tailored to each chapter, including internet links, additional text and kml files for Google Earth (enabling readers with Google Earth to look at places or examples of the features discussed in some of the chapters).

You can contribute to the website too. Please tweet recommendations of journal articles (or other resources) that are good examples of the philosophies and theories discussed in the book to @DrPaulineCouper using the hashtag #GeoThought.

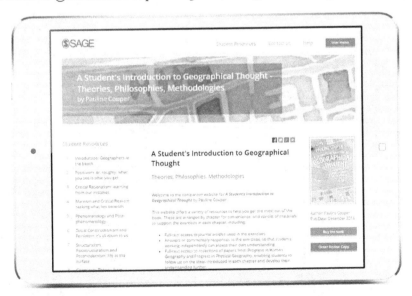

Introduction: Geographers at the Beach

1.1 Before we get there: Introducing philosophy and theory

> We begin in late autumn, with a geography field trip to the beach. The students climb into the bus, which then leaves the university and threads its way through the countryside towards the coast. Looking out of the bus window, Nikki says to Adam, 'The leaves are really turning brown now.'

Nikki's simple statement is a claim to knowledge, a claim to know something about the leaves on the trees. It is the kind of knowledge claim that we all make in our everyday lives, but it provides a good starting point for thinking about the more specialised knowledge that we develop within geography. At the broadest level of generalisation, geographers seek to know the world around us. If we want to have confidence in our knowledge – of glaciers, transport systems, flooding, poverty, biodiversity, pollution, inequality, landscapes and all the other things that geographers are interested in – then it is important to interrogate how we develop such knowledge. In effect, the question at the heart of this book is 'How do we know?'

A simple response to that question is to make reference to sources of evidence. We know something because we have evidence of it; we have seen (or heard, or measured) it for ourselves, or we have read it somewhere and accept that someone else has evidence of it. We know what the weather was like yesterday because we experienced it for ourselves. We know the Earth is spherical because we have seen satellite images of it. We know that health and wealth inequalities in the UK have increased since the 1970s, because we can read research that provides evidence of this (Dorling, 2010, 2013). Geography students everywhere are taught to acknowledge their sources of evidence early in their studies through conventions of academic referencing, and this is an important part of the *discipline* of geography. Being clear about evidence, though, is only the first step in answering the question 'How do we know?'

Every claim to knowledge involves making assumptions. These are assumptions about things such as: what exists; what knowledge is; how we can know; and what counts as 'evidence'. In our everyday lives we usually take these things for granted without really thinking about them. Nikki's observation about the leaves turning brown is one example. This is a claim that the colours of the leaves on the trees are changing. There are some broader, unspoken implications, but if we leave those aside for a moment and focus just on the spoken claim to knowledge it is possible to identify at least three assumptions hidden in it:

1. That leaves are 'real' objects, existing independently of us.

2. That our senses – in this case, sight – provide us with knowledge of leaves.

3. That Nikki's memory that the leaves have not always been brown is accurate.

It would probably be difficult to live our lives if we did not take these kinds of things for granted. If we spent all day worrying about whether objects are real we would find it quite difficult to do anything, including eat and drink. But it does not take too much effort to realise that we can be mistaken in our assumptions. If ever you have forgotten something (as we all have), you know your memory is not infallible. If ever you have waved at somebody thinking it was a friend and then realised you were waving at a complete stranger, you know your senses are not infallible. There may seem less reason to doubt whether objects really exist, but many people have experienced hallucinations, seeing or hearing things that are not really there. Each of the three assumptions above could be unfounded. These issues – about what exists, what we know and how we know – fall within the realm of **philosophy**.

There are three philosophical terms that are often used in literature relating to how we do research. These are:

Metaphysics, the branch of philosophy concerned with the 'first principles' (or, broadly speaking, the fundamentals) of things like existence, time, space and identity.

Ontology, which is about what exists and what it means to exist.

Epistemology, which is the study of how we know.

Metaphysics therefore encompasses ontology. Philosophy texts often refer to metaphysics, whereas geography texts use the terms ontology and epistemology more often.

If we look again at the three assumptions identified in Nikki's comment about the leaves, the first (that leaves exist independently of us) is an ontological assumption. The second, that our senses provide knowledge of the leaves, is an epistemological position. The third is more complex. Nikki is relying on her memory of the leaves, and this involves an assumption about herself; that she is a discrete entity (a 'self') whose existence has been continuous over the timescale in which the leaves have changed colour. In other words, she is assuming that she was not just invented yesterday, with things that seem like memories programmed into her mind. (This may seem far-fetched, but films like *The Matrix* and *Avatar* play on this kind of idea.) Nikki is also relying on her memory to store 'true' knowledge of the leaves. The third assumption is therefore a metaphysical assumption, containing both ontological and epistemological claims.

Although Nikki's statement referred only to the observable colour of leaves, she was really commenting on something bigger. The implication of her comment is that the seasons are progressing and autumn is turning to winter. There are assumptions here too, but these are of a different kind. Rather than being assumptions about what exists or how we know, the implied meaning of Nikki's statement involves ideas about how the changing colour of leaves is connected to the seasons. These ideas are along the lines of the following:

> As the autumn turns to winter, daylight hours shorten and the temperature falls. The potential for photosynthesis is reduced and chlorophyll within the leaves breaks down, causing the leaves to lose their green colour and turn yellow and brown before falling to the ground. The changing colour of leaves is therefore an indicator of changing light and weather conditions, letting us know that winter is coming.

This brief explanation is a **theory**; a generalised, abstract idea about the relations between phenomena. Nikki has applied this generalised idea to the particular trees she can see through the bus window.

Trying to move beyond a simple answer to the question 'How do we know?', then, takes us into the realms of philosophy and theory. If the knowledge that we rely on in our everyday lives is dependent upon philosophical and theoretical assumptions or ideas, then it follows that our claims to specialist geographic knowledge also involve such assumptions and ideas. The study of 'geographic thought' is the study of the philosophical and theoretical assumptions we make in developing geographical knowledge, and how different philosophies and theories have become dominant within geography at different times.

Students often find studying 'geographic thought' difficult, not least because philosophy and theory are, by definition, rather abstract. Many geographers are more interested in doing 'proper' geography, learning about society, culture and the natural environment. Concrete issues such as wealth inequalities, flooding or habitat conservation can seem far more interesting, and more *relevant*, than abstract philosophy and theory. There are at least two good reasons for persisting with the difficult abstract ideas though.

Firstly, as we have seen with Nikki's comment about the leaves, there are hidden assumptions in all claims to knowledge. Ignoring philosophy and theory does not make these assumptions go away; it just means that we are oblivious to them. As geomorphologist Colin Thorn pointed out in 1988, learning and thinking about philosophy and theory puts us in a position to make choices about what philosophies and theories we use. The alternative is to blindly rely on assumptions without being aware of them.

Secondly, assumptions about what exists and how we can know, and ideas about how phenomena are (or could possibly be) related to each other directly connect to the ways we do research. In choosing to use a particular method of data collection, we are implicitly, perhaps subconsciously, making a decision about what counts as knowledge. Our own methodological practices and our ability to judge the reliability of evidence presented by others are enhanced by an awareness of philosophy and theory.

The first of these reasons provides a justification for books such as this one, examining the key philosophical and theoretical positions that have been significant in the development of geographical knowledge. The second reason guides the particular approach taken here: the aim of this book is not just to consider philosophy and theory, but also to make the connections between these philosophical and theoretical positions and research **methodology**, the specific practices by which geographers produce knowledge.

The rest of this chapter returns to the beach to reveal some key differences among philosophical approaches. This chapter is designed to be read before the others in the book. Chapters 2 to 8 then address ideas that have been significant in the development of geographic thought since the '**Quantitative Revolution**' of the mid-twentieth century. Each chapter seeks to establish what the ideas are, where they have come from and how geographers have used them. In each we then return to the beach to consider what kinds of research questions might be asked and what kinds of methods might be possible, making the connections to research 'in practice'. These chapters are organised in roughly chronological order, in that those appearing later in the book address ideas that became influential in geography more recently that those appearing earlier. However, none of these chapters assumes prior knowledge of the others, so each can be read on its own.

Finally, Chapters 9 and 10 address issues that cut across all of the others. Chapter 9 makes the move from questions of how we know (epistemology) to how we judge right from wrong, examining moral philosophy and ethics. Chapter 10 summarises all the different ways of looking at a beach covered in the book, and considers the connections and tensions between human geography and physical geography. Some prior understanding of the different approaches to geography covered in Chapters 2 to 8 is probably useful for these last two chapters.

Geographic thought is sometimes alternatively referred to as 'history and philosophy of geography' (as, for example, in the Royal Geographical Society's research group of that name). This book is intended as a 'philosophy of geography' rather than a 'history of geography' book. Really the two are entangled, but other histories of geography, such as those by Unwin (1992) or Holt-Jensen (2009), already exist and their coverage extends further back in time than this text. The aim here is to take up the significant '-isms' (ways of thinking) referred to in books such as those, and explore what they are, where they come from, and what they mean for geographical research. Without further ado, let us return to the beach.

1.2 On arrival: What are we studying?

> The geography students arrive at the beach, but what, exactly, are they studying? What is a beach?

The question 'What is a beach?' might seem trivial. Just the mention of the word 'beach' probably conjures up some image or idea of a beach in your mind, whether this is a memory of a specific beach you have been to or a more general idea of 'beach-ness'. But the geography students on our field trip could each have a very different focus to their studies. We will explore five different responses to the question, 'What is a beach?' to illustrate some different assumptions about what is real and how we can know. These assumptions lend themselves to different research questions and the use of different methods to address those questions.

1. *A beach is a coastal deposition of sand and gravel particles lying between mean tide and the inland extent of the highest storm waves.*

This defines a beach in terms of what we can see, where. It recognises only the existence of physical, or material, features (as opposed to, say, spiritual dimensions of the beach). This means it is a **materialist** response. It would give rise to questions about the form of the beach and its constituent sediments – in other words, questions that also focus on what we can see, where. We might, for example, seek to identify and delineate patterns of fine and coarse sediments such as those in Figure 1.1.

The methods necessary for this kind of study would be likely to involve observation, including surveying and measuring the material objects forming the beach. The whole focus, then, from research question to methods, is on the evidence of our senses (and predominantly the sense of sight). It is worth noting here that even when we use instruments, such as remotely controlled cameras flown over the beach for an aerial view, or laser range-finders to measure long distances, these are extensions of our senses. The assertion that our senses provide our only secure source of knowledge is known as **empiricism**. So our first definition of the beach is both materialist and empiricist.

Figure 1.1 Sediment sorting in beach cusps at the eastern end of Seaton Beach, Cornwall, UK (Photograph by Kevin Couper)

2.   *A beach is an active part of the **morphodynamic** coastal system of energy transfers and sediment movement. As the boundary between water and land, a beach is the transitional area between aquatic and terrestrial ecosystems, where continual change creates hostile environments for life.*

Here we again have a definition that depends on observable, material phenomena, but this time prioritising the relations between them, and the functioning of geomorphological and biogeographical processes. This perspective lends itself to questions about what happens, where, when, at what rate, and how the different components of the beach interact. Looking at the beach in Figure 1.2, we see there are three possible sources of sediment in the picture: the sea to the left, the cliffs in the background, and the river cutting across the beach in the centre of the photograph. So we might ask questions about the relative influences of these on sediment supply to the beach, and to different parts of the beach. Subsequent processes of sediment transport and the resulting changes in beach form could also be of interest.

Some processes are (more or less) directly observable. We could, for example, paint some beach clasts (rock fragments) to mark them and then track their movement across or along the beach by re-locating them regularly over a period of time. Empiricism and materialism are still relevant here then. However, some processes, or the causes of processes, are not directly observable. We know that things (sediments, water) move downhill, yet we cannot actually see gravity, we can only observe its effects. In such cases we use reasoning to infer the existence of processes or mechanisms, and the idea that knowledge can be legitimately based on reason is known as rationalism. In practice, geographers' theories are then tested against empirical evidence, so we still retain an empiricist approach.

Figure 1.2 Three sources of sediment: sea, cliffs and river at the western end of Seaton Beach, Cornwall, UK (Photograph by Kevin Couper)

3. *A beach is a place that people visit primarily for recreational purposes (e.g. sunbathing, swimming), often in social groups. Beaches are busiest in the summer months, when people may travel considerable distances to visit.*

The obvious difference between this response and the first two is that we have switched from physical geography to human geography. However, philosophically there is little change. The focus is still empirical phenomena, such as numbers of people and their observable behaviour, the things they are physically doing. Other observable phenomena associated with humans at the beach would include visitor input to the local economy, the informal economy that can develop around beaches (Figure 1.3) and material impacts on the beach such as littering. Research questions might focus on identifying relations between empirical phenomena. A simple (and rather dull!) example would be whether people who have travelled furthest spend the longest on the beach.

Figure 1.3   The informal economy in operation at Charlestown, Cornwall, UK

It might seem odd to include travel distance among 'observable phenomena'. It would not be possible for an individual researcher to physically watch the journey of every beachgoer on any given day. However, we noted earlier that our senses can be extended by research instruments. The examples given were remotely controlled cameras and laser range-finders, but, for the social sciences, questionnaire surveys serve a similar purpose. Somebody's travel distance is, in principle, observable even if we did not see it directly for ourselves (we might say it is 'empirically verifiable', in a sense that is explained in Chapter 2).

So far, then, our third response assumes that society can be studied in the same ways as the natural world, using methodological approaches identical to those in the natural sciences, albeit with different methods of observation and measurement. This is sometimes referred to as **naturalism**, although it is specifically a form of methodological naturalism (as the word 'naturalism' is used in many different ways by philosophers).

More complex questions arising in human geography might again focus on relations between phenomena. Some beach resorts are patronised predominantly by wealthy visitors, and so we might be interested in identifying any disparity in household income or socio-economic class between visitors and local residents, and the degree of dependency of the local economy on beach tourism. Examples of such locations within Britain would include Padstow and Rock in Cornwall. Internationally, many of the island beach resorts in the Caribbean would be of interest, marketed as 'paradise' holiday destinations for American and European tourists.

This kind of study would probably lead us to consider the economic and political structures of society, and how these structures shape relations between beach visitors and local residents. This would, then, become a **structuralist** analysis such as those addressed in Chapter 4 (though noting that this is distinct from Saussure's linguistic Structuralism, which is discussed in Chapter 7 and denoted in this book with a capital 'S'). The starting point, though, is the empirical economic conditions of the two social groups.

Like Nikki's comment about the leaves on the trees earlier in the chapter, these first three responses to the question 'What is a beach?' all assume that a real world exists, independently of us as individuals. This means they are all **realist**, broadly speaking. However, there are many variations of realism, and this can lead to confusion – indeed, it does appear to have led to confusion in geography at times. Box 1.1 explains some of the different versions. These three descriptions of a beach also prioritise empirical data, at least as the 'acid test' of our theories, if not as the source of all of our knowledge.

BOX 1.1 REALISM AND SOME OF ITS VARIANTS

Realism in its broadest sense is the assumption that we know objects really exist, independently of us. The directly opposing view is **idealism** which, strictly defined, is the view that nothing exists outside of our minds (although see Box 1.2 for more on this).

Scientific realism is a particular form of realism, and a central topic of debate in the philosophy of science. Scientific realism involves commitment to three ideas:

1. That there are 'real' observable and unobservable objects, which exist independently of our minds. This is a **metaphysical** commitment. In other words, the beach is real.

2. That our scientific theories about observable and unobservable objects are true – that is, they correspond to how the world really is. This is a **semantic** commitment (semantic being associated with meaning). In other words, the theories geographers hold about beaches really reflect the nature of the beach.

3. That we can know the truth about these observable and unobservable objects, and so we can know that our theories are true (or, at least, that our best theories are approximately true). This is an **epistemological** commitment. In other words, we can know what the beach is really like.

(Continued)

(Continued)

Scientific anti-realism involves the rejection of one or more of these com-
mitments (Ladyman, 2002). Some people claim that we have no grounds
for assuming that a mind-independent world exists (as it is impossible to
step outside of our minds to find out), and so they reject the metaphysical
commitment. Historians and sociologists of scientific knowledge have long
pointed out that our theories have been found to be wrong in the past, and
whether or not a theory is accepted by the scientific community is influenced by social factors as much as 'scientific' factors (see Chapter 6 for an
example). This raises doubts about the semantic commitment. Some people
argue that we can never know the world as it really is, but only as it appears
to us; the point of scientific theories is not that they are 'true', but that they
seem to work (for example, enabling us to make predictions about things
as they appear to us). This is an **instrumentalist** view, and challenges the
epistemological commitment. It is perfectly possible for a scientist – whether
physicist, chemist, biologist, or geomorphologist, hydrologist or glaciologist –
to doubt the claims of scientific realism. So in our discussion of the beach,
the first three responses to the question 'What is a beach?' can be seen as
broadly realist, but it would be wrong to assume that they adopt the position
of scientific realism.

Structural realism is a response to two key arguments in debates about scientific realism. On one hand, if scientific realism were not true, it would be a
miracle that our scientific theories are so successful. On the other hand, many of
our scientific theories have been proven incorrect in the past, so it is perfectly
possible – or even probable – that our current theories will be proven incorrect
in the future. Structural realism offers a way out of this stalemate by arguing
that our best theories describe real relations between phenomena (structures),
rather than being correct in every detail. Approaches that seek to describe relations between phenomena are **structuralist**.

A point of confusion in the geographical literature is that the term 'realism' is
often – but not always – used to refer to Bhaskar's **critical realism** (Chapter 4).
This is a specific form of structural realism that has become popular in the social
sciences, with some advocates in physical geography too.

4. *A beach is sand between your toes, the sound of the surf surging towards you, the smell
    and taste of sea salt, momentary weightlessness as each wave lifts your body and rolls
    past, hot sunshine on your skin, cold water. It is a place for relaxation, or for adrenaline-
    fuelled, surf-induced excitement; splashing out through the shallows, watching the
    incoming surf, launching yourself ahead of the wave. A beach is escape, banishing every-
    day pressures from your mind. For some, though, a beach is a place of fear
    (eremikophobia is a fear of sand).*

This depiction of a beach is significantly different from the first three. Rather than assume a beach is a mind-independent object, it defines the beach solely in terms of our senses, experiences and meanings as individuals. Here the focus is on our perception of the beach, rather than the object of our perception (the beach itself).

In the eighteenth century, German philosopher Immanuel Kant (1724–1804) distinguished between things as they are in themselves, which he called 'noumena', and things as we perceive them, or 'phenomena'. Kant argued that we can never know things as they are in themselves. Our knowledge is restricted to phenomena. In Kantian terms, all geographers – even physical geographers – study phenomena. Through the twentieth century, though, a philosophical movement known as **phenomenology** (the word derives from 'phenomena' and 'ology') developed to specifically focus on studying human experience and things as we experience them. Our fourth description of a beach fits with this perspective, which is explained further in Chapter 5.

For geographers one of the key questions arising from a phenomenological perspective is about place and sense of place: what does the beach mean for us, and why? A phenomenological study might encompass the things we do at the beach, the embodied experience of being at the beach and meanings associated with the beach. Such issues are best addressed through qualitative research methods, which could include capturing and reflecting on our own beach experiences as well as using methods such as diaries or interviews to provide insights into the experiences of others.

5. *A beach is a 'liminal' place, where normal rules – such as rules about dress – do not apply. But a beach can also be a regulated space. Behaviour may be formally controlled by 'safe swimming' flags and sun-lounger hire rules, constantly under the surveillance of lifeguards and vendors, but also informally controlled as we conform to social expectations of what is normal. A beach is a site in which identities of gender, health, wealth and fitness are performed, exhibited or inhibited.*

Like response 4, the focus here is on our experiences and perception of beaches. However, there has been a shift in emphasis. Response 4 was about personal, subjective perceptions and meanings. Our fifth response pays attention to social rules and expectations that are external to us as individuals.

EXERCISE 1.1

Things not to do at the beach

There are some things that it would just seem wrong to do at the beach. Setting up a drum kit and practising for an hour or two would certainly be rather odd. We do not expect to see suit-clad insurance company representatives trying to sell us their insurance policies at the beach. Those are quite extreme examples. Try to think of other things that would seem wrong to do.

If there are socially defined rules or expectations about what a beach is for, and what behaviour is acceptable or unacceptable at a beach, then the kinds of research questions we might pursue relate to how these rules or expectations come about. We could look at how beaches are represented in the media. We might be interested in who (or what) 'polices' these rules, and how deviation from the expected norms – looking or behaving out of place – is rectified. Questions of inclusion, exclusion and power arise, and these are associated with issues of identity, difference and representation. We could also examine the unwritten rules around space, for example in the way that British families delineate beach territory through the use of wind breaks and sun shades (Figure 1.4).

Figure 1.4 Beach territory defined through the erection of wind breaks and sun shades. Bantham Beach, Devon, UK (Photograph by Kevin Couper)

Responses 4 and 5 share a concern with our understanding and experiences of the beach. The emphasis is on meaning, rather than on empirical phenomena. The fourth focuses primarily on individual perceptions, while the fifth pays regard to social context. This means there is a subtle difference in the metaphysical assumptions. Response 4 does not make any assumptions about whether or not a 'real' world exists independently of us. Its sole focus is the world as it appears to us. In response 5, the 'social facts' of appropriate or inappropriate behaviour and appearance at a beach derive from human thoughts and actions, but they appear as 'objective reality' to each of us as individuals. This is inherently a **social constructionist** position (see Chapter 6), though it is a theme that also runs through **poststructuralist** and **postmodernist** theories (Chapter 7). Human geographers (and other social scientists) often refer to this as idealist. As with realism, the term **idealism** offers scope for confusion, and Box 1.2 provides more detailed information on this.

BOX 1.2 INTERPRETATIONS OF IDEALISM

Human geographers and social scientists use the term 'idealism' in the sense that there are aspects of society that appear to each of us as external, independent objects or facts, and yet are defined solely by human agents, by our ideas and actions.

For philosophers, idealism is mostly understood to mean the doctrine that all that exists is mental or spiritual in nature (Ladyman, 2002). This is an 'immaterial-ist' metaphysical perspective, opposed to the belief that material objects exist. This kind of idealism is particularly associated with philosopher Bishop George Berkeley (1685–1753).

Redding (2012) points out that this is not the only kind of idealism, and not all forms are against the possibility of a mind-independent reality. 'German idealism' is a movement among German philosophers of the 1780s to 1840s. Beginning with the ideas of Kant, the German idealists focused on things as they appear to us. Their work (and particularly that of Georg Hegel) was an important influence on the French theorists of the mid-twentieth century, who in turn have had substantial influence on the development of social theory (McQuillan, 2012).

When we use or come across the term 'idealism' we thus need to be clear about which kind of idealism is meant.

1.3 Conclusion: -isms and geography

The development of knowledge in geography, as in any other subject, always involves assumptions about what exists and how we can know. In this chapter we asked a simple question: 'What is a beach?', and considered five possible responses to that question, to examine the metaphysical assumptions associated with them. This has entailed an encounter with lots of '-isms', and a glance at the contents list of this book reveals that there are more to come. Box 1.3 lists them all. In the context of philosophy and theory, the suffix '-ism' simply denotes a doctrine or way of thinking (although we come across other kinds of '-ism' in geography, such as tourism).

BOX 1.3   -ISMs ENCOUNTERED IN THIS BOOK

Listed in the order (or at least, roughly in the order) in which they appear, the -isms mentioned in this book include:

Empiricism
Materialism
Rationalism
Naturalism
Realism
Structuralism
Idealism
Positivism
Social constructionism
Feminism
Poststructuralism
Postmodernism

EXERCISE 1.2

Revising -isms

From the -isms above, list those which appear in this chapter and (without looking at the glossary) try to summarise each of them for yourself.

It can be helpful to think of '-isms' as points of similarity. Any approaches to geographical research that are empiricist, for example, will share an assumption that we can know the world through our senses. Any materialist geographies pay attention to physically (materially) existing objects. There are two important (and related) points to make here. Firstly, not all '-isms' are mutually exclusive and conflicting. Any research project could fit with, or draw on, multiple perspectives. The ways in which '-isms' are discussed in the literature can sometimes make it seem as though one or another must be 'right', but it is a mistake to think that way. This is probably another reason that geographic thought can seem confusing and difficult.

The second point is more broadly about philosophies and theories in geography. When you read chapters on **positivism, critical rationalism,** Marxism and the other positions introduced in this book, it is tempting to think of these as fixed, static, unchanging things that underlie (implying 'come before') our research practices. But research is a messy and unpredictable business. Ideas are developed, borrowed and adapted by living, breathing people, each individual bringing their own interpretation, within the context of their particular research project, prior experience and the other ideas they are working with.

It is perhaps more useful to think of philosophies (and maybe theories too) as more like musical genres. Songs within any single genre, such as urban, reggae, blues, folk or punk, do not sound exactly the same but there are commonalities between them. These commonalities make up the genre, but musicians find room to do their own thing, develop their own interpretation, and bring their own ideas. In the same way, researchers may take inspiration from particular philosophies or theories, perhaps more than one, and develop their own interpretation and add their own ideas. Some researchers are committed to a particular philosophical or theoretical outlook. David Harvey's longstanding association with Marxist geography is a prominent example. But many do not start with a distinct philosophical position, and this is perhaps particularly true among physical geographers. Just as it can be difficult to place some songs within any given musical genre, some research can be difficult to place within a particular philosophical movement.

This book, then, aims to explain some of the key ideas that have influenced geography and what they mean for research in practice. Like all geographers, take note of the ideas, decide which you find convincing or relevant to your interests, and see if you can use them for yourself.

Contribute to the Companion Website!

Chapters 2 to 8 of this book include examples of research (journal articles) to illustrate the research practices associated with the philosophy or theory being discussed in that chapter. They also include an exercise that directs you to read a specific journal article and answer some questions about it. For all of these exercises the journal article can be accessed via the book's companion website, along with some answers to the questions so that you can check whether you were along the right lines. Go to **https://study.sagepub.com/ couper**

Do not stop at this though. The 'secret' to academic success is reading, so try to find more examples for yourself.

If you come across a recent journal article that you think is a good example of research fitting with a particular chapter, let me know. I will look at it and (if I agree with you) will add the reference to the website, along with an acknowledgement that it was your suggestion. Tweet a web link, or preferably the article's Digital Object Identifier (doi), along with the relevant chapter number (e.g. 'C4' for Chapter 4) to @DrPaulineCouper, using the hashtag #Geothought.

FURTHER READING

For further explanations

Clifford, N., French, S. and Valentine, G. (eds) (2010) *Key Methods in Geography*, 2nd edition. London: Sage.

Clifford, N., Holloway, S., Rice, S.P. and Valentine, G. (eds) (2009) *Key Concepts in Geography*, 2nd edition. London: Sage.

Creswell, T. (2013) *Geographic Thought: A Critical Introduction*. Chichester: Wiley-Blackwell.

Holt-Jensen, A. (2009) *Geography: History and Concepts*. 4th edition. London: Sage.

Hubbard, P. and Kitchin, R. (eds) (2011) *Key Thinkers on Space and Place* (2nd edition). London: Sage.

Inkpen, R. and Wilson, G. (2013) *Science, Philosophy and Physical Geography*. 2nd edition. London: Routledge.

Johnston, R. and Sidaway, J. (2004) *Geography and Geographers: Anglo-North American Human Geography since 1945*. London: Routledge.

Montello, D.R. and Sutton, P.C. (2013) *An Introduction to Scientific Research Methods in Geography and Environmental Studies*. London: Sage.

Warburton, N. (1999) *Philosophy: The Basics*. 3rd edition. London: Routledge.

Progress in Human Geography and *Progress in Physical Geography* resources (available on the companion website)

Barnes, T. (2010) 'Taking the pulse of the dead: history and philosophy of geography, 2008–2009', *Progress in Human Geography* 34 (5): 668–77. doi: 10.1177/0309132509355352.

Bassett, K. (1999) 'Is there progress in human geography? The problem of progress in the light of recent work in the philosophy and sociology of science', *Progress in Human Geography* 23 (1): 27–47. doi: 10.1191/030913299669363669.

Mather, P. (1979) 'Theory and quantitative methods in geomorphology', *Progress in Physical Geography* 3 (4): 471–87. doi: 10.1177/030913337900030040.

Trudgill, S. (2012) 'Do theories tell us what to see? The 19th-century observations of Darwin, Ramsay and Bonney on glacial features', *Progress in Physical Geography* 36 (4): 558–66. doi: 10.1177/0309133312439593.

Positivism: *Or*, Roughly, What You See is the Knowledge You Get

2.1 Introduction: Geography and 'science'

The set of philosophical ideas known as positivism has long been associated with 'scientific' geography, and has been a focus for much debate in the discipline. Geography has a rather uneasy relationship with science. For a start, geographers are not all the same. A geomorphologist working on the dynamics of sediment movement in periglacial environments may be in no doubt that their research falls within the domain of science. A cultural geographer studying film festivals may specifically not identify with 'science', and yet still refer to human geography as a social science subject. So it is not really clear whether geography is a science or not. What is 'science' anyway?

EXERCISE 2.1

What do you think of as 'science'?

The instructions for this exercise are simple:

What is science? Without looking it up anywhere, try to write down your own definition of 'science'.

(Continued)

(Continued)

When trying to define something, sometimes it can help to think about what
it is *not*. In other words, you could ask yourself: How is science different from
other ways of knowing?

  When you have had a go at this, look at the companion website for some
comments.

Geography first became a university subject in the late 1800s. Right from the outset
its practitioners aligned the subject (at least to some degree) with science, and we
have continued to do so ever since in one way or another. A prominent reason for
this is that the word 'science' carries political weight. Science has credibility. Science
gets funding. People are impressed by science. It follows that a subject which can
call itself 'science' also has prestige, credibility and status.

  The early university geographers tended to use the term 'science' quite loosely,
in a non-technical and non-specific manner (Castree, 2005). Every academic discipline needs some definable intellectual 'territory', distinguishing it from other
disciplines. For geography this was being established through two core themes:
human/environment relations; and the concept of the region. The two overlap as
the region provides a convenient framing for understanding how people interact
with their environment. Significantly, this focus on 'the region' also offered a means
of classification, and classification was considered to be a central and necessary
feature of any science in the early twentieth century (Unwin, 1992).

  The ultimate aim of regional geography was to develop a comprehensive synthesis of everything in a given area. This directly contrasts with 'systematic' (**nomothetic**) geography, whose end goal is generalisable knowledge, transferable from one
place to another. Systematic approaches to study had long been popular in physical
geography, yet even physical geographers valued regional description. One of the
most prominent and influential physical geographers of the early twentieth century,
William Morris Davis, was an advocate of regional geography. Davis is most famous
for the '**cycle of erosion**' model of landscape development. This was proposed as
a universally applicable model, depicting the trajectory of development of *all* landscapes, and yet Davis saw such systematic work simply as a preparation for regional
geography. He depicted 'the description of existing landscapes, districts, and regions
of the earth's surface' as the ultimate goal, towards which all other kinds of geography aimed (Davis, 1915, p. 62). The first decades of the twentieth century were thus
dominated by regional geography.

  By the 1950s, things were changing. Geographers had played a substantial part
in the Second World War. British geographers found themselves working in various Government ministries and military organisations. War requires information
about places, and a war conducted in the air and at sea as much as on land requires

information about those places, too. The Central Interpretation Unit (CIU) is a good illustration. Its origins lay in 1939 as a small unit associated with the British Expeditionary Force, just three men who had been trained in the interpretation of aerial photographs, later combined with the efforts of civilian Sidney Cotton. Rapidly growing in work and workforce, it was named the CIU in 1941 (later becoming the Allied CIU, reflecting the involvement of US personnel). By 1942 it had amassed over 3 million aerial photographs of Europe (Pearson, 2002), and by 1945 was taking in 25,000 negatives and 60,000 prints every day. Photogrammetry and the production of terrain models were essential to the war effort. Alongside aerial photographs, geological data, tide data and oceanographic data all needed interpretation. There was more cartographic activity during World War II than in whole of the previous decade (Corson and Palka, 2004). Meteorology was just as important, with accurate weather forecasts crucial for targeted exercises such as D-Day. German geographers were similarly analysing coastal geomorphology, water supplies and terrain (Rose and Willig, 2004). Geographical skills and knowledge were in demand.

The degree to which geographers were able to meet such demand is less clear, with particular critiques emerging in the USA. Colonel Poole (1944), a university professor who spent the war years in the American army, argued that geographers had an invaluable understanding of terrain but (perhaps understandably) lacked any appreciation of military strategy and operations. Of greater consequence was Ackerman's (1945) critique. He was clear that geographers had contributed much to the war effort and achieved greater professional standing for the discipline as a result. But they lacked competence in systematic methods of study and found their degree of specialist knowledge wanting. The geographers who performed most strongly during the war effort, Ackerman claimed, were those who had a systematic specialism already. Regional geography was of little consequence.

At the same time, doubts were surfacing about whether regions really existed as independent entities, and arguments were made that regional description did not actually provide *explanation*. In 1948, political wrangling within Harvard University led to accusations that geography was unscientific and lacking intellectual rigour. Harvard closed its geography department. Both Castree (2005) and Creswell (2013) highlight this as a significant moment in the discipline's history.

The outcome of such developments, undoubtedly in combination with technological advancements made during wartime (Church, 2010), was a renewed drive towards systematic studies. Geography would adopt the methods of science, the goals of science. Geographers would develop **theory** – implying generalisable rather than place-specific knowledge – and would do so using quantitative methods of measurement and statistical analysis.

The substantial transition in aims and style that occurred through the 1950s and 1960s (see Box 2.1) later became known as the '**Quantitative Revolution**'. In human geography this meant the development of spatial science. Space was conceived of in terms of **Euclidean geometry**, a blank surface on which the organisation of objects was analysed, relationships were mapped and modelled, and causal influences identified. Distance, direction, connection, nodes and networks became important (Hubbard et al., 2002; Flowerdew, 2011). Physical geography was similarly changing, adopting methods and mathematical techniques from hydraulic engineering, grounded in Newtonian physics. Church (2010, pp. 266–7) explains that this was accompanied by a shift in focal scale. Rather than trying to explain long-term, large-scale landscape development, the 'everyday human scales' at which processes could be observed and measured became the focus of attention.

BOX 2.1   CHANGING GEOGRAPHICAL STYLE

Textbook descriptions of geography's history necessarily over-simplify things, so it can seem as though the transition from regional geography to system-atic, quantitative geography happened suddenly, all at once. If you trace through the contents pages of journals (such as *Annals of the Association of American Geographers* or *Transactions of the Institute of British Geographers*) from the 1950s to the 1970s it soon becomes apparent that it was a gradual change. Many issues contain articles with titles that sound like regional geographies alongside more systematic studies, so the shift in style was not as sudden as it is sometimes por-trayed, but it was a significant shift all the same. The two extracts below present the first paragraph of two articles published in the same journal, ten years apart. The first is illustrative of the descriptive style associated with regional geography. The second, is … well, see for yourself.

Hunter, J.M. (1961) 'Akotuakrom: a case study of a devastated cocoa village in Ghana', *Transactions and Papers (Institute of British Geographers)* **29: 161–86.**

Despite efforts at diversification, cocoa remains the mainspring of Ghana's economy, accounting for some two-thirds of the aggregate value of its exports. Ghana's position of eminence as the world's largest producer has been attained through the private and uncoordinated efforts of peasant cultivators who have rapidly and successfully incorporated a semi-permanent tree crop into their traditional system of fallow farming. (p. 161)

Blaikie, P. (1971) 'Spatial organization of agriculture in some North Indian villages: Part I', *Transactions and Papers (Institute of British Geographers)* **52: 1–40.**

It is the purpose of this analysis to investigate the spatial organization of four selected villages in northern India. It will be in two parts. The first (this issue of *Transactions*) will briefly describe the sites and give a general theoretical background to the analysis. A familiar model of the local agricultural production will be presented and modified to apply to local conditions. Data sources and method will briefly be reviewed. The model will then be tested by a variety of statistical procedures. Part I will deal with the distribution of input levels and crop zones within the villages followed by a conclusion. Part II (to be published in *Transactions* Number 53) will deal with farm structure and land-use patterns from a disaggregated viewpoint, ending with some general comments on the implications of this analysis for agricultural geography. (p. 1)

EXERCISE 2.2

What does 'scientific' geography look like?

Through the middle decades of the twentieth century geography was transformed, moving from an emphasis on regional synthesis and description to one of systematic analysis aiming to produce generalisable knowledge. Re-read the second abstract above (by Blaikie, 1971), and identify as many characteristics of this 'scientific' geography as you can. (It might help to re-read both abstracts and consider how they differ.) There are notes on the companion website to compare with your answers.

When you have finished, have another look at Exercise 2.1. How would you describe 'science' now?

The **Quantitative Revolution** is also generally regarded as a positivist revolution, although few of the early examples explicitly discussed positivist philosophy. It is probably true to say that most geographers were more concerned with being 'scientific', and they focused on scientific methods rather than on the philosophical assumptions those methods might entail. Interpretation of this as positivist tended to come later. Nevertheless, positivism remains a reference point for discussion of 'scientific' and quantitative geography.

This should not be taken to mean that all quantitative research is necessarily positivist, although some social scientists (geographers and otherwise) seem to assume that to be the case. **Critical rationalism** (Chapter 3) and **critical realism** (Chapter 4) equally offer a philosophical backdrop for quantitative research. This potential for confusion, along with the strength of anti-positivist thought in some quarters, provides good reason for developing an understanding of what positivism actually entails. The rest of this chapter explains the basic tenets of positivism and where they came from, along with further consideration of positivist research in geography. Criticisms will be acknowledged, but along with some acknowledgement of the ways in which positivist geographies can still be of value today.

2.2 The positive philosophy of Auguste Comte

'Ideas govern and revolutionise the world' (Comte, 1830, p. 37).

If you could change the world, where would you start? This was pretty much the question that a young French intellectual attempted to tackle in the 1820s. Dismayed at the problems around him, Auguste Comte attempted to develop a means of understanding and organising society in a way that would provide for stability and peace.

The context for Comte's concerns stemmed from the French Revolution, 1789–1799. In just a decade, the basic principles for organisation of one of the most powerful countries in Europe were radically altered. Before the revolution, power lay in the hands of the King, nobility and the Church; a minority of the populace. Ordinary people had to pay taxes to the King, tithes to the Church, and rent to the noblemen who owned land and property. Those who resisted or rebelled against such authority were tortured and executed in public. Fear ensured obedience and conformity. The French Revolution changed everything. The all-powerful monarchy was replaced with the constitution of a republic, founded upon the notion of self-government by citizens.

The effect was profound. The democratic ideals of liberty and equality spread rapidly beyond the borders of France. The very ideas on which society was based had been challenged, and the result was political and social turmoil. The Revolutionary and Napoleonic Wars (1792–1815) encompassed the whole of Europe. Ordinary people were encountering other cultures and languages, as men were recruited into armies and transported to countries far from home (Bavendamm et al., 2004). Globally, colonial territories were fought over, economies were affected, and the balance of power shifted (O'Rourke, 2006). It was in the aftermath of such profound change that Auguste Comte (1798–1857) developed his 'positive philosophy'.

The *Course de Philosophie Positive* (Course of Positive Philosophy) began as a series of sixty-three lectures, first delivered to an audience in Comte's Paris apartment during 1826–7 before being published in 1830. This was an enormously ambitious work: addressing both philosophy of science and political philosophy, it encompassed all branches of the natural sciences, provided a foundation for the establishment of the social sciences and ultimately aimed to create the conditions for a stable and harmonious society. Comte was just 28 when he delivered the first of these lectures. As an aside, it is interesting to note that his audience included one

Alexander von Humboldt (Andreski, 1974), a highly influential figure in early academic geography (Unwin, 1992).

2.2.1 The development and organisation of knowledge

Comte set the scene for his positive philosophy by arguing that society develops through three successive stages:

1. The 'theological' or fictitious stage. In this stage a society seeks to explain phenomena through supernatural agents, or 'personified gods'. Earthquakes may be caused by one god, lightning by another; a good harvest requires offerings to a god; every stone, every river, every animal has a spirit to be respected, revered and appeased.

2. The 'metaphysical' stage. This is little more than a modification of the first stage. The world is still explained through reference to the supernatural, but this has become more abstract: a single, all-encompassing entity (whether known as God, Allah, Mother Nature, or any other name), rather than many gods or spirits manifest in the world around us.

3. The 'positive' stage. Finally, society no longer seeks to explain the world or invokes supernatural agents to provide those explanations. Attention shifts instead to developing an understanding of the world around us in terms of relations between phenomena and the natural laws that govern their behaviour – in other words, describing the world and how it works. This understanding is founded on observation and reason.

This development of society is paralleled by the development of the individual mind, which also progresses from the theological (the child frightened of monsters under the bed), and then the metaphysical, to the more grown-up and intellectually sophisticated positive state. Comte termed this the 'law of three stages', and in defining this law he was practising the positive philosophy himself: his law was based upon observation and reason, and described the relation between the three modes of thinking thus identified.

Comte then turned his attention to the organisation of knowledge, presenting a new classification of the branches of knowledge. Again, he was following the positive philosophy by developing a classification based on observation (or study) of the objects to be classified. He took the principles of classification that had been established in botany and zoology and applied them, classifying the 'positive sciences' according to their relation to one another, moving from the simplest and most general to the complex and most particular.

Imagine a **drainage basin**, consisting of the physical hills and valley(s), the single river that it eventually drains into, and all of the plants, animals and people living in it. If we begin with the physical features, the processes that shape the erosion of the river basin are hillslope processes (such as creep and mass failure) and the velocity – and hence eroding and transporting force – of the water. These processes are largely determined by gravity. The Earth's gravity is a function of 'universal gravitation', which is simpler to describe and more generally applicable (universal gravitation applies to all objects in the Universe). Here we have the first two branches in Comte's classification of knowledge: astronomical physics (astronomy) as the simplest, and terrestrial physics as dependent upon astronomical physics.

If we were to look more closely at erosion processes, we would find that they are influenced by mechanical properties, such as friction between soil particles, and chemical properties, such as those determining the chemical bonding between clay particles within the soil. Chemical activity is dependent upon physical properties, and so Comte's class of 'terrestrial physics' breaks down into physics (the simplest) and chemistry (dependent on physics). His three branches of knowledge relating to inorganic phenomena are thus: Astronomy → Physics → Chemistry.

Plants in our river basin need soil and water to live; organic phenomena are dependent upon inorganic, and so come later in Comte's classification. If we understand the light and nutrient needs of a single plant, we will be able to develop an understanding of the distribution of that plant species across our river basin. The study of an individual living organism, physiology, is thus simpler and more generally applicable than the study of a whole species, which Comte termed 'Social Physics'. These form the two most complex branches of knowledge.

Finally, Comte argued that mathematical science is the purest, simplest and most general science, and provides the foundation for all the rest. Formed on the principle of moving from the simplest and most general to the most complex and particular, Comte's classification of the sciences was defined: Mathematics → Astronomy → Physics → Chemistry → Physiology → Social Physics (Figure 2.1).

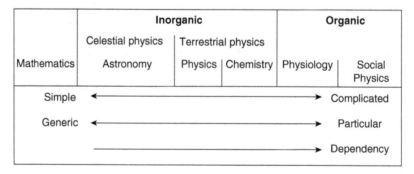

Figure 2.1 Auguste Comte's classification of the branches of knowledge, moving from the most simple and generic on the left, to the most complicated and particular on the right. As we move to through that sequence, each branch of knowledge is dependent upon the branch before it.

Bringing the classification of knowledge and the law of three stages together, Comte recognised that branches of knowledge have not all developed through the three stages he described at the same rates or times. Astronomy, being the simplest and most general, was the first to reach the positive state, with physics, chemistry and physiology following in succession.

2.2.2 Method in the natural sciences and the foundation of 'social physics'

The law of three stages and the classification of knowledge provide a foundation for understanding Comte's positivism, but the real key to the positivist philosophy lies in method. Again, Comte was practising what he preached, as his discussions of method are based on observation. He described how science is done, and not how it should be done.

Comte observed that in the most advanced sciences, knowledge is based on observation and reason. In his view, we cannot know the 'essences' of facts or phenomena, only their relation to other facts or phenomena. By identifying the constant relations that link phenomena together, we reveal the laws of nature. An example would be Horton's laws of drainage composition (Horton, 1945), which described geometric relations in stream networks. These relations were identified solely through empirical analysis of many stream basins, finding a constant pattern (Scheidegger, 1968).

This emphasis on observation removes subjectivity, in that any human preconceptions about phenomena are subordinate to the evidence provided by the external world (Comte, 1830). Two points follow from this. Firstly, there is an assumption that the human mind can observe all phenomena directly (except for those internal to itself, as observation would be compromised by emotion). This echoes the epistemological commitment of scientific realism (explained in Chapter 1, Box 1.1). Secondly, the positivist study of humans is based on knowledge of the external world. This puts positivist science in contrast with theological and metaphysical forms of knowledge, which Comte argued are centred on human concerns. The importance of observation in the positivist method also means that knowledge is relative, as knowledge can be expected to progress as our observations of (or means of observing) phenomena improve.

This positive method based on observation and reason is common to all science, but Comte (1830) identified that it can involve different procedures, in the form of observation, experiment and comparison. The emphasis between these will be different in the different sciences, but the foundational importance of mathematics should not be forgotten. Comte considered maths to be the most powerful means of searching for natural laws.

Auguste Comte's understanding of science, then, is that it involves observation (in its broad sense, encompassing experimentation and comparison) combined with mathematics to reveal the laws by which phenomena operate. The whole point of understanding laws – and, indeed, the ultimate test of our understanding – is prediction. Progress in science is characterised by greater precision and confidence in the predictions we can make, and if we can predict phenomena, we can then intervene. As Comte (1830, p. 44) himself put it, 'In short: *science = foresight, foresight = action*' (emphasis in original). He was not suggesting that scientific endeavour should be dictated by society's immediate practical needs (indeed, he argued against this quite vociferously) but, to Comte, positivist science would ultimately make the world a better place.

Now we return to the classification of the sciences and the law of three stages. If astronomy, physics, chemistry and physiology had been identified as having reached the positivist stage, all that remained to achieve a unification of the whole of knowledge was the development of positivist social physics. Comte's next step was to advocate the application of positivist methods to the study of society. Unwin (1992, p. 31) therefore describes positivism as being 'founded on the belief that phenomena of the social world are no different from the natural world…, and they can therefore be investigated through similar means'. Positivism is a **naturalist** doctrine. Whereas Comte was descriptive in his treatment of the natural sciences, he was now being prescriptive, defining how social science *should* be done.

In developing social physics – or Sociology, as he came to call it – Comte was not just seeking to achieve a unity of all branches of knowledge. He was consistent in his position that the ultimate aim of science was action, and hence the purpose of the positivist study of society was to improve social order and stability. He explained how the 'deplorable ills' (p. 126) of society around him stemmed from a continued adherence to religious thinking as the basis for society. Put into action, Comte believed that all such political doctrines eventually result in some kind of contradiction with their own principles, and this resulted in the social and political upheaval that was widespread throughout Europe at the time. To Comte, the point of positive social physics was that it would reveal the natural laws by which society functioned. A 'positive politics' could then be based on these natural laws, and so it would remain consistent when put into practice. This would enable the achievement of social consensus, thereby providing a stable foundation for progress and social order (Ferrarotti, 1999).

In discussion of the positivist method Comte distinguished between 'static' science, which focuses on existing conditions, and 'dynamic' science, examining change. In relation to Sociology he paid most attention to the latter, which is perhaps understandable given his optimism that social physics could bring about badly needed improvements to society. Inevitably, Comte thought such social changes would involve a progression, as described by the law of three stages, from the theological and metaphysical to the positive state. The central method of positivism is observation, and so developing a positivist understanding of social *change* would require a historical observational method. It is here that reading Comte's work, from a twenty-first-century perspective, becomes uncomfortable.

Comte argued that to fully understand the development of a society through history it would be necessary to examine a single society (or, in scientific terms, one 'social series'). To maximise the knowledge to be gained, the object of study should be the most advanced society and Comte went on to argue that this pinnacle society would be that of a white Western European nation. Such study could then be used to guide political relationships with other nations, ensuring that 'our intervention in the development of more or less backward peoples' (p. 201) was regulated towards 'wise and benevolent protection' rather than disturbance and oppression. As in all sciences, Comte argued that the emphasis in such study should be on the commonly occurring phenomena (the most likely to be amenable to generalisation), rather than on exceptional events and minuscule details.

Andreski (1974) identifies that Comte's most significant contribution was as a 'methodologist' rather than as a scientist, philosopher, sociologist or reformer. The *Course de Philosophie Positive* was pivotal in establishing **naturalism**, the idea that society could be studied through the methods of the natural sciences, and the significance of this should not be underestimated. Comte coined the term sociology in preference to social physics, and introduced general concepts such as structure, function, system and equilibrium to the study of society. Comte's ideas were adopted (and adapted) by John Stuart Mill in England, and eventually had a worldwide influence (Nussbaum, 2011, makes reference to a positivist group in Bengal in the early twentieth century). However his later writings, focusing on religion, were less popular, and critics soon made a distinction between his earlier and later works.

Comte's underpinning aim for the *Course de Philosophie Positive* was the achievement of social stability and harmony, but his ideas on social physics emphasise **normativity** rather than diversity, and the superiority of white Western European civilisation. It seems likely that such factors contributed to the later neglect of his ideas.

2.3 The Vienna Circle: Logical positivism

While Comte provides a foundation for understanding positivism, for its twentieth-century manifestation – and hence applications within geography – we need to turn to the Vienna Circle.

The Vienna Circle was a group of philosophers, scientists and mathematicians based at the University of Vienna in the 1920s and early 1930s. Led (at least in name) by Moritz Schlick, its central members included Rudolf Carnap, Hans Hahn, Otto Neurath, Olga Hahn-Neurath (Hahn's sister and Neurath's wife), Philipp Frank and Friedrich Waismann. There were other members, as well as a number of sympathisers around the fringes, and other individuals who interacted with and influenced the Vienna Circle – Austrian philosopher Ludwig Wittgenstein being one of the most notable. It is important to recognise that the 'Vienna Circle philosophy' is not a single, uncontested entity. Members of the group did not all agree on everything, and their views changed over time. What they did share was a commitment to the scientific world-view and, to a greater or lesser degree, its political potential (Okruhlik, 2004). Science could provide a rational basis for the organisation of social and economic life.

While such political ambition and commitment were not necessarily the main focus of the Vienna Circle, and certainly not for all of its members, it did make life difficult for them. They advocated a discourse based on evidence and reason, and this directly challenged the assumptions that underpinned racist and fascist politics (Ubel, 2012). As the influence of the Nazi party in Europe increased through the 1930s many members of the Vienna Circle left Austria, dispersing throughout Europe and, in most cases, eventually relocating to the United States or the UK. In order to fit in with the intellectual and cultural environment of their new homes, their teaching largely became depoliticised, focusing on philosophy of science in a more restricted sense. The logical empiricism that became known in North America was therefore, Giere (1996) argues, quite different in character from its European origins (the term 'logical empiricism' is sometimes used interchangeably with 'logical positivism'). As if to underline the political danger that had befallen the Vienna Circle, Moritz Schlick, who was still in Vienna, was murdered in 1936.

2.3.1 On language and meaning: Basic principles of logical positivism

Broadly speaking, the Vienna Circle's philosophy was positivist and **empiricist**, accompanied by a rejection of **metaphysics**. Some parallels with elements of Comte's positivism can be seen, although Unwin (1992) suggests that his influence was relatively minor. Logical positivism's primary focus is on language and meaning. To explain, we need to look at what Frost-Arnold (2005) calls its two 'central planks'.

First is the 'unity of science'. In Comte's positivism, unity was to be found in the dependence of each branch of knowledge on the laws of the branch preceding it (so chemistry is dependent upon physics, physiology dependent upon chemistry and physics), and in unity of method. Frost-Arnold (2005) refers to this as the 'pyramid' view of science (with mathematics as the base of the pyramid, and sociology the pinnacle). The logical positivists' unity, in contrast, was not a unity of law or theories, but a unity of language: it should be possible to derive a single language in which to express all of the sciences. For Neurath the relevant analogy was that of an encyclopedia of knowledge, rather than a pyramid (Okruhlik, 2004), and the unity of science lay in cooperation and coordination across disciplinary boundaries.

The second principle is often referred to as the 'verification principle of meaning'. Put in its simplest form, this is the notion that 'the meaning of a statement is its method of verification' (Hanfling, 1981, p. 5). The logical positivists' attention was focused on statements (or 'propositions'), as distinct from other kinds of sentences like questions or orders. Statements express the way things are. A statement can be true in one of two ways:

1. An *analytic* statement is one that is logically true, simply by virtue of its meaning. Examples would be: 'The Earth is a planet'; 'reggae is a form of music'; 'a boulder is made of rock'; or 'the All Blacks are New Zealand's national rugby team'. This kind of statement is sometimes referred to as *a priori* knowledge: it is independent of (and so 'prior to') experience. Discussion of *a priori* statements is the domain of logic and maths.

2. A *synthetic* statement is one whose truth or falsity is dependent upon the state of the world. Examples would be: 'the river is frozen'; 'the Rolling Stones are the longest running rock band'; 'global population is increasing'; and 'the climate is changing'. This kind of statement is *a posteriori* knowledge, meaning that it is dependent upon experience, and so this is the domain of empirical science.

To the logical positivists, a synthetic statement only has cognitive meaning if its truth or falsity makes a difference in the world. (Cognitive meaning is distinguished from emotional meaning.) We understand a statement when we understand what it says about the world around us, and when we understand what it says about the world around us, we know how the statement could be verified. So if your friend says to you, 'It is raining outside', you know that this means there are water droplets falling from the sky, and that if you went outside you would both see and feel those water droplets. That experience would provide the empirical evidence that would confirm the statement as true. The logical positivists argued that if this kind of verification of a statement is not possible, then the statement has no cognitive meaning. To the logical positivists, the statement that God exists is neither true nor false; it is simply meaningless, because there is no way of verifying it. It is not difficult to see why this might get them into trouble, but this is the essence of their rejection of **metaphysics**. Metaphysical statements have no cognitive meaning.

Now imagine your friend had said, 'There is gold in the Earth 300 metres below the University building' (adapting an example from Schlick, 1925-1936). Is this a verifiable statement or not? We might not *actually* be able to verify the statement, but it is not difficult to imagine how it could be done. This tells us that it is still a meaningful statement. It is the underlying principle that is important; we know what difference we would see in the world if the statement were true. There is another parallel with Comte here, because Schlick makes it clear that this principle is commonly used in science (and in everyday life, for that matter). In that sense the logical positivists began by describing how science works, rather than prescribing how it should work, just as Comte had done.

EXERCISE 2.3

The verification principle of meaning in practice

The verification principle of meaning asserts that a synthetic statement has meaning when we know what difference we would see in the world if it is true. Synthetic statements are used all the time in everyday life, not least in the news. Look through some news articles (whether in a newspaper or online) and try to identify some synthetic statements.

One of the implications of this principle is that science can never comment on what *ought* to be the case, only what *is* the case. This is a problem that was first identified by Scottish philosopher David Hume (1711–1776) (Ladyman, 2002). Identifying how things are cannot tell us how we *ought* to act. It sounds as though we are in danger of saying that moral or ethical statements are meaningless, but Hanfling (1981) claims that the logical positivists' common response to this was to claim that they are not really statements, but directives or instructions. When we describe something as morally right or wrong, we are really offering a directive as to how a person should behave (see Chapter 9 for more on moral philosophy and ethics).

In summary, the logical positivists focused on language, with the two principles of the unity of science and the verification principle of meaning being central. What we know is based on what we experience, and only statements that relate to what we experience have any cognitive meaning. Recognition of this is perhaps the first step in defining a common language for science.

2.4 Positivist geography and its critics

Two key points follow from the account of positivism above. The first is that positivism encompasses **naturalism**, the notion that social phenomena can be studied using the same methods that are used to study natural (physical/chemical/biological) phenomena. For geography, being a discipline that encompasses both, this is particularly convenient. The second point is that positivism's starting point was a description of how (natural) science works, which then led to prescriptions for how social science *should* work. This means that positivism has been rather less contentious for physical geographers than for human geographers.

Geographers turned to positivism in the 1950s and 1960s, in what has long been referred to as the **Quantitative Revolution**. In practice, this shift was a rather more gradual diffusion of ideas and approaches than the term 'revolution' might imply. It began with particular people (such as Schaefer, Hartshorne, Haggett) in a limited number of universities (Washington, Bristol, Lund, Iowa, Michigan,

Chicago, Columbia and Cambridge, though lists vary slightly). Key papers are often cited, including those by Horton (1945), Mackin (1948) and Strahler (1950, 1952) in physical geography, and Schaefer (1953), Berry and Garrison (1958) and Haggett (1961) in human geography. The general trend, though, was a move away from regional geography towards systematic geography, transforming the discipline to become more 'scientific'. This was important for political reasons, as both academics and politicians were increasingly equating knowledge with science (Unwin, 1992). Equally, Church (2010) suggests that technological developments drove change in geomorphology, with new techniques for measurement and analysis becoming available.

It may be a mistake to assume that the Quantitative Revolution was necessarily entirely a positivist revolution (see Chapter 3), but it brought profound methodological changes at all levels, with definite positivist themes. The move towards a systematic geography was accompanied by an emphasis on **empiricism**, and on the use of quantitative methods to identify and analyse spatial patterns and causal relations which, at least in some cases, may reveal generally applicable 'laws'. Geography as 'spatial science' developed, based on an understanding of space as an objective, empirical entity (described by **Euclidean geometry**, mathematics being the foundation of all sciences) within which observable phenomena are distributed. Physical geography was increasingly turning to physics to understand the operation of natural processes. Unwin (1992) suggests that the increasing array of techniques for observation was accompanied by a proliferation of technical solutions to environmental and social problems; the new geographical science could, like all good positivist sciences, be used to predict and hence to control.

The Quantitative Revolution was both lasting and short-lived: lasting because quantitative geographers have continued their practices (in both physical and human geography) into the twenty-first century, but short-lived because criticisms of positivist quantitative human geography began to appear from the late 1960s.

At the heart of these critiques is a concern for humans as individuals, for people's lives and experiences. Quantitative methods are dependent upon quantifiable attributes or phenomena, but not all human experiences can be quantified. Categorising people, their behaviours and experiences in order to quantify them necessarily involves generalisation, which renders the details of individuals and their lives invisible. If ever you have answered a multiple choice question in a questionnaire and not been able to answer in the way you want, you will have some sense of the limiting nature of such generalisation. As Kwan and Schwanen (2009) point out, such predetermined categories tend to be predicated on the experiences of the majority or powerful groups. This means that the very 'facts' on which positivist knowledge is based tend to reflect the interests of the dominant groups, in terms of class, culture, race and gender. The positivist search for universally applicable laws adds a further normalising dimension (Johnston, 2009), as such laws are assumed to apply to everyone. The aim of positivist science was prediction, and prediction enables control, and so it followed that positivist social science was doing nothing more than serving the interests of those dominant groups, maintaining their dominance and perpetuating inequalities. What was needed was a more politically engaged, critical social science.

The effect of such criticism was to herald a significant shift away from quantitative methods in human geography, with the development of critical and **humanistic geographies** (see Chapters 4 and 5), such that perception of a binary divide between positivist and anti-positivist positions became the norm (Barnes, 2009). These debates were not just restricted to human geography, but reflected the social sciences more broadly (Ferarrotti, 1999).

At the same time, Thomas Kuhn's (1962) illustration of the ways in which science is a social activity was rapidly gaining influence. Kuhn demonstrated that 'scientific knowledge' is not just a matter of synthetic statements based on empirical evidence. The acceptance of knowledge, its legitimation and validation by the scientific community, is very much a social process. Kuhn's work (see Chapter 6) particularly challenged the assumption that the development of scientific knowledge progresses in a linear, cumulative fashion.

A further criticism of positivist geographies addresses the implications of Comte's hierarchy of disciplines. Positivist science tends to be **reductionist**, seeking to reduce phenomena to the underlying, simpler and more generally applicable, components. In physical geography this tends to mean physics and chemistry. Such 'physics envy' (Massey, 1999; Lane, 2001) can act to underplay the spatio-temporal particularities of specific places (specific meanders in specific rivers, for example), and to limit our abilities to understand and explain the particularities of phenomena. In other words, the 'natural laws' of physics may offer generalisable explanations, but limit our capacity to acknowledge and explain geographical differences.

Since the late 1990s, though, there appears to have been growing appreciation, in geography and elsewhere, that a blanket notion of positivism as inherently bad is misguided. As Okruhlik (a philosopher of science) puts it, 'logical empiricists have functioned chiefly as foils and bogeymen' (2004, p. 48) in discussions of epistemology, providing convenient 'demons' that serve to underline the virtues of alternative positions. Okruhlik goes on to examine Otto Neurath's writings on logical positivism, identifying themes that are not too dissimilar from feminist philosophies of science: a recognition of the role that researchers' decisions play in science (choosing what theory to apply, for example), and that a diversity of scientists from different backgrounds, bringing different assumptions, may lead to a diversity of observations and, ultimately, to better science.

Among geographers, Barnes (2009) points out that Marx (whose work informed the development of radical geography, as discussed in Chapter 4) used quantitative methods, and Sheppard (2001) and Poon (2003, 2004, 2005) explain that quantitative methods have developed considerably beyond those that were available in the 1960s, being now better able to allow for local difference, diversity and multiplicity. Such methodological advancement leads Wyly (2009) to argue for a re-recognition of the contribution that positivist research could make to a critical geography, not least in terms of developing the kinds of arguments that policymakers will notice.

Finally, we should not forget that both Comte and the Vienna Circle were ultimately concerned with positive political and social change, seeing positivist science as a tool which could be put to use in working towards such ends.

2.5 Positivism in practice

2.5.1 A spatial analysis of civil war

O'Loughlin and Witmer's (2011) study of violent events in civil war in Chechnya during the period 1999–2007 could be interpreted as broadly positivist. The aim here is to demonstrate how elements of positivism can be seen 'in practice' in their work.

O'Loughlin and Witmer provide a contextual account of the civil war, identifying that it involves different types of conflict, between different parties, at different times and places. This includes conflict between government forces and rebel troops, local territorial disputes between ethnic minorities, and reactions against military and police actions. They identify (on p. 180) three aims for the paper, which are: i) to provide a descriptive account of the 'ebb and flow of conflict', based on cartographic and geostatistical analysis; ii) to test the hypothesis that the conflict has diffused outwards from Chechnya; and iii) to examine the ratio of violence, in terms of numbers of events per head of population, in 143 spatial units (counties and cities) across the region, establishing how this ratio is related to political and environmental factors. At various points the authors make reference to claims from the Russian and Chechen government officials and other commentators about the changing nature of the war; claims that it is 'diffusing from Chechnya' (p. 187), and that significant violence has ended but the conflict has spread (p. 191). O'Loughlin and Witmer's methods enable them to examine the evidence for these claims. This perhaps indicates a critical rationalist hypothesis-testing approach (see Chapter 3), rather than positivism, but they also use data to identify patterns as we would expect in positivist research.

Using a data set of over 14,000 violent events that took place between 1 August 1999 and 31 August 2007, they coded each event according to the target of the violence, the actor perpetrating the violence, the date on which it occurred, its location, numbers of casualties, the source of this information and any corroborating reports. Violent events were then categorised as military actions, police actions, rebel actions, or arrests (in effect, classifying observations). Alongside this information, the researchers used data on land use/land cover, population and ethnicity, and mean elevation of the land surface.

Geostatistical analysis identified that violent events were clustered along the main Federal highway and in other 'hotspot' areas such as cities and major towns. The intensity of violence had reduced in the last three years of the time period under study. Two statistical methods were used to examine the spatio-temporal distribution of violent events, one of these being the construction of 'standard deviation ellipses', identifying the spatial mean and distribution of events (Figure 2.2). This revealed that the spatial distribution of arrests throughout the time period of study was wider than that of the other event types examined, but comparison of annual data revealed that this distribution decreased over time. In other words, the authorities were becoming more targeted in their efforts to arrest those involved in violence. In contrast, the spatial distribution of military actions, police actions and rebel actions remained fairly constant. All the ellipses are centred on Chechnya, and their North-West to South-East orientation (see Figure 2.2) corresponds to the direction of the Federal highway through the region. This is consistent with the idea that violence is diffusing from Chechnya into neighbouring regions. Examination of the relations between violent events and other factors identified that violence was negatively correlated with the proportion of Russians in the local population (i.e. localities with a lower ethnic diversity in the population experienced less violence), and that land elevation was not a significant factor, but forest cover was. The predictive power of such variables was also identified.

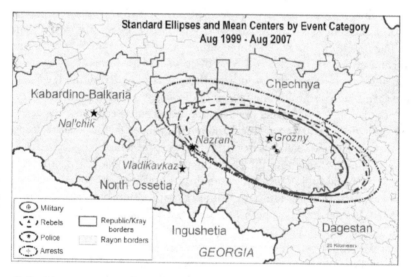

Figure 2.2 Mean centres and standard deviations of violent events in the North Caucasus, August 1999–August 2007, by type of event (O'Loughlin and Witmer, 2011, p. 192). The North-West to South-East orientation of the spread of events is clearly visible. The ellipses are all centred on Chechnya, extending into neighbouring territories.

Returning to our discussion of positivism, the logical positivists' understanding of meaning is clearly evident here. O'Loughlin and Witmer (2011) are examining the claims of Chechen and Russian governments, rebels and other commentators, and these claims are synthetic statements. Government officials are reported to have made claims 'about the ending of significant violence in the region' (p. 191). Taking the principle that the meaning of a statement lies in its method of verification, the corresponding evidence that would support this claim is a reduction in the recorded severity (such as number of casualties) of violent events and/or a decrease in the number of violent events. Similarly, the authors cite an earlier paper on the region by Lyell (2006, p. 16, quoted on p. 191 of O'Loughlin and Witmer, 2011):

> it is clear, however, that violence is spreading: war touched only eleven districts … in 1999, principally in Chechnya and (briefly) Dagestan, but reached nineteen by 2003, twenty-five by 2004, and thirty-two in 2005.

Here the synthetic statement is 'violence is spreading'. The increase in the number of districts experiencing war is both its meaning and the evidence by which it is verified. In essence, O'Loughlin and Witmer are assessing the truth claims of synthetic statements on the basis of empirical evidence. The large data set (over 14,000 events) used to provide this evidence is characteristic of positivism, which seeks generalisations rather than focusing on individual instances and their specificities.

The researchers also examine the relation between phenomena: between violent events and population density; violent events and forest cover; violent events and transport links (the Federal highway). They do this using the principles of mathematics (statistics), with the aim of describing predictive relations, noting that 'by connecting the local impacts of wars to the immediate and contextual nature of the communities affected, aid programs can be properly targeted and distribution points located' (p. 181). The Comtean project of using mathematical reasoning to establish relational 'laws', thereby enabling prediction and ultimately action, is clearly in evidence.

We should also note the geospatial nature of the analysis, examining the distribution of events across 'objective' (Euclidean) space. In effect, space is a 'blank canvas' on which characteristics such as land cover, elevation and population density are painted, and in which violent events occur. Finally, O'Loughlin and Witmer have studied an area for which the reliability of data is problematic and they clearly acknowledge this, saying that 'the limitations of data access make the modelling of violence in the North Caucasus a challenging exercise' (p. 197). This echoes Comte's emphasis that knowledge is relative, increasing in certainty as our observations improve.

EXERCISE 2.4

Identifying some positivist characteristics in physical geography research

Diolaiuti et al. (2012) present a study of glacier changes over time in the Italian Alps, identifying the influence of climate change. Read their article and try to identify:

(Continued)

(Continued)

i) Some synthetic statements. You should look for these in both the introduction (where the authors draw on other literature) and in sections reporting and discussing their results.

ii) The data used, and their methods of analysis. How do the authors look for patterns or trends in their data?

iii) Any references to underlying physical processes.

As with any research, if you have not studied any glaciology before you may find some parts difficult to follow. You should still be able to find answers to the three tasks above though, and you can look up any terms you are not familiar with. Diolaiuti et al.'s paper is available via the companion website, along with some notes that you can compare your responses to the questions to. The full reference for the paper is:

Diolaiuti, G.A., Bocchiola, D., Vagliasindi, M., D'Agata, C. and Smiraglia, C. (2012) 'The 1975–2005 glacier changes in Aosta Valley (Italy) and the relations with climate evolution', *Progress in Physical Geography* 36 (6): 764–85. doi: 10.1177/0309133312456413.

2.6 Positivism at the beach

Through this chapter we have seen that positivist research involves assessment of the truth claims of synthetic statements on the basis of the empirical events or circumstances those statements point to. This does not mean that research must always begin with such statements: it is equally likely that research may begin with examination of observable phenomena to identify synthetic statements that are empirically true. Indeed, Comte (1830, p. 32) recognised that we 'sometimes go from facts to principles, sometimes from principles to facts'. Characteristically, positivist research makes use of large, quantitative data sets to reveal generally applicable patterns and relations, assessing such relations between variables through mathematical analysis and thereby identifying 'laws' or predictive causal relations between phenomena. The treatment of space as an objective, Euclidean surface on which events occur lends itself to such analysis. It follows from this that, taking a positivist perspective, the possibilities for research are defined by the synthetic statements that could be made about the phenomena of interest. The meaning of a synthetic statement is the 'difference in the world' that we would expect to see if the statement is true or false, and so the starting point for positivist research (in one way or another) is necessarily observable phenomena.

It is not difficult to think of potentially observable phenomena at the beach. In the style of Comte, we might begin with the physical phenomena, observing the morphological characteristics of the beach: its gradient, width and height. We might study specific morphological features, such as the **berm** or **beach cusps** (as in Chapter 8). On a gravel beach we may look at the particle size and shape characteristics of beach materials, identifying variation from the seaward to the landward side, or along the length of the beach. We could seek relations between particle size and beach gradient, examine changes in beach morphology through the year, or paint selected particles and track their movement over time (as Bluck, 2011, did on six beaches in the UK) to identify patterns of development. The outcome of such research would be synthetic statements about the relations between such variables.

Similarly, we could choose to observe and document the distribution or behaviour of a particular faunal species, relating this to data describing the physical characteristics of the beach or its tidal environment. Schlacher and Lucrezi (2010) examined the behaviour of ghost crabs (Genus *Ocypode*) on an island beach in South East Queensland, Australia. They used spool-and-line tracking, by which a spool of thread is attached to the crab's shell, each crab leaving a thread as it moves across the beach and thereby enabling observation of its route of movement. Comparing the behaviour of crabs on areas of beach frequented by off-road vehicles with that of crabs in areas from which all vehicles are banned revealed significant differences between the two. All of this seems relatively straightforward 'natural science' stuff – but then Comte and the logical positivists both began by describing how science works.

To apply a similar approach to the human geography dimensions of the beach, observable phenomena could include the number of visitors on the beach at any one time, and their spatial distribution across the beach. We might relate that distribution to observable features of the beach environment; proximity to the sea or to café/toilet/car park facilities, for example. Equally, we might be interested in the spatial patterns formed by social groups on the beach. Patterns of activity through the year could be monitored, identifying seasonal trends in visitor numbers or activities, or the (self-reported) distances that visitors have travelled to get to the beach. Such research, enabling prediction of seasonal demand patterns, might then inform decisions about service provision (when the café should open, what lifeguarding services should be present, or looking beyond the beach to local emergency service provision).

2.7 Positivism in summary

To summarise, Comte's 'positive philosophy' (or positivism) and the Vienna Circle's Logical Positivism provided the backdrop to the **Quantitative Revolution** in geography. Positivist science can be broadly characterised as:

- Defining knowledge as based on the empirical evidence of observable phenomena
- Using (at least, wherever possible) mathematical analysis of data
- Identifying patterns indicative of generalised causal relations and thereby enabling prediction
- Promoting the unity of the sciences, either through method or language.

As with any philosophical position, its key proponents did not all share a single view. Logical positivism differs from Comte's positivism, for example by assuming the sciences are (or have potential to be) unified by language rather than methods. There were differences between the individual members of the Vienna Circle. It is important to recognise that philosophical theories are ideas, and ideas can be interpreted, adapted and developed in different ways by different people at different times.

Among geographers, the **Quantitative Revolution** of the mid-twentieth century is often thought of as a turn to positivist approaches, although few of the geographers publishing at that time specifically identified their work as positivist. Within human geography, a reaction against quantitative geographies and 'spatial science' from the 1970s meant that positivism has had negative connotations for many. Increasingly some geographers are arguing that there is a place for positivist geographies in the twenty-first century, but its aim should not necessarily be the identification of universal laws. Finally, while positivism does emphasise quantitative methods, this does not mean that all quantitative research is necessarily positivist, or that all positivist research is necessarily quantitative.

FURTHER READING

For further explanations

Kwan, M.-P. and Schwanen, T. (2009) 'Quantitative Revolution 2: the critical (re)turn', *The Professional Geographer* 61 (3): 283–91.

Richards, K. (2009) 'Geography and the physical sciences tradition', in N.J. Clifford, S.L. Holloway, S.P. Rice, and G. Valentine (eds) *Key Concepts in Geography*, 2nd edition. London: Sage. pp. 21–45.

Wyly, E. (2009) 'Strategic positivism', *The Professional Geographer* 61 (3): 310–22.

Progress in Human Geography and *Progress in Physical Geography* resources (available on the companion website)

Church, M. (2010) 'The trajectory of geomorphology', *Progress in Physical Geography* 34 (3): 265–86. doi: 10.1177/0309133310363992.

Lake, R.W. (1993) 'Planning and applied geography: positivism, ethics, and geographic information systems', *Progress in Human Geography* 17 (3): 404–13. doi: 10.1177/030913259301700309.

Mather, P. (1979) 'Theory and quantitative methods in geomorphology', *Progress in Physical Geography* 3 (4): 471–87. [Note that the 'realism' described early in this paper is Bhaskar's **critical realism** – see Chapter 4 – rather than scientific realism in general.]

Schurman, N. (2000) 'Trouble in the heartland: GIS and its critics in the 1990s', *Progress in Human Geography* 24 (4): 569–90. doi: 10.1191/030913200100189111. [The focus here is on GIS, but this includes some discussion of (debates about) positivism and GIS.]

Smith, N. (1979) 'Geography, science and post-positivist modes of explanation', *Progress in Human Geography* 3 (3): 356–83. doi: 10.1177/030913257900300302. [This also addresses phenomenological and Marxist geographies.]

Examples

Diolaiuti, G.A., Bocchiola, D., Vagliasindi, M., D'Agata, C. and Smiraglia, C. (2012) 'The 1975–2005 glacier changes in Aosta Valley (Italy) and the relations with climate evolution', *Progress in Physical Geography* 36 (6): 764–85. doi: 10.1177/0309133312456413.

Mitchell, L., Frank, M.R., Harris, K.D., Dodds, P.S. and Danforth, C.M. (2013) 'The geography of happiness: connecting Twitter sentiment and expression, demographics, and objective characteristics of place', *PLoS ONE* 8 (5): e64417. doi:10.1371/journal.pone.0064417. [Note that, although this paper has a geographical theme, its authors are based in an applied mathematics department, rather than a geography department.]

O'Loughlin, J. and Witmer, F.D. (2011) 'The localized geographies of violence in the North Caucasus of Russia, 1999–2007', *Annals of the Association of American Geographers* 101 (1): 178–201.

3

Critical Rationalism: Learning From Our Mistakes

> It might be well for all of us to remember that, while differing widely in the various little bits we know, in our infinite ignorance we are all equal. (Popper, 1974, p. 29)

Is geography a science? The question of what distinguishes science from other ways of knowing was central to the development of Karl Popper's critical rationalism. Although geography's **Quantitative Revolution** tends to be associated with **positivism** (Chapter 2), much quantitative geographical research reflects critical rationalism as much as positivism. This chapter will explain critical rationalism as defined by Popper, identify its influence and use within geography, and consider some strands of criticism.

3.1 Popper's critical rationalism

Karl Popper was probably one of the most influential philosophers of science of the twentieth century. Born in Vienna in 1902, he attended the University of Vienna in the 1920s, and interacted with the Vienna Circle of logical positivists (see Chapter 2), although he became very critical of positivism as his own ideas developed. He later worked in New Zealand before settling in England. Popper's philosophical interests throughout his career spanned **epistemology**, science, and society/politics – Thornton (2011) comments on the coherence of his philosophy across these domains – but it is his philosophy of science that is of greatest interest to us here.

Popper observed that many previous philosophers of science had been preoccupied with identifying the *source* of scientific knowledge. Put simply, some (the 'British empiricists', including Bacon, Locke, Berkeley, Hume, and Mill) argued that the source of knowledge is observation, while others (Continental philosophers such as Descartes, Spinoza and Leibniz) argued that it is our intellect. Popper's view was that both positions were mistaken, and that the question about the source of our knowledge was the wrong question to ask. All sources of knowledge can lead us to error and so, Popper argued, the more important question to ask is how we can be sure of the *validity* of our knowledge. To Popper, 'objective truth' represents a standard that we will always fall short of in our efforts to develop knowledge. It is therefore important to recognise our fallibility and make every effort to find our mistakes. While Popper's works span several volumes, we can understand this basic idea through examination of two problems: the 'problem of demarcation' (how we distinguish science from other forms of knowledge), and the 'problem of induction'. These are addressed in turn below, before we look at some examples of critical rationalist geography research.

3.1.1 The problem of demarcation

One of the central problems of the philosophy of knowledge – and the problem that exercised Karl Popper throughout his career – is how to understand the growth of knowledge (O'Hear, 1980). Science is seen as a prime example of the growth of knowledge, because scientific knowledge has advanced so rapidly. It follows that if we can isolate science, delimiting it from other forms of knowledge, then it becomes possible to examine how the growth of scientific knowledge works. This gives rise to the problem of demarcation: distinguishing between science and non-scientific knowledge.

Chapter 1 of Popper's *Conjectures and Refutations* (1974, but first published in 1963) provides a very readable account of the development of his thinking on this. He began working on the problem of demarcation in 1919. At this time, the commonly accepted view was that science is based upon an **empirical** method, proceeding from observation to **theory**. This progression from observation of specific instances to generally applicable theories is called **inductive** reasoning. Popper could see that this formulation for delimiting science was not satisfactory; after all, he argued, astrologists had amassed a large amount of empirical evidence based on observation, but somehow astrology still did not meet 'scientific' standards. He became interested in four theories that were prominent at the time: Einstein's theory of relativity, Marx's theory of history, Freud's theory of psychoanalysis, and Adler's theory of individual psychology. Popper noticed that, in the latter three cases, any and every observation could be interpreted in light of the theory, and through such interpretation any and every observation provided additional confirmation of the theory. It was impossible to prove such a theory wrong. In contrast, Einstein's theory of relativity was 'risky'. It led Einstein to make predictions about the universe which, if they turned out to be false, would mean his whole theory was wrong. To

Popper, this provided the key to the problem of demarcation. He argued that it is easy to find observations that verify any theory if we only ever look for such confirmation. A scientific theory should be prohibitive, identifying that certain things should not happen. This allows us to make 'risky predictions', as any observation of the phenomena prohibited by the theory would mean the theory is wrong. In other words, Popper argued that scientific theories are falsifiable, and this falsifiability is what distinguishes science from pseudo-science. Any real test of a scientific theory should be an attempt to refute it.

3.1.2 The problem of induction

The problem of induction is related to the problem of demarcation. We noted above that, prior to Popper's work, the common view was that science was based upon inductive reasoning, proceeding from observations to theory. There are two problems with this classical view of science (which dates back to Francis Bacon, 1561–1626). Firstly, Popper argued that observation cannot come before theory. Every observation is dependent upon some kind of theory, whether conscious or subconscious. In observing something, our attention is always directed by some kind of aim or problem, some kind of idea about *what* to observe. Another way of looking at it is that what we see is influenced by what we expect to see, shaped by our background knowledge. Trudgill (2012) illustrates this through Charles Darwin's visits to North Wales in 1831 and 1842. He explains that 'Darwin did not see [evidence of glaciation] at all on his first visit but, tellingly, on his second visit when he knew about glaciation he then saw it all around him' (p. 559). Science cannot proceed from observation to theory, as observation is itself determined by theory.

Secondly, inductive reasoning was identified by Scottish philosopher David Hume (1711–1776) to be logically unjustifiable. There is no logical basis for assuming that our future experiences will conform to our past experiences. In relation to scientific theories, Popper pointed out that no matter how many times we observe phenomena that confirm a theory, this does not provide grounds to assume that the theory will hold for all future instances of the phenomena under question. In his words 'Theories are…never empirically verifiable' (Popper, 1972, p. 40).

3.1.3 Deductive falsification of theories

Bringing the problem of demarcation and the problem of induction together, Popper argued that the logical basis for the growth of knowledge in science is the *falsification* of theories based on **deductive** reasoning. Whereas induction proceeds from singular observation(s) to universal theory, deduction involves the opposite, moving from universal theory to singular observation (see Box 3.1). Using Popper's approach, we take a (proposed) theory, make a risky prediction from it, and then examine specific instances to look for evidence that the prediction (and hence the theory) is wrong. The advantage of this method is that just one observation contradicting our risky prediction will falsify the theory.

The classic example used to illustrate this is the theory that 'all swans are white'. It would be possible to make many hundreds of observations of individual swans that would all seem to confirm this theory, but it takes only one observation of a single black swan to refute it. Popper summarises his critical rationalism as being based around the theme that 'we can learn from our mistakes' (1974, p. vii). (In practice, Popper was conscious that a single contradictory observation might not be sufficient to warrant discarding a theory, as a single instance could be the result of experimental error.) If, on the other hand, our attempt at falsification fails and we only find evidence that conforms to our prediction, then we can say that the theory has been corroborated. In this case it must be allowed to stand for the time being, until it is falsified by new evidence. Popper emphasised that such corroboratory evidence should only be accepted if it has arisen from a genuine attempt to falsify the theory, a 'severe test' of the theory. As a theory passes more and more such tests, we can have greater confidence that it is approaching the 'truth'.

BOX 3.1   INDUCTIVE AND DEDUCTIVE ARGUMENTS IN GEOGRAPHY

I: Inductive and deductive arguments

	A: Inductive argument	B: Deductive argument
Premise 1:	Antony, Golant and Devoran are all villages in Cornwall, England.	Golant village Post Office was closed in 2008, meaning that Golant's residents have to travel to another village or town to use a Post Office.
	⬇	⬇
Premise 2:	Antony, Golant and Devoran all had their Post Offices closed in 2008.	Bryony lives in Golant village.
	⬇	⬇
Conclusion:	All villages in Cornwall had their Post Offices closed in 2008.	Bryony has to travel to another village or town to use a Post Office.

(Note: around 2,500 Post Office branches in Britain were closed in 2008 in the 'Network Change Programme', because technological developments had rendered them unsustainable. Langford and Higgs (2010) provide contextual information on the closures and assessment of the impacts in Wales.)

(Continued)

(Continued)

In **A**, we move from two observations about specific cases (the two premises) to a more general conclusion. This conclusion does not necessarily follow from the premises. In other words, premise 1 and premise 2 may be true (and they are), but this in itself does not mean the conclusion must be true. The conclusion is, in fact, incorrect. Many villages in Cornwall still have functioning Post Offices. It is worth noting that this is a weak (overly simplistic) example of an inductive argument, which has been constructed for the purposes of explanation. A better inductive argument is one in which the initial premises provide some likelihood that the conclusion is true. So if researchers had sampled a number of villages in Cornwall, identified the proportion that have had their Post Offices closed, and made an inductive move to assume that the same proportion of *all* Cornish villages had experienced Post Office closure, this would be a more convincing inductive argument. The case remains, though, that inductive arguments provide no guarantee of the conclusion being true.

In **B**, we move from a general case in premise 1 (general because it tells us something about all of Golant's residents) to a particular case in premise 2 and in the conclusion. As long as premise 1 and premise 2 are true, then the conclusion must be true, because it contains no new information. Bryony, as an individual resident, is a particular example of the general case specified in premise 1.

II: An example of inductive and deductive arguments being used in combination

In practice, it is not unusual to see inductive and deductive arguments used in combination. Huggel et al.'s (2012) examination of the possible effects of climate change on landslides in high mountains provides one such example. They explain that their research takes a 'hybrid approach', reviewing relevant literature and theory, and presenting case studies of particular landslides, in order to identify whether there may be potential signals of climate change in the record of large landslide events.

In their introduction, Huggel et al. (2012, p. 77) state that 'observations of recent large landslides in some mountain regions suggest that climate change is having an effect on slope stability'. This represents a move from particular cases to a (possible) general case, and so is an inductive move.

The main body of the paper is then divided into three sections, each addressing particular types of landslide events: i) catastrophic landslides involving bedrock and ice; ii) debris flows in periglacial environments; iii) process coupling among landslides, glaciers and rivers. In each of these sections, the authors review relevant theory before examining particular cases in light of that theory. Here they are moving from the general to the particular; a deductive move.

In their concluding section (p. 88), they state that 'the case studies presented here raise the question of whether there are tipping points in geomorphic systems related to climate change.' This is a broadly inductive move, using particular cases (the individual landslide events) to suggest a possible general theory in the existence of tipping points in geomorphic systems. We should note that, while Popper argued against the use of inductive logic in science, his issue was with the use of induction in testing theories. He was ambivalent about where those theories came from, recognising that there could be many possible sources; indeed, in Popper's view, 'every source, every suggestion, is welcome' (1974, p. 27). For a critical rationalist, the essential next step would be to derive falsifiable hypotheses from the idea that there might be tipping points in geomorphic systems associated with climate change, and to test those hypotheses.

3.1.4 Science's social dimension

Popper was conscious that science is a social activity – indeed, this is central to his idea of critical rationalism. Scientific theories should be subject to criticism in the form of attempts to falsify those theories. Recognising that no theory is ever proven, all scientific theories are open to rational debate about which is best. While we should strive to criticise our own ideas, Popper stresses that such criticism is a collective effort. The social dimension of science is also evident in relation to the problem of demarcation, as Popper argues that the delimitation of science is based upon convention or agreement about what constitutes science; in effect he was proposing falsifiability as a criterion for the scientific community to use. Finally, his understanding of the objectivity of science is that it stems from inter-subjectivity; both the inter-subjective criticism involved in rational debate about our theories, and the fact that science's risky predictions can be tested by anyone (which Popper, 1972 describes as a particular form of inter-subjective criticism).

Regarding the progress of scientific knowledge, Bortolotti (2008) characterises the critical rationalist view as one in which new theories are both conservative and revolutionary. They are conservative because they preserve successful elements of previous theories, and revolutionary because new theories must conflict in some way with those they replace. Ultimately, the growth of knowledge is cumulative, as new theories build on those that come before them.

3.2 Critical rationalism in practice

Within geography, explicit discussion of critical rationalism or adoption of a critical rationalist position seems to be mostly confined to physical geography. This is not to imply that human geography cannot be practised in a critical rationalist vein, or indeed that it is not, but there has been more overt discussion of Popper's ideas within physical geography, and particularly geomorphology. This can be largely attributed to the efforts of Roy Haines-Young and James Petch (Haines-Young and Petch, 1980, 1981, 1983, 1986). They noted in 1980 that physical geographers were making reference to critical rationalism and yet inductive approaches still dominated the practices of research. Haines-Young and Petch (1980) argued that Popper's critical rationalism and its methodological prescriptions offered a means for physical geographers to become more conscious of the philosophical and theoretical basis of their work, and more rigorous in their methodological design. They followed this with a book-length treatment in *Physical Geography: Its Nature and Methods* (1986), which Whalley (1987, p. 678) described as 'both pedagogic and polemic', aiming to both teach and persuade. This became a standard text for physical geography students. Indeed, as Lane (2001, p. 245) explains, by the early 1990s 'critical rationalism was presented as *the* methodological approach that should be adopted'. Critical rationalism was upheld as an ideal, then, but it is less clear whether the practices of geographical research strictly adhered to this ideal.

Research using a strictly critical rationalist perspective would be expected to proceed through the following sequence:

1. identifying or proposing a theory;

2. developing falsifiable predictions from that theory;

3. making observations, for example through field data collection or experiment;

4. examining the data to establish whether the predictions were false, thereby falsifying the theory.

In the following two examples of geographical research, the first follows this sequence quite closely, while the second has clearly identifiable critical rationalist elements. It is important to recognise, though, that the researchers do not specifically identify their approach as critical rationalist in either case.

3.2.1 Effects of beaver dams on stream ecosystem

Beavers are particularly known for altering their habitat, using wood (along with mud and leaves) to build dams across streams and small rivers, thereby creating pools of deep, slow-moving water. While specific effects of beaver ponds had been observed previously, Fuller and Peckarsky's (2011) study aimed to establish whether or not the beaver ponds systematically alter in-stream habitats. They note from literature that beaver ponds can vary in morphology, and that ponds affect nutrient dynamics and hence impact on the food web. Previous authors have encountered effects of beaver ponds on groundwater flows, on 'streambed substrate hydraulic conductivity' (the ability of water to move between the streambed particles) and hence on nutrient availability. Fuller and Peckarsky (2011, p. 48) state: 'If varying beaver pond morphology results in different rates of upwelling downstream of the ponds, then nutrient availability should vary predictably downstream of beaver ponds.' Here they have taken the first step in defining testable hypotheses. This is, in effect, the overall theory that is being tested. They develop this further by adding that if beaver ponds alter the movement of nutrients and organic matter, then this may affect other organisms in the food web. In the quote above, though, the term 'varying beaver pond morphology' is quite vague. The authors therefore need to break their theory into more clearly defined, testable hypotheses. They summarise these hypotheses in three sentences (p. 36), presented here with commentary between each:

> We hypothesized that stream reaches below ponds with high-hydraulic head dams and small surface areas would have higher nutrient concentrations due to greater groundwater upwelling into the downstream reach.

This sentence identifies specific observable phenomena. We can now see that the previously vague term, 'pond morphology', is made up of: i) hydraulic head, that is, the potential energy created by the difference between water levels in the pond and in the stream reach below, and ii) pond surface area. Fuller and Peckarsky have made a 'risky prediction', setting out an expectation that higher nutrient concentrations will occur below beaver ponds with high hydraulic head and small cross-section area. They go on to state:

> Additionally, we tested for relationships between pond morphology and downstream nutrient limitation, periphyton, benthic organic matter, and pond spillover phytoplankton as potential resources for invertebrate consumers.

The authors are not explaining their hypotheses in the same detail here, but this sentence represents a series of hypotheses similar to that above. In place of high nutrient concentrations they have substituted the variables of: i) nutrient limitation; ii) periphyton (a mixture of algae and microbes living on streambed particles); iii) organic matter at the streambed; and iv) phytoplankton. They expect to see differences in each of these phenomena between ponds of different morphology.

> Finally, we tested effects of beaver ponds in general and pond morphology in specific on invertebrate consumers downstream.

This provides clue to the authors' final two hypotheses: that invertebrates living downstream of beaver ponds would be different from elsewhere in the stream, and invertebrates living downstream of ponds with particular morphology would be different from elsewhere (remembering that pond morphology refers to hydraulic head and pond surface area).

Fuller and Peckarsky then go on to explain the observations used to test their hypotheses. Collecting data from 22 field sites over two years, they examined conditions upstream of the beaver pond, in the pond itself, and downstream of the pond in each case. Specifically, stream water nutrients were identified, and stream bottom (benthic) conditions examined, calculating the biomass of algae, and identifying the organic matter and invertebrates present. For each variable, a hypothesis that there would be a difference between conditions upstream and downstream of the beaver pond was tested statistically against a null hypothesis of no difference. In a similar manner, the authors examined whether pond morphology had any systematic effect on the habitat downstream of the pond.

On analysing the data, Fuller and Peckarsky report that there were no significant differences between conditions upstream and downstream of the beaver ponds in most of the variables tested. Some significant relationships between specific aspects of pond morphology and downstream conditions were identified, but overall, pond morphology was found not to provide a universally applicable explanation of such variation. In essence, the hypotheses were falsified, leading Fuller and Peckarsky to conclude that the current body of theory is insufficient to understand the impacts of beaver dams. They suggest that 'a new conceptual framework focusing on smaller temporal and spatial scales is needed' (p. 46). Fuller and Peckarsky (2011), then, provide quite a clear example of falsifiable hypotheses (risky predictions) being developed from theory and tested against observable phenomena, and so being used to criticise current theory.

3.2.2 The myth of Martin Luther King Street

In our next example, the empirical research appears to follow a critical rationalist approach, but this is situated within other perspectives. The focus of Mitchelson et al.'s (2007) research is streets in the USA named to commemorate the Reverend Dr Martin Luther King Jr ('MLK Streets', for brevity).

The authors begin by using a specific case study to illustrate the contested nature of MLK Street naming. Here their work fits a broadly **poststructuralist** vein (see Chapter 7), recognising that space is socially produced, and places have specific cultural meanings and identities. They point out that streets occupy and connect (or divide) both **Euclidean geometric** ('objective') space and socio-culturally symbolic places. They go on to explain that the name MLK Street (including its derivatives, such as MLK Boulevard, Avenue or Drive) has become a 'negative brand', associated in the public imagination with economically deprived areas. This association is reproduced in popular media, comedy and in **grey literature**, and has been recognised in the authors' previous research. It is important to acknowledge that the issue of MLK Street-naming is also highly racialised, given Martin Luther King's iconic status as an African-American leader. Debates about whether or not a street should be so named, or which street in a town should bear the name, often have racial undercurrents. MLK Streets are often located in predominantly African-American areas, and associated with these areas in the collective consciousness of the public.

We should perhaps pause here for a moment's reflection: the underlying argument here is that examples of particular MLK Streets have been assumed to represent MLK Streets in general. This move from particular instances to a general case is an example of **induction**, which Popper (and Hume before him) flagged up as logically flawed. The purpose of Mitchelson et al.'s (2007) research is to critically examine this popular perception. In Popperian terms, they are taking the popular understanding of MLK Streets as a theory, and testing this theory against the empirical evidence of the 'economic vitality' of the streets.

The authors' next step is to explain the data by which they can assess economic vitality. They use the number of employees, levels of sales, and the business type of individual organisations on each street as indicators of economic vitality, accessing the data from national databases. Economic deprivation here is a relative term; MLK Streets are imagined to be economically deprived compared to other places, and so Mitchelson et al. then identify a means of making the comparisons needed. 'John F Kennedy (JFK) Streets' provide an equivalent named in honour of a prominent white figure from the same era, and 'Main Streets' present a 'neutral', also frequently occurring, alternative. A broader comparison is enabled through use of aggregate data for the USA as a whole. The authors also note the importance of assessing the economic vitality of a street relative to its host town/city, and so aggregate data for individual settlements are obtained. This explanation clarifies the assumptions and decisions underpinning the data, illustrating Popper's assertion that all observations are theory-dependent.

Mitchelson et al. then provide (on pp. 130–3) some descriptive statistics about MLK Streets, and this section of the paper could almost be interpreted as **positivist**. For example, the statements, 'most of these streets (85 per cent of the total) are found in the South. Georgia alone is home to 117 MLK Streets' (p. 130) are synthetic statements, empirically verifiable. We know what they mean because we know what observations would verify them as true (see Chapter 2). Both positivism and critical rationalism assume the existence of an empirically observable reality, and so perhaps we should not be surprised to see this kind of alignment. In the case of Mitchelson et al.'s research, though, this section just provides contextual information.

The paper then sets out a series of hypotheses (e.g. on pp. 134, 136 and 138), testing these through statistical analysis of the data. In each case, the hypothesis is subjected to a number of tests via more specific hypotheses. For example, for the broad hypothesis: 'given popular conceptions, we expect to find a negative correlation between the MLK label and the level of economic development' (p. 134), specific tests involve examination of the annual sales of establishments on MLK Streets compared to JFK Streets, Main Streets, and the total United States, and analysis of the employment levels of establishments on those streets.

Their analysis enables Mitchelson et al. to falsify their overall theory, identifying that the image of MLK Streets as consistently economically marginalised is largely

a myth. At the same time, they do note there is some evidence of economic marginalisation among MLK Streets in the Southern states. They also identify that MLK
Streets, nationally, do tend to have a particular economic function, being dominated
by churches, schools and Government offices (termed 'No Sales Function' premises),
and they proffer possible reasons for this.

   Finally, the authors re-emphasise the importance of the particularity of each individual street and the lives of the people in them. Here they are moving back from
the critical rationalist, 'objective', quantitative approach to a more poststructuralist
philosophy and recognising the richness of understanding of particular cases that
qualitative studies can provide. Mitchelson et al.'s work, then, illustrates that researchers may draw on different philosophical perspectives (either explicitly or implicitly)
at different times. While their paper provides quite clear shifts between perspectives,
it is not always possible to identify distinct philosophical positions quite this clearly.

EXERCISE 3.1

Ethnic diversity and social trust in urban neighbourhoods

Gundelach and Freitag (2014) present a study of neighbourhood ethnic diversity
and social trust in the city of Konstanz, Germany. Read their article and try to
answer the following questions:

1 What are the two theories that the authors use, from which they develop
   their hypotheses?

2 What are their three hypotheses, and which theory does each come from?

3 Why is the city of Konstanz a suitable location for conducting a severe test
   of those hypotheses? (note that the authors do not use the term 'severe test'
   themselves. If you are not sure about this one, come back to it when you have
   read the rest of this chapter.)

4 The authors try to ensure that they are subjecting their hypotheses to a severe
   test by controlling for the effects of other variables. What are these variables?

5 Why do the authors suggest their method for measuring 'social trust' is more
   appropriate for neighbourhood studies than methods other researchers have
   used?

6 Looking at the results of the research:

   a. Was each hypothesis rejected or not?

   b. What are the implications of their findings for the two theories that the
       authors started out with?

> Gundelach and Freitag's paper is available via the companion website, along with answers to the questions. The full reference for the paper is:
> Gundelach, B. and Freitag, M. (2014) 'Neighbourhood diversity and social trust: an empirical analysis of interethnic contact and group-specific effect', *Urban Studies* 51 (6): 1236–56.

3.3 Critical rationalism at the beach

The examples above provide illustration of the **methodology** of critical rationalist research, that is: identifying or proposing a theory; developing falsifiable predictions from that theory; gathering data; and analysing the data to establish whether the predictions were false. Devising a research project at the beach would therefore first require the identification of a theory to test. Popper was unconcerned where this theory might come from. It could be from first-hand observation, perhaps spotting a phenomenon that there is no obvious explanation for. It could be from a chance comment made by someone else; something that leaves you thinking. It might be triggered by some imposed change on a particular beach, such as the implementation of a new management practice. In practice, it is probably most likely to involve reading previous research, following up on others' ideas and taking them further. The key criterion, from a critical rationalist perspective, is that the theory is falsifiable. It must enable you to make predictions that could be proven wrong by empirical evidence, and ideally that would be unexpected from other theories.

Ariza and Leatherman (2012) review the use of smoking bans on beaches. They explain that beaches are particularly important for tourism revenue, with coastal states in the US generating 85 per cent of total tourist revenue, and that litter is a primary factor in tourists' choice of beach. Proposals to implement smoking bans on beaches are not viewed positively by everyone, and so Ariza and Leatherman (2012, p. 145) conclude that 'more studies need to be undertaken on the economic implications of smoking bans, especially since beach tourism is often the principal economic engine of coastal communities'. They imply that a smoking ban on beaches is good for tourism and, more specifically, that it will: decrease litter on the beach; increase the number of tourists using a beach (because of the cleaner beach); and have a positive impact on the local economy, because of higher visitor numbers and reduced litter collection costs. Here we have some 'theories' that could be tested in a critical rationalist vein.

If a critical rationalist approach to research involves deductive logic, moving from a general theory to particular cases, then the next step to take would be to develop more specific 'risky predictions' from our theories. Two possible approaches spring to mind. We could adopt a comparative approach, examining all beaches in a region where some have smoking bans in place and some do not. If the theories are correct, we would expect the beaches with smoking bans to have less litter, and higher visitor numbers, than beaches without. This comparative approach would require us to consider what other factors might affect litter, visitor numbers and local tourism income, in order to take these into account in our analysis and 'isolate' the effects of a smoking ban. (Visitor numbers might be influenced by the size of the beach, the amenities available, and other visitor attractions close by, for example.) Alternatively, we could undertake a 'longitudinal' study over time, by examining an individual beach or beaches before and after the introduction of a smoking ban. If our theories are correct, we would expect a decrease in litter, increase in visitor numbers, and increase in local tourism income after the smoking ban.

The next step would be to define the observations (data) that would enable us to test these predictions more precisely. This would include identifying a procedure and sampling strategy for a litter count, for example, and a means of counting visitor numbers. The notion of 'local tourism income' would need refining. (What do we mean by 'local'? What kinds of businesses might be included?) Planning a research methodology also requires identification of appropriate methods of data analysis. This would include considering any assumptions underlying statistical tests, and identifying whether or not those assumptions would be valid for the data collected. In practice, such considerations may well influence decisions about the data to be collected. Once all such decisions are made, we would then be in a position to collect the data and identify whether or not the predictions arising from our theories are true. If the predictions are false, then the theories would be falsified. If the predictions are found to be true, we would have to accept the theories until such a time as they are falsified by other data.

3.4 Critical rationalism's place in geography

Histories of geography often seem to provide rather limited discussion of critical rationalism – perhaps surprisingly, given the status accorded to it within physical geography in the 1980s and early 1990s. Hubbard et al. (2002), Johnston and Sidaway (2004) and Creswell (2013) all note the critical rationalist's rejection of induction and emphasis on falsification, but situate this within discussion of positivism, quantification and spatial science. Johnston and Sidaway (2004) point out that the ultimate goal of both positivism and critical rationalism is to establish theories or laws enabling prediction of the world around us, and they present this as justification for treating the two together. In practice, research that may be critical rationalist does not always follow the critical rationalist path obviously. It is not uncommon, for example, for hypotheses to be proposed, tested and verified (see Boschma et al.'s 2008 study of labour mobility and skills for an example), and it can be difficult to tell whether this is adopting a positivist or critical rationalist perspective unless you are familiar with the technicalities and underpinning assumptions of the specific statistical tests involved. (In truth, it is just as likely that the researchers have not made a conscious decision on this point either.) On this basis, it is not entirely unreasonable to lump positivist and critical rationalist research together.

However, treating positivism and critical rationalism together puts us at risk of overlooking other facets of Popper's work. His assertion that observation is always theory-dependent was in direct contrast with the positivists, and his emphasis on critical debate is also important. This is without paying attention to the social philosophies of Comte (positivism) and Popper (critical rationalism), which differed significantly. Pedynowski (2003) argues that it is not uncommon for authors to erroneously portray 'science' as a singular entity against which alternative perspectives are presented. While she was specifically concerned with discourse around the **social construction** of nature, to some degree perhaps the same has happened here. Critical rationalism has been subsumed into a homogeneous (and positivist) **Quantitative Revolution**, imagined as a singular movement against which critical geographers reacted (see Chapter 4). This is not to deny that critical rationalism has its limitations, of course, and criticisms will be explored in the next section.

3.5 Criticisms of critical rationalism

The merits and problems of critical rationalism are still much debated by philosophers. Putting aside the difficulty of explaining the origin of theories (an issue which Popper argued was irrelevant as the key concern is testing any theory, regardless of its origin), we will consider four key criticisms here. These are explained below, and summarised in Box 3.2.

BOX 3.2 SUMMARY OF KEY PROBLEMS WITH CRITICAL RATIONALISM

1. *The problem of identifying the source of error:* According to the Duhem problem, it is impossible to test a scientific theory in isolation. Any empirical test also makes use of additional theories, such as those underpinning the methods of measurement used. If a test result contradicts the theory being tested, it may not be possible to determine whether it is the theory of interest that is at fault, or one of these additional theories.

2. *The problem of theory preference:* there may be two or more competing theories proposed to explain the phenomenon of interest. We can then find ourselves in a situation where none of the competing theories is falsified, or even where all are recognised as being false to some degree but no better

(Continued)

(Continued)

alternative has yet been found. In such situations critical rationalism provides no means of deciding between them.

3. **The problem of defining a 'severe test':** Popper argued that a confirmatory test result should only be accepted as corroborating a theory if it results from a genuine attempt to falsify the theory – that is, a 'severe test' of the theory. Philosophers of science have yet to establish how a severe test should be defined or identified.

4. **The social nature of scientific practice:** The social dimension of science is central to Popper's critical rationalism, in that rational debate and criticism (of our own ideas and each other's) is essential. However, others (most notably Kuhn, discussed in Chapter 6, and Feyerabend, 1975) argue that the status of science as a social activity is more important than Popper recognised, and the acceptance or rejection of a theory is not made solely on the basis of deductive logic; it is influenced by the preferences, allegiances and aims of members of the scientific community.

3.5.1 The problem of identifying the source of error

For any empirical test of a theory, the test outcome is not solely dependent upon that theory alone; other factors (including other theories) are always involved. These will include the initial and boundary conditions of the test (and how these have been defined), theories underpinning the method(s) of measurement used, and possible sources of error in the conduct of the test (Bouillon, 1998; Brown, 1999). So, for example, in biogeography Frick et al. (2008) report on a study of bat colonies in 37 islands of Baja California, Mexico. Their research had two aims:

1. To determine whether the bat colonies throughout the archipelago conform to predictions of the equilibrium theory of island biogeography. The predictions of interest specify relations between the number of species on an island and island size (area), and between the number of species and the degree of isolation of the island (defined in this context as the shortest distance to the mainland peninsula). Note that, in saying they sought confirmation rather than falsification, the researchers appear not to be taking a strictly critical rationalist approach, but this may be just a matter of presentation and language used; Whalley (1987) comments on the likelihood of such mis-match between research practice and presentation.

2. To explore how the two variables of island size and habitat diversity might each independently influence bat species richness.

The methods used in the study include characterisation of 32 islands (calculating their area and degree of isolation) across the archipelago, along with presence/

absence surveys of bat species on these islands to determine which species inhabit each. These surveys were conducted by a combination of passive and active acoustic sampling to detect bat sounds, and mist-net surveys. Passive acoustic sampling at 113 sites across the 32 islands involved leaving broadband ultrasonic bat detectors *in situ*, attached to high-frequency microphones in waterproof housing, connected to a recording device. Active acoustic sampling was carried out using hand-held ultra-sonic bat detectors, enabling confirmation of species by visual identification. This allowed the researchers to build up a reference library of bat sounds of known species, enabling identification of species from the passive sample data. Mist-net surveys, where nets are set up to catch bats in flight, also contributed to the reference library by enabling the researchers to catch bats, identify species and make recordings of their calls as they were released. A key for identifying bat species by their calls was then established.

The results of these bat surveys, then, will be dependent upon: the technology used (the ultrasonic bat detectors, microphones, recording devices, etc.), which is itself dependent upon underlying theories of acoustics and sound recording; the sampling strategy used to identify sites for data collection, which will have been influenced by the researchers' prior understanding of the theories being tested and knowledge of the local area(s); the placing of mist-nets, and underpinning ideas about known bat behaviour; and the reliability of species identification. This is without considering the methods of data analysis and theories underpinning those methods.

Given that any such **empirical** test (including in social science research) will involve this kind of range of factors, if the test results contradict the theory being tested, it may not be clear whether this really represents a problem with the theory or with one of these other elements. This notion, that a scientific theory can never be tested in complete isolation from others, is commonly known as the Duhem problem (after physicist Pierre Duhem, 1861–1916). However, there is some merit in the argument that scientists will often have a pretty good idea of the likely source of problems if a theory is falsified. In Frick et al.'s research they acknowledge that the ultrasonic bat detectors can be susceptible to both 'false positive' data (detecting species that are not present) and 'false negative' data (not detecting species that are present), and so their research design aimed to minimise such errors. Hence Gower's (1997) view is that a falsifying claim can still provide good reason to reject a theory despite this potential problem, as researchers are likely to have a sense of whether the source of error is the theory being tested or another aspect of the research.

3.5.2 The problem of theory preference

Popper's arguments for the deductive falsification of a theory can seem relatively unproblematic if it is assumed that only one theory for a problem exists at a time. As each theory is falsified, it is amended or discarded and so replaced by a new theory. However, in practice it is just as likely that there are two or more theories proposed as possible explanations for a particular phenomenon. If neither theory has (yet) been falsified – or, conversely, if both theories are known to be problematic but no other theory has been developed to replace them – then it is not clear how we should decide which is the best. Bouillon (1998) calls this the 'problem of theory preference'.

Haines-Young and Petch (1986) point out that geographers often work with two competing hypotheses, assessing them against each other (indeed, geographer Chamberlin first proposed the use of 'multiple working hypotheses' in 1890). These may take the following form, for example:

Hypothesis a): variable x has a direct effect on variable y

Hypothesis b): variable x has no direct effect on variable y

Hypothesis b), specifying no relationship, would normally be termed the 'null hypothesis', and hypothesis a), the 'alternative hypothesis'. Each effectively prohibits the observations that would corroborate the other, and so falsification of one of these hypotheses means that we can accept the other for the time being (unless or until further tests prove it false). This approach can help us to decide between theories, but it only works if all relevant theories can be judged using the same test. If that is not possible, we are left with no clear means of deciding between theories.

The problem of theory preference can also be illustrated with an example from biogeography. As Baker (2007) explains, examining two areas in two different regions of the world will reveal a different set of species in each, even if environmental conditions are similar. This was first noticed by French naturalist Comte de Buffon in 1761, and became known as Buffon's law. Baker summarises this law as: 'areas separated by natural barriers have distinct species' (p. 206). It was also known that there are some exceptions to this general law; 'cosmopolitan species' that can be found in two or more regions at long distances from each other. The problem was how to explain these two seemingly contradictory phenomena, and two competing theories were developed:

1. According to Charles Darwin and Alfred Russell Wallace, two causal mechanisms are involved. Firstly species migrate into new areas (dispersal). Through the process of evolution by natural selection, some of these species then become extinct and others adapt into new forms. Gradually, over a long period of time, different species develop in different places. The existence of cosmopolitan species can be explained by a notion of 'improbable dispersal'; transport assisted in rare circumstances by means such as wind or ocean currents or ice floes. Where this has occurred in the relatively recent past, leaving insufficient time for evolution by natural selection, the same species can be found in two locations at a distance from each other. Baker (2007) points out that this theory involves an assumption that the configuration of topographic features (such as mountain ranges) and oceans is stable.

2. Léon Croizat offered an alternative theory in the 1950s. Having studied the global distribution of species, his view was that species in different regions stemmed from a shared ancestral history. Rather than having dispersed through migration from a localised centre, this ancestral population was widespread over a large area but was subjected to spatially differing environmental changes across that area, leading to different evolutionary trajectories (Colacino and Grehan, 2003). Crucially, Croizat used theories that were emerging in geology at the time, arguing that tectonic change (such as continental drift, sea floor spreading and the uplift of mountain ranges) created natural barriers between populations that were once not so distant, and this was the main mechanism behind the existence of cosmopolitan species.

As Baker (2007) explains, at the time that Croizat put forward his theory there was insufficient geological evidence to really choose between the two, and 'both theories were very much in the running' (p. 209). Advances in geology since the 1950s have lent further weight to Croizat's theory, rather than to the Darwin-Wallace theory of dispersal.

Popper attempted to provide a means of identifying progress in science by proposing the concept of 'verisimilitude', the degree to which a theory approximates to the truth. In essence, this is the idea that a better theory is one that is closer to the truth than others, and so it could provide a means of deciding between competing theories as well. However, the concept of verisimilitude is still widely criticised, not least because it raises questions about how we know what 'truth' is (Heyt, 1999) and how we can tell when one theory is closer to it than another. Some argue that verisimilitude also involves an inductive argument, as claims about the degree to which a theory is close to the truth inevitably imply claims about unknown events and circumstances in the future, and so it is out of step with critical rationalism's anti-inductionism (Bird, 2000).

Other attempts to provide a means of distinguishing between competing theories have been made – Baker (2007) discusses 'Ockham's razor' (also written as 'Occam's razor'), a principle by which the theory involving the fewest assumptions is preferred. Given that our purpose here is to understand critical rationalism, it is sufficient to note that the problem of theory preference may not be easy to resolve.

3.5.3 The problem of what constitutes a 'severe test'

Key to critical rationalism is the idea of criticism, in that we should submit our scientific theories to serious attempts to falsify them. Popper was clear that where a test yielded results that support a theory, we should only accept such results as providing corroboration for the theory if they arise from a genuine attempt at falsification – that is, from a 'severe test' of the theory (Bortolotti, 2008). Mayo (2010; 2013) explains that one of the problems of critical rationalism is a lack of clarity around what constitutes a severe test. In essence, we have no definition or rules that enable us to demonstrate that a test is severe. Mayo (2010) argues that it is not sufficient that a test *could* reveal that a hypothesis is false by an expected result not occurring; in such circumstances, it might be that the result predicted by the hypothesis occurs, but for reasons that are nothing to do with (or only weakly related to) the original hypothesis. In such a case, the test has given us corroborating evidence for the theory, but the theory has not really been tested. This is illustrated in Box 3.3. This problem is still the subject of debate, Musgrave (2010) arguing that Mayo seems to want to believe that a theory which has not been falsified is 'true', which is not the critical rationalist position. To a critical rationalist, when a theory passes a test it simply means that the theory must be allowed to stand until it has been subjected to further testing. Either way, this problem emphasises the need for careful thought in research design, if we are to try to avoid the kind of problem illustrated in Box 3.3.

BOX 3.3   WHAT CONSTITUTES A 'SEVERE TEST' OF A THEORY?

Darren is a (fictional) geography student who is interested in the leisure activities of young people in rural areas. He develops a hypothesis (largely based on his own experience) that there is less skateboarding among 11–15-year-olds living in rural areas than in urban areas because the rural youths have more 'natural' open spaces, and so do other things instead. He designs a questionnaire for young people asking how they spend their leisure time and, with the cooperation of a school, he collects data from young people who live in five villages around the town of Slipford, and in Slipford itself. His results indicate that there certainly is more skateboarding activity among the young people who live in Slipford than among those who live in the rural locations. His data thus corroborate his theory, but was this a severe test of the theory?

The information not included in the description above is that there is a skate park in Slipford, but none of the villages has one. The rural 11–15-year-olds are too young to drive, they live too far from the town to cycle there, and bus fares are expensive. This means that their access to a suitable environment for skateboarding is limited. Does this change or confirm your view of Darren's test of his theory?

In this example, the hypothesis specifies a particular set of circumstances, and the research finds that those circumstances do occur. However, they occur for reasons that are not directly related to the hypothesis that Darren is trying to test. This was not a 'severe test' of the hypothesis – in fact, it was not really a test of the hypothesis at all.

The flaw in Darren's research was obvious when additional information was provided, but for some research it may not be obvious what the relevant additional information (or other factors) might be. That would make it much harder to identify whether or not a theory has stood up to a 'severe' test.

3.5.4 The social nature of scientific practice

Possibly the strongest criticism of Popper's ideas came from philosopher Thomas Kuhn (1922–1996). By Kuhn's thinking (see Chapter 6 for a more detailed discussion), Popper did not entirely recognise the significance of the scientific community, in that acceptance or rejection of a scientific theory is not solely determined by logic. Rather, the scientific community develops a particular frame of reference, a way of looking at the world, and scientific problems are determined and solved within that frame of reference. As inadequacies in that 'normal' way of looking at the world are revealed and accumulated, a crisis is reached whereby the taken-for-granted assumptions and principles underlying it are challenged. A new frame of reference, a new set of assumptions – in Kuhn's terminology, a new 'paradigm' – is needed, and such a shift represents a revolution in science. From this perspective, acceptance or rejection of a theory involves the scientific community making judgements about what kinds of problems are important and what kinds of theories count as explanations. According to Kuhn, the social influences of the research community are more pervasive than Popper accounted for.

3.6 Critical rationalism in summary

In developing critical rationalism, Karl Popper was prescribing how science should work. Rather than beginning with observations and trying to identify patterns in them (thereby revealing causal influences), as a positivist would advocate, Popper's view was that science is about subjecting our theories to rigorous testing. Regardless of where an idea for a theory stems from, science should proceed by using deductive logic (moving from the general to the specific) to make risky predictions from that theory, and then testing these predictions with empirical data. Popper recognised that all observations are theory-dependent. Crucially to his critical rationalism, all theories are open to critical debate, and such inter-subjective assessment is the root of science's objectivity.

Critical rationalism was promoted within physical geography in the 1980s (particularly by Haines-Young and Petch, 1986), and it is a mistake to assume that all quantitative geography is necessarily positivist. Positivism and critical rationalism are quite different; after all, Popper was openly critical of the logical positivists. In practice, though, it may be difficult to identify a piece of research as one or the other. Critical rationalism, as a prescription for how research *should* be done, is an ideal that does not entirely reflect how research *is* done. Geographers use a mixture of **induction, deduction**, and also **abduction** (sometimes referred to as 'inference to the best explanation'). Simandan (2012) points out that, for applied geographic research at least, the ever-changing nature of the world means that it would be impossible for us to rely on deductive reasoning alone. New situations arise, and new information becomes relevant. As the world changes, our ideas must change.

FURTHER READING

For further explanations

Haines-Young, R.H. and Petch, J.R. (1981) 'Causal and functional relationships in geomorphology: a reply', *Earth Surface Processes* 6: 207–9.

Haines-Young, R.H. and Petch, J.R. (1983) 'Multiple working hypotheses: equifinality and the study of landforms', *Transactions of the Institute of British Geographers* 8 (4): 458–66.

Haines-Young, R.H. and Petch, J.R. (1986) *Physical Geography: Its Nature and Methods.* London: Harper & Row Ltd. [Note that this is now out of print, but your University library may have it.]

Popper, K.R. (1974) *Conjectures and Refutations: The Growth of Scientific Knowledge,* 5th edition. Abingdon: Routledge. [The first chapter after the Introduction provides a good summary.]

Progress in Human/Physical Geography resources

Bassett, K. (1999) 'Is there progress in human geography? The problem of progress in the light of recent work in the philosophy and sociology of science', *Progress in Human Geography* 23 (1): 27–47. doi: 10.1191/030913299669363669. [This is a broad-ranging discussion, but refers to Popper's critical rationalism among others.]

Bird, J. (1977) 'Methodology and philosophy', *Progress in Human Geography* 1 (1): 103–10. doi: 10.1177/030913257700100106.

Edwards, K.J. (1983) 'Quaternary palynology: consideration of a discipline', *Progress in Physical Geography* 7 (1): 113–25. doi: 10.1177/030913338300700106.

Haines-Young, R.H. and Petch, J.R. (1980) 'The challenge of critical rationalism for methodology in physical geography', *Progress in Physical Geography* 4 (1): 63–77. doi: 10.1177/030913338000400104.

Moss, R.P. (1977) 'Deductive strategies in geographical generalization', *Progress in Human Geography* 1 (1): 23–39. doi: 10.1177/030913337700100103.

Examples

Blekesaune, A. and Rønningen, K. (2010) 'Bears and fears: cultural capital, geography and attitudes towards large carnivores in Norway', *Norsk Geografisk Tidsskrift – Norwegian Journal of Geography* 64: 185–98. [This paper sets out some theoretical background from literature and develops hypotheses. Its conclusions are not overtly written in a critical rationalist framing though.]

Brantley, S.L., Megonigal, J.P., Scatena, F.N., Balogh-Brunstad, Z., Barnes, R.T., Bruns, M.A., van Cappellen, P., Dontsova, K., Hartnett, H.E., Hartshorn, A.S., Heimsath, A., Herndon, E., Jin, L., Keller, CK., Leake, J.R., McDowell, W.H., Meinzer, F.C., Mozdzer, T.J., Petsch, S., Pett-Ridge, J., Pregitzer, K.S., Raymond, P.A., Riebe, C.S., Shumaker, K., Sutton-Grier, A., Walter, R. and Yoo, K. (2011) 'Twelve testable hypotheses on the geobiology of weathering', *Geobiology* 9: 140–65. [This is not an example of critical rationalism in practice, but presents a review of the geobiology and promotes particular strands of research, implicitly assuming a critical realist approach.]

Gundelach, B. and Freitag, M. (2014) 'Neighbourhood diversity and social trust: an empirical analysis of interethnic contact and group-specific effect', *Urban Studies* 51 (6): 1236–56.

Marxism and Critical Realism: Seeking What Lies Beneath

...the problems of nature, of space, and of uneven development are tied together by capital itself. (Smith, 1984/2010, p. 8)

This quote from geographer Neil Smith (1954-2012) offers a nice start for this chapter because it points at two things: firstly, at Marxist geography's core concern to understand how economic production shapes places, spaces and lives; secondly, in his reference to 'nature' Smith hints that this is a mode of thought which can begin to connect human and physical geography. As Marxian **political economy** came to dominate human geography, the emergence of **political ecology** in the 1980s offered a means of understanding issues of human-induced environmental degradation and associated inequalities. The influence of Roy Bhaskar's **critical realism** followed Marxism in the discipline, gaining favour with human geographers in the 1980s and physical geographers in the 1990s.

Marxism and critical realism are treated in a single chapter here because of an underlying similarity, in that both are concerned to identify the structures behind events in the world. However, it is worth noting that the exact nature of the relation between the two is contested, with similarities, differences and compatibilities identified by different commentators. Some of this debate may be due to a difference in focus: Fleetwood (in Brown et al., 2001) points out that critical realism is 'located at the level of philosophy' (p. 2), whereas Marxism places more emphasis on **theory** and political practice. Nevertheless, it is clear that Bhaskar was influenced by Marx. It is also not unusual for geographers to frame their work as both Marxist and critical realist. This chapter aims to provide introduction to both of these theories sufficient to draw out the philosophical similarities, in order to examine the methodologies appropriate to this spectrum of thought.

4.1 Marxism

In the twenty-first century it is not uncommon for students to have to work through their degree, earning money to pay rent and bills, and to buy food, clothes, entertainment and books. You might work in a fast food outlet, a shop, or a factory; you might be cleaning offices, serving behind a bar, or driving a delivery van. According to Marxists, whatever the nature of the job, if you work for a private company (as opposed to, say, a charity or government department) then the value of the work you do is more than you are paid. If your employer had to give you every pound, dollar or euro that your labour made, then he or she would be just as well off without you, and without going to all the bother of employing someone. So your work produces value over and above the amount you are paid, and this 'surplus labour' is the source of your employer's profit. Equally, you having that job is dependent upon your employer owning the shop, factory, bar or restaurant where you work. There is a basic inequality here: your employer owns the means of creating wealth, and that wealth is created through the surplus labour provided by you and any other employees. This inequality is fundamental to capitalist societies.

Karl Marx (1818–1883) was trained as a philosopher but turned his attention to economics and politics in his mid-twenties. He was a prolific writer whose works (including some produced in collaboration with Friedrich Engels) have been influential in many disciplines and have given rise to a variety of competing theories and political programmes (Brown et al., 2001). Marx argued that the foundation of a society is its 'mode of production'. To understand a society, we need to understand how it produces the means of survival (such as food and shelter) and, beyond that, how it produces wealth. Throughout history, different modes of production have given rise to different social structures, such as feudal societies, slave societies, capitalist societies and communist societies. This is a **materialist** position, assuming that human uses of the physical (material) world provide the basis for understanding the character of whole societies.

In *Capital* (volume I, first published in 1867) Marx undertook an analysis of capitalist commodity production, identifying that it is dependent on two things: the 'relations of production' and the market. The relations of production have been identified above, in that some people in society (the capitalists) own the means of production, for example in the form of machinery, land and know-how, while others (the workers) provide the labour. But once a commodity is produced it needs a market. The products of labour must be sold, and sold for more than the workers have been paid to produce them, in order for the capitalist to make a profit. The competitive nature of the market means that she or he cannot sell products for more than other companies are selling comparable products; if you can buy a pair of jeans for £30 from one shop you are unlikely to spend £40 on the same jeans in another shop. The capitalist can drop the price of his/her product to undercut competing companies, but can only do so to a limited extent, as the workers still need to be paid for their labour and a profit still needs to be made. The only way to drop the price of the commodity without losing profit is to reduce the labour costs. It is therefore in the capitalist's interests to constantly seek new ways of reducing labour costs, for example through new technology. The introduction of self-service check-outs in UK supermarkets in recent years is one illustration of this. Where every till once had a member of staff at it, one member of staff can oversee 4, 6 or 8 self-service tills, reducing the need for so many employees. In this way, Marx pointed out, capitalism involves an inherent conflict of interests between worker and capital-ist, with every employer working labourers as hard as they can or for as little pay as possible. Fundamentally, capitalism generates exploitative social relations.

For Marx, the means of production (productive forces; the machines etc. that are the engines of production) and the associated social relations (the relations of pro-duction) provide the foundations or 'base' of society. This then gives rise to society's 'superstructure', which encompasses facets such as politics, law, religion, media, culture; all the things inherent to our daily lives. Marx argued that the superstructure tends to normalise the relations inherent within the economic structure. In other words, the TV and movies we watch, the magazines and newspapers we read, the sports teams we follow, are all artefacts arising from the base, but all reproduce its norms and values. The result is that the exploitative relations inherent in capitalism go unnoticed, appearing to us simply as the way the world is. As Harman (2000) explains, to Marx and Engels explanations of society must *begin with* the means of material production, even though they appear to be just one realm among others. These give rise to social relations (or social forms), which in turn give rise to forms of consciousness (ideas).

This is a simplified version of a very large and complex body of work, but it is enough to highlight two important points. Firstly, Marx's work is essentially **realist**, accepting that the world exists independently of our minds. Although his ideas are **materialist**, in the notion that society is shaped by its material conditions, he was critical of earlier forms of materialism, arguing that they ignored the active role of human subjects. For Marx, people can make their own history and geography to a considerable degree. He was also critical of **idealism**. Marx agreed that humans intervene in and transform the world, but argued that we do so through our mat-erial actions, not our thoughts. Secondly, his realism is essentially **structuralist**. In seeking to explain society we need to look to the structure (of modes and relations of production) that underlies appearances.

Methodologically, the key to Marx's work is his process of **abstraction**. In every-day we life we tend to use the term 'abstract' to mean something vague, or contrasting with 'concrete' reality. This is not what Marx meant by abstraction. Marxian abstraction is a process by which we isolate a particular aspect of a phe-nomenon in thought, analysing it in depth. Ollman (2003) provides a good explanation of this (albeit across several chapters). He stresses Marx's emphasis on processes and relations. Capitalism, for example, is not just how capitalism *appears* and how it *functions*. Marx's understanding of capitalism also encompasses processes of change, past and future. In other words, how capitalism has developed and its tendencies (Ollman cites the tendencies towards concentration and centralisation) are seen by Marx as integral parts of the phenomenon that is capitalism. Similarly, the inherent relations (for example, between capitalist and labourer) are seen as integral to capitalism. Abstraction is a way of thinking that draws attention to such processes and relations. The starting point is always the real, 'concrete' phenomenon. Through abstraction, we break the phenomenon down into parts, carefully identifying the processes and relations at work. Ollman (2003) identifies four kinds of relations, as a way of aiding abstraction:

1. Identity/difference, establishing similarities and differences between things. This is, in its simplest form, 'common sense' abstraction, in that we use it every day to think about the world around us, classifying and distinguishing cars from buses, uncles from aunts, or pets from wild animals. Marx goes beyond this 'either/or' binary, to establish *both* identity and difference. Dogs and cats are different, but both are pets, which involves a particular kind of relation to humans.

2. Interpenetration of opposites. This is a recognition that one phenomenon may appear very differently (even opposite) from a different perspective. A two-week holiday on a Greek Island may be a relaxing break, but for the workers in the hotels, restaurants, bars and nightclubs it is just another two weeks in their six months of seven-days-a-week, 14-hours-a-day, working season. Recognising these different perspectives is not to suggest that reality is dependent on perspective. Rather, it highlights the real relations between holidaymakers and those working in the tourism industry.

3. Quantity and quality, as two 'moments' in the same process. The development of UK indie rock bank the Arctic Monkeys provides an example. They began playing local gigs to small audiences around Sheffield in 2003. Having recorded some songs onto writable CDs, their fans began to file-share these, so more and more people found their songs on the Internet. This is quantitative change. The band's first single then reached the top of the UK charts, and their first album was one of the fastest selling albums of all time (Rolling Stone, undated). In 2013 the Arctic Monkeys were one of the headline acts at the Glastonbury Festival, the world's largest green-field music festival. Gradual quantitative change led to a qualitative change in status, from little-known cult to mainstream.

4. Contradiction. The classic Marxian example here is the capitalist always seeking to reduce labour costs, but the labourer seeking a wage sufficient to live on. The two tendencies work against each other. It is in the capitalist's interests to ensure that the labourer is paid enough to live and retain health, in order to be able to work. It is also in the capitalist's interests to decrease costs in order to maximise profit.

Each of these four kinds of relations involves some kind of 'opposite' or tension (sameness and difference; opposing perspectives; quality and quantity; contradicting forces). This mode of examining first one thing, then its (seemingly) opposite, to arrive at a third understanding, is referred to as **'dialectical'** thinking. Guided by these kinds of notions, then, dialectic abstraction moves beyond identifying the obvious, to a deep examination of processes and relations. Putting all of the abstracted elements back together then moves us to what Ollman (2003) calls 'thought concrete'. That is, the whole phenomenon (rather than the abstracted parts) as we understand it in our theory. This theory thus offers us a window through which we can see our everyday lives differently from how they appear.

4.2 Marxism in geography

The description of Marxism above really focuses only on one aspect of Karl Marx's work, but it is sufficient to provide a starting point for understanding Marxist geographies. We have seen that capitalism is inherently contradictory. On the one hand, capitalism acts to maximise profit, pursuing profit for its own sake. Market competition between companies ensures that the capitalist must seek to reduce costs in order to maintain or maximise profit, and this cost reduction often takes place through technical innovation and mechanisation. On the other hand, significant technical innovation can result in workers being made redundant, which then reduces the market for commodities as redundant workers cannot afford to buy them. This inherent contradiction periodically results in a 'crisis of over-accumulation', with pools of workers unemployed and pools of commodities unused (Castree, 2011). Global recession in the 1930s and again from 2008 can be seen as examples of such crises. However, Marx's analysis of capitalism focused on its historical development, and was essentially 'a-spatial'. Marxist geographers, led by David Harvey, demonstrated that the contradictions of capitalism also have spatial dimensions.

In 1969 Harvey published *Explanation in Geography*, a treatise on the scientific approach to geography that was characteristic of **positivist** spatial science (see Chapter 2 on positivism). By 1973, Harvey was on a different tack altogether. The emphasis of positivist science on observable phenomena meant that, to Harvey, such geography could only ever describe surface problems. It lacked any means to offer explanation for those problems. In *Social Justice and the City* (1973), Harvey drew on Marx's writings to explore the causes of social conditions in cities. In doing so, he challenged the (positivist) notion that 'facts' are distinct from 'values' (a dichotomoy that is further discussed in Chapter 9), and argued instead for a more politically moti-vated and engaged geography. Harvey continued to develop his Marxist geography throughout the 1970s, producing another landmark text, *The Limits to Capital*, in 1982. Castree (2011, p. 235) describes this as 'nothing less than a reconstruction and exten-sion of Marx's theory of capitalism', the extension being primarily geographical.

The big risk presented by economic crisis – aside from loss of profit – is that it may lead to political instability and social chaos. In *The Limits to Capital* Harvey identified that the risk of a crisis occurring in the first place could be temporarily staved off by investment of capital. Profitable companies can invest surplus finance in long-term and short-term savings, enabling banks to lend funds to start-up companies. Similarly, finance can be invested in stocks and shares in emerging economies. Such activities tie up capital, removing it from circulation by investing it in future commodity production and profit (Castree, 2008). Harvey referred to this as the 'temporal fix'.

Similarly, the circulation of capital requires a built environment, consisting of the factories (environments of production), shopping malls (environments of consumption), homes for the workers (environments of reproduction), and means of transporting goods (environments of distribution and communication). Such environments are expensive to develop, and this kind of investment only yields returns in the long term. This means that periodic 'splurges' of investment (Castree, 2011) in the built environment also tie up surplus capital, removing it from circulation. However, this kind of infrastructure can be costly to replace, and later on this can present a barrier to further investment. Periodically, it becomes more economical to move investment out of developed towns and into less developed or run-down areas. Harvey calls this the 'spatial fix', and this means that spatial inequalities are as much a part of capitalism as inequalities in social status. Capitalism 'produces' space, rather than simply operating within it.

Neil Smith, once a student of Harvey, added to this understanding of space as central to capitalism in his (1984) book, *Uneven Development*. This book addresses both political economy and society/nature relations, explaining that both nature and space are socially produced. Among these ideas, Smith explained that capitalism has contradictory tendencies towards spatial differentiation and spatial equalisation. Differentiation occurs through the differentiation of labour. To some degree this may be influenced by the natural environment, in that cotton production (for example) is easier in some places than others, and coal production is possible in some places and not others. Smith also pointed out the rural/urban differentiation between industry and agriculture. Another example would be the regional concentration of particular industries, such as the automobile industry that developed around Coventry and Birmingham in the UK, or Detroit in the US. Similarly, high-tech industries are associated with the West Coast in the US, and the 'golden triangle' of Oxford–Cambridge–London.

At the same time, the capitalist drive for continued profit has a globalising impulse, constantly expanding markets. This brings a tendency towards equalisation of the conditions of production and level of development of productive forces, in the universalisation of the wage–labour relation. Improved efficiency of production in one sector requires improved efficiency in other, related sectors. Here Smith (1984) cites Marx's example of the mechanisation of spinning, which necessitated the mechanisation of weaving, and the two together provided impetus for the mechanical and chemical revolution in dyeing. Similarly, the development of the computer industry triggered revolutions in microelectronics. If labour is spatially differentiated, then capitalist relations are spatially diffuse, places interconnected with other places through market relations, an equalising force.

David Harvey and Neil Smith were thus influential in arguing that space is not just a 'container' within which things happen. Space is produced by social processes and practices, and those processes and practices are shaped by space. This also means that space – or geographical phenomena – could be theorised, rather than geography being restricted to empirical investigations of seemingly contingent (place- and time-specific) phenomena.

Marxian political economy became somewhat dominant in human geography in the 1970s and 1980s, and Castree (2011) explains that Harvey (in particular) established a precedent for radical geography more generally in being politically motivated and engaged. This paved the way for geographers to respond to the oppression or marginalisation of other social groups, defined by gender, sexuality and ethnicity. More recently geographers' attentions turned elsewhere. Hudson (2006) suggests this was driven by three factors: recognition of limitations of Marxist thought, with concern that it neglected social divisions other than class; a desire among newly qualified geographers to establish their own intellectual territories and make their own mark on the discipline; and a perception that engagement in such overtly political work may not be conducive to career progression. Phillips (2008) and Castree (2008) point out that Marxist geographies can be seen as aspiring to meta-theory, a 'grand theory' that seeks to explain everything, and this kind of aim fell out of favour with the development of postmodern geographies (Chapter 7). Nevertheless, Hudson (2006) and others emphasise that Marxian political economy still has value for human/economic geography, and Glassman (2011) describes the interweaving of Marxian political economy and postcolonial theory as providing fruitful insights in development geography.

The account presented here is rather singular, and it is worth pointing out that there is probably no such thing as 'Marxist geography'. Rather, there is a range of different approaches influenced by Marxian ideas (Castree, 1994). A further strand that developed from the 1980s fused Marxian political economy with studies of environmental issues; **political ecology** addresses the intersections between capitalist production, politics and the environment. This move was pioneered by Piers Blaikie's (1985) study of soil erosion, based primarily on work in Nepal, with Blaikie and Brookfield's following *Land Degradation and Society* (1987) often cited as a key text. Forsyth (2008) argues that Blaikie's key contribution was to reorient thinking about environmental policy, in that 'rather than seeking to demonstrate how a particular approach to "politics" could be applied to predefined notions of "environment", Blaikie sought instead to demonstrate how social values and environmental knowledge are co-produced' (pp. 756–7). Issues of inequality, justice, poverty and exploitation are central to political ecology (Walker, 2006). An example of political ecology research is discussed later in the chapter. Next, though, we consider an example of research that illustrates the intersections of capitalist production and space.

4.2.1 The globalisation of wine production

If you browse the wine section of your local supermarket, probably in most cases you will find some degree of geographical organisation and labelling of the shelves. White wines are usually separated from red, of course, but within either of those, French wines will be grouped together, Chilean wines grouped in a different area, and South African wines grouped separately again. Wine is a globalised commodity, yet one in which place clearly matters.

Overton et al. (2012) present a very readable account of the globalisation of the wine industry. They begin with themes characteristic of Marxian political economy, although without mentioning Marx directly. Wine is described as almost universal, consumed by a range of social classes. As an example of globalised agribusiness, the value chains of wine production extend across the globe, yet at the same time are grounded in specific places, and the lives of specific rural communities. Wine manufacturing involves a range of modes of production. At one end of the spectrum, small-scale and labour-intensive peasant production is largely for subsistence; at the other, large-scale industrial production is the domain of global multi-beverage corporations.

According to Overton et al., wine has symbolic value. It is not just about drinking alcohol, but is often associated with sophistication and affluence. At the same time, throughout much of Western and Southern Europe wine is cheap, and so accessible to the poor. It is inclusive and exclusive at once, with a high degree of price differentiation. 'Place' is central to this.

In contrast with other products such as cars or beer, wine is considered to be place-specific in two important ways. Firstly, grapes (the raw material) are thought to vary in flavour on the basis of local environmental characteristics such as soil, slope and climate. Secondly, there is a widespread acceptance that different places make different wines in different ways. These natural and cultural differences come together in the notion of *terroir*, whereby place is seen as a distinctive element of the quality of wine. Place is even central to the legal description of wine in France, through the *appellation d'origine contrôlée* (AOC) system. An AOC designation is an indicator of the origin, quality and often even style of a wine, protecting 'the label and the integrity of the wine's geographical origin' (Overton et al., 2012, p. 276).

The notion of *terroir* is said to divide the global wine industry in two. There are producers who operate on the basis that place is important, and reinforce this through geographical descriptors on their wine labels. Such producers are associated with production techniques and styles of wine that have evolved in a particular region. These are usually small- to medium-sized enterprises, using artisanal methods, emphasising the individuality of wines and wine-makers, and targeting the higher end of the wine market. Their marketing strategies use stories and myths that align with this image of place specificity.

Other producers do not use the *terroir* concept explicitly, although they may still identify the geographical origin of their wines, at least at a regional scale. For these producers, the emphasis is on 'modern' and 'industrial' methods of wine-making that produce a consistent product at an affordable price.

Overton et al. then turn their attention to the globalisation of wine production. Here they identify two contradictory, yet connected, features of wine production worldwide: concentration and spread.

Concentration is associated with the notion of *terroir*. In most globalised markets producers will necessarily seek to minimise the costs of labour and raw materials, locating their production where it is cheapest. In contrast, wine-makers want to be associated with the locations that are known for producing the best grapes. Upgrading in the global value chain is achieved by concentrating in particular locations and qualitatively refining production. In New Zealand, trade reform in the mid-1980s exposed the national wine industry to international competition. This led to a shift in production from 'bulk white varieties' (cheap and largely sweet) to a focus on new varieties and styles that proved popular in an international market. New Zealand's wine export had increased from 0.8 million litres in 1985 to 112.6 million litres in 2009, with almost two thirds of the total national production being Sauvignon Blanc, and just over two thirds from the Marlborough region. Concentration is space differentiation. Capitalism *produces* space.

While some subsectors of the global wine industry have shifted towards concentration, industrialised wine-making has seen a tendency towards spreading. An increase in demand for 'moderately priced' wine is 'associated with the rise of the middle classes, economic growth, wine tourism, and increased travel' (Overton et al., 2012, p. 278). New vineyards tend to be associated with this mass market production. In Australia, a focus on reliability of product and low production costs led to an increase in vineyard area of 143 per cent in ten years. China has similarly experienced a rapid expansion of vineyards.

In the 'old world' wine regions of Europe there have also been comparable shifts. France, for example, has experienced both concentration of wine production into the AOC regions, moving away from the cheaper end of the market, *and* an expansion of production in some areas outside of the AOC regions. These latter wine-makers are utilising methods and producing styles more characteristic of the large Australian wine producers, targeting international markets.

Specialisation and homogenisation have thus occurred simultaneously in the global wine industry. Global companies are prominent, but they retain regionally distinctive brands within a multi-national portfolio. Overton et al. (2012, p. 283) conclude that 'The evolution of the global wine sector illustrates the dialectical and often contradictory nature of globalization, as well as making clear the centrality and importance of geography in the evolution of the space-economy… space is differentiated, scale is collapsed, and place reconstructed.'

EXERCISE 4.1

The political economy of aggregates extraction: 'Pits, quarries and climate change'

Sandberg and Wallace (2013) use political economy and Actor Network Theory (which is described in Chapter 5) to consider the global aggregates extraction industry. Read their article and try to answer the following questions:

1) Why is aggregates extraction considered to be an important (integral) part of the global capitalist economy?

2) Companies in the aggregates industry often emphasise their efforts to reduce carbon emissions during the production of aggregates products, and to restore/rehabilitate land once a quarry is abandoned. Why is this described as 'environmental rhetoric'? What would need to be included for a fuller picture of environmental impact?

3) What is the 'spatial fix' described in the paper, and what is it 'fixing'?

4) The authors discuss examples of aggregate extraction in India, Southern Ontario, and Northern Scotland. Although they do not explain it directly in these terms, their analysis reveals the contradictory tendencies of spatial differentiation and equalisation that Neil Smith identified as inherent in capitalism. How are these tendencies manifest in the aggregates industry?

Sandberg and Wallace's paper is freely available online, with a link to it on the companion website, along with answers to the questions. The full reference for the paper is:

Sandberg, L.A. and Wallace, L. (2013) 'Leave the sand in the land, let the stone alone: pits, quarries and climate change', *ACME: An International E-Journal for Critical Geographies* 12 (1): 65–87.

4.3 Critical realism

Bhaskar's **critical realism** became popular in Anglo–American human geography in the 1980s, with Andrew Sayer being particularly influential in its promotion. Physical geographers picked up on critical realism a little later, Keith Richards (1990) first demonstrating its potential within geomorphology. While Bhaskar's influence has probably been greatest in the social sciences (Collier, 1994), it is important to appreciate that critical realism represents a combination of two (related) sets of ideas: Bhaskar's (1975) philosophy of science, which he termed 'transcendental realism', and his (1979) philosophy of social science, 'critical naturalism'. Others later combined the two terms into 'critical realism' (Bhaskar, 1998).

Much of Bhaskar's writing makes for difficult reading, and it is perhaps because of this that accounts of critical realism within geography can also be somewhat confusing. Clarity is not helped by a tendency among geographers to refer simply to 'realism', without explicitly identifying that they mean critical realism (examples include Richards, 1990, 1999; Rhoads and Thorn, 1992; Harrison, 2001; Hubbard et al., 2002; Holt-Jensen, 2009). This has led to some misinterpretations and misunderstandings (such as the exchange between Lawson and Staeheli, 1991, and Chappell, 1991). Rhoads and Thorn (1994) go so far as to claim that scientific realism is 'normally' associated with critical realism. This may be true among geographers, but Bhaskar's work does not really feature in mainstream philosophy of science so it seems less true elsewhere. An ability to identify critical realism by its constituent principles and assumptions is therefore helpful in interpreting the geographical literature. The following sections provide introductions to Bhaskar's transcendental realism (in the natural sciences) and critical naturalism (in the social sciences) in turn, before further considering their influence and use within geography.

4.3.1 Transcendental realism: Understanding science

The positivists (see Chapter 2) had been concerned with questions about the *source* of our knowledge, and Popper (see Chapter 3 on critical rationalism) was concerned about the *validity* of our knowledge. Roy Bhaskar adopted a different starting point again, asking 'how must the world be, for science to be possible?'

To start with, Bhaskar argued that the **empiricist** view, which assumes that the world is as we experience it, is mistaken. This confuses our knowledge with the world, effectively saying that if we do not know something, it does not exist. This is the 'empiricist fallacy'. While science is a social activity and scientific knowledge is a social product, it is crucial to remember that sometimes our scientific knowledge is mistaken. Our capacity to make mistakes in science must mean that the *object* of our knowledge is independent of what we know about it. This led Bhaskar to the idea that science has two dimensions:

- The *intransitive* dimension consists of the objects of scientific knowledge, which exist independently of us. It is when we notice a mismatch between the objects of science and our knowledge that we realise our mistakes. These objects are unchanging (hence the term, 'intransitive').

- The *transitive* dimension to science lies in the theories, ideas, paradigms, methods and techniques that we use to understand the world. These are our constructions, and they may be developed, modified or replaced over time, as our understanding changes. Even 'facts' reside in the transitive dimension, as what we consider to be a fact is determined by us.

If the objects of science are independent of our knowledge of them, it follows that there must be events that we do not perceive. If Bhaskar had been asked the question, 'Does a tree falling in the woods make a sound if there is no one to hear it?', he would surely have answered that it does.

Bhaskar focused his attention on experimental science, and noted that experiments involve scientists controlling conditions to make some 'event' happen. In effect, the scientist creates a **closed system**, isolating particular phenomena from the messiness of the natural world in order to understand them. The core of a laboratory experiment is often the production of a pattern of events, enabling us to see how events relate to each other (in other words, 'if we do X, then Y happens'). In the **open systems** of the natural world the same pattern of events rarely, if ever, occurs. There would be no need for the experiment if it did. However, we then assume that what we learn from the experiment tells us something about what happens in the world. Indeed, the value of the experiment rests on this kind of translation being possible. An example is provided by flume experiments in fluvial geomorphology, such as those performed by Papanicolaou et al. (2011) to examine the effects of submerged gravel clasts on bedload transport in high gradient streams. Working in the laboratory the researchers were able to control the flume gradient, discharge and bed materials (size and packing density), and then examine the streambed sediment transport rates and occurrences, and the bedforms that developed as a result. These bedforms and sediment transport behaviours are the 'events' observed. While recognising limitations to their work and the need for further experiments, the researchers then highlight the potential utility of their work to stream restoration design. This kind of claim can only be based on an assumption that the laboratory results bear some relation to processes operating naturally. An important point here is that Papanicolaou et al. created the conditions in which particular events occurred, but they did not create the events themselves. The fact that they did not create these events suggests that there is some mechanism at work that is independent of the researchers, which *did* cause the events to happen. Given that we can use experiments to learn something about the world, the mechanisms at work in experiments must also operate naturally. These causal mechanisms provide the connection between the controlled, closed system of the experiment and the open systems of the world around us. Whether or not the events observed in the experiment actually happen in nature will depend on the particular conditions (including other mechanisms at work) in particular places at particular times – the contingent conditions.

Putting all of this together (the transitive and intransitive dimensions of science, and the possibility of experimental science), Bhaskar argued that there are three 'domains' of reality:

- The 'real', consisting of mechanisms (or tendencies) with the potential to produce events;

- The 'actual', consisting of events caused by those mechanisms in particular circumstances;

- The 'empirical', consisting of our observations of events.

Events may occur without us observing them, and mechanisms may exist without resulting in actual events (if contingent conditions are not conducive to the events). To Bhaskar, the ultimate goal of science must be to understand the causal mechanisms that generate the events we experience. In order to do this, he suggests that science utilises a dialectical method, whereby: i) a regularity is identified on the basis of empirical experience; ii) a possible explanation (causal mechanism) is proposed, and; iii) the reality of this explanation is checked against further empirical evidence. Bhaskar goes on to explain that reality is structured and differentiated. Starting with empirical experience, we identify the causal mechanism accounting for the particular event(s) of interest, but then that raises questions about a 'deeper' level of casual mechanisms or tendencies to explain the mechanisms we have identified. Through an iterative process, then, we gradually achieve deeper explanation (noting that 'deeper' does not mean 'more true' or 'more accurate'). This deeper explanation posits unobservable causal mechanisms that can explain observed events.

4.3.2 Critical naturalism: A cautious application of natural science methods to social science

Having examined the natural sciences, Bhaskar then tackled the question of whether society can be studied in the same way. As before, his analysis hinged upon consideration of how the world – in this case, society – is, that we can know it. He identified three broad conceptual models of society commonly used by others, and considered the problems presented by each.

Model I is an individualistic conception of society, in which social phenomena are considered to be the result of the intentional actions of individual people. This is a position characteristic of Max Weber's sociology. The problem, as Bhaskar points out, is that explanations for our actions as individuals always presuppose social structures or phenomena: 'A tribesman implies a tribe, the cashing of a cheque a banking system' (Bhaskar, 1989, p. 209).

Model II is a collectivist conception of society. Here the emphasis is on social phenomena, which exist 'externally' to individuals and exert a coercive, controlling or conditioning force on them. Things happen in society the way they do precisely because of the social structures that exist. To be a student you need a subject to study; to sell something you need a market. Moreover, your position in society largely determines what you do (Collier, 1994): if you want to be a student, you need to study. The problem here is that this can result in reification – a kind of 'thingification', where abstract concepts are seen as real entities. The 'market' is nothing more than the result of lots of individual actions of exchange, and it cannot exist independently of those individual actions. Similarly, an academic subject such as geography is the result of many individual acts of knowledge production and exchange. Model II is said to be characteristic of Durkheim's sociology.

Model III represents an attempt to find a middle ground between these, but it is an attempt that Bhaskar argues is misguided. This is a dialectical model, whereby society influences individual actions, which influence society, which influences individual

actions, and so on and so on. This sounds as though it makes sense, but it implies a
linear sequence of causes switching from one to the other (Bhaskar, 1979/2005) and,
in doing so, it diminishes the relative autonomy of each (Harvey, 2002).

Bhaskar argues that, instead, societies and people are two distinct kinds of entity,
both existing at the same time, and each influencing the other. Our actions are
always in the context of social structures that pre-exist, but our actions have the
effect of reproducing or transforming those structures. People do not work to reproduce a capitalist economy, and people do not get married to reproduce the nuclear
family, but the reproduction of these social structures is the effect of our individual
acts of working and marrying. Collier (1994, p. 146) illustrates this using the example of language:

> Unless we have learnt a pre-existent language with rules that exist inde-
> pendently of us we could not talk at all (structure as condition). We talk
> not as a rule to reproduce or transform the language but for personal
> ends of which we are conscious (practice as production). But our lan-
> guage only continues to exist because we talk, for it has no existence
> apart from people talking (structure as outcome).

Bhaskar (1979/2005) calls his model the 'Transformational Model of Social
Activity'.

We saw earlier that transcendental realism recognises three domains of reality: the
real, the actual and the empirical. For the study of society, the 'real' consists in social
structures; the 'actual' in the actions of individuals; and the 'empirical' is observed
phenomena (Table 4.1). This parallel in the structuring and differentiation of the
natural and social worlds gives us the 'naturalism' in critical naturalism: the notion
that the ideas of natural science apply to social phenomena. The 'critical' lies in
recognition that there are limits to naturalism, and Bhaskar emphasises three:

1. Unlike in the natural sciences, where 'mechanisms' (the real) operate inde-
    pendently of 'events' (the actual), social structures are *not* independent of the
    activities they govern.

2. Social structures are also *not* independent of agents' (people's) conceptions of
    what they are doing in their activities. The purpose or function of our social
    structures is determined by us.

3. In the natural sciences, the mechanisms of the 'real' are timeless, enduring,
    intransient. Social structures, in contrast, are only *relatively* enduring, because
    they can be transformed by our activities. This allows for history and change,
    and it means that social science explanations are always space- and time-specific.

These three caveats mean that there are real differences between the natural sciences
and the social sciences, as well as parallels. Ultimately, the aim of both is to identify
the generative mechanisms or causal structures at work.

Table 4.1 Comparison of the natural sciences (transcendental realism) and social sciences (critical naturalism)

	Natural science	**Social science**
Real	Mechanisms	Social structures
Actual	Events	Actions
Empirical	Observations	Observations
Intransitive dimension	Objects of science	Social relations
Transitive dimension	Our knowledge (theories, facts, paradigms, etc.)	Our knowledge (including the knowledge held by the individuals or groups being studied)

4.4 Critical realist geographies

We noted earlier in the chapter that critical realism became popular within human geography in the 1980s, spreading to physical geography in the 1990s. A number of possible reasons for this popularity have been proposed. Rose (1990) identifies critical realists' insistence on the 'ontological depth' of the social world as a particular strength, moving beyond the (superficial) observable phenomena that provide the focus of positivist and critical rationalist studies. A degree of affinity with Marxist approaches added to the attraction. Both seek to understand structures, tendencies and relations, and critical realism lent itself to investigation of themes of class, gender, race and ethnicity, and their production, combination and reproduction in specific contexts and places. Johnston and Sidaway (2004) and Roberts (2001) identify critical realism as offering a critique of both **positivist** and **humanistic** geographies, overcoming a seemingly intractable opposition between them. Critical realism allows for both structure and agency, recognising the interactions of the two.

For physical geographers, Richards (1990) suggested that many geomorphologists were already working in a critical realist vein, but the conscious emphasis on explanatory power rather than predictive success was seen as welcome. Richards et al. (2002) point out that critical realism enabled human and physical geographers to explore common methodological values. Indeed, the potential for making connections between the two halves of geography is not simply methodological. Like social systems, the natural systems of interest to physical geographers are open systems, requiring explanation at an appropriate scale, along with recognition of contingent, space-time-specific, influences (Richards, 1990; Lane and Richards, 1997).

4.5 Critical realism in practice

Methodologically, critical realism demands a combination of abstraction with both intensive (case study) and extensive empirical research. Abstraction, as we saw in

Marxism, involves isolating a particular aspect or dimension of the object of interest in thought, thereby distinguishing between its essential and incidental characteristics. This could include identifying different kinds of relations between objects: *substantial* relations of connection and interaction; and *formal* relations of similarity or dissimilarity (Sayer, 1992). As a student you have substantial relations with the academics who teach you, interacting with them in the exchange of ideas. In this you share a similarity (a formal relation) with other students elsewhere, though you may have no direct connection or interaction with those students individually.

Similarly, abstraction may involve distinguishing between 'internal' and 'necessary' relations, and 'external' and 'contingent' relations. Your relation with the chair you are sitting on is external and contingent, as both you and the chair would exist without the relation between you. A daughter's relation with her father is internal and necessary, as neither would be what they are (daughter or father) without the other.

Abstraction, then, is a means of carefully thinking through the phenomenon of interest in order to identify the necessary causal mechanisms and generative structures at work. Yeung (1997) argues that the first stage of abstraction should always be a critique and reconceptualisation of existing work on the subject. Intensive empirical research can then be used to test and refine our ideas, such that abstraction becomes an iterative process. Extensive (large-scale) research can be used prior to abstraction, identifying empirical regularities that may help guide our thinking (Yeung, 1997; Richards, 1999), or to establish the regularity of the phenomena under study and further test our ideas (Unwin, 1992). Thus Richards (1999) explains that geomorphological research spirals between extensive and intensive and back again; and Roberts (2001) emphasises that critical realist research moves from concrete to abstract, and abstract to concrete. Both are captured within Yeung's (1997) flow-chart depiction of critical realist research in practice (reproduced as Figure 4.1). The ultimate aim is to differentiate between the necessary causal mechanisms and the contingencies in operation, thereby informing our understanding of the phenomenon in question (hence the feedback to 'literature review' in Figure 4.1). Critical realism may not entail using different methods than in other approaches – human geography, for example, may still use interviews, or focus groups or participant observation – but it requires close attention to **methodology** (Bakewell, 2010).

4.5.1 Violation of national pesticide regulations in the global food chain

At the time of writing this chapter, one of the dominant news stories has been about horse meat being sold as beef within the European Union. Tests are identifying more and more processed food products containing horse DNA, and supermarkets and major food manufacturers are withdrawing products from sale. Questions have been raised about the prospect of equine medicines finding their

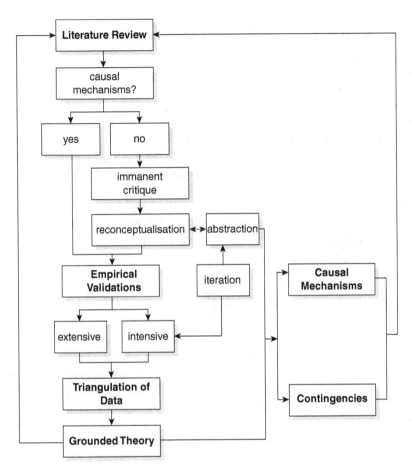

Figure 4.1 Yeung's (1997) conceptualisation of critical realist research in practice

way into human food but it seems that, in this case, the greater concern is food-related fraud rather than food security. Horse meat is eaten in some parts of Europe, though generally not in Britain. Whether you are against eating horse meat or not, these food products have been sold as something they are not. Horse meat is cheaper than beef, so it seems that some unscrupulous meat dealers have sought to increase profits by substituting one for the other. The metaphorical finger has been pointed at one or two Eastern European countries, while foods containing horse DNA have been found in Britain, Ireland, Italy, Germany and the Czech Republic. This has served to highlight the complex routes that food may take from the primary producers to the supermarket shelves in an era of globalised food production.

Galt (2010) demonstrates that these kinds of issues can be understood through a political ecology perspective. His research focused on fresh vegetable imports to the Unites States, examining the extent to which US food safety regulations relating to pesticide residues on the vegetables are met. Galt specifically identifies that he is working from a critical realist perspective, developing a framework to explain why vegetables from some countries have particularly high rates of violating US regulations.

The first step in this research was an exercise in global-scale empirical data analysis (extensive research). Two large databases on vegetable imports were obtained from the US Food and Drug Administration, and analysed to identify patterns of compliance with, and violation of, the pesticide residue regulations. Galt identified which countries are major sources of fresh vegetable imports, noting considerable variation in their levels of regulatory compliance. Generally, domestic vegetables (produced within the US) showed a higher rate of compliance with regulations than those produced elsewhere. Galt points out that this may be because of between-country differences in regulatory regimes, but also that some countries (for example, in tropical regions) are more susceptible to pest problems, which result in farmers applying pesticide more frequently. His analysis reveals that developing countries are not more likely to produce food with adverse levels of pesticide residue than developed countries. Rather, there is 'high variability in adverse residue rates among countries, different types of vegetable, and vegetable-country combinations' (p. 333).

Having first dealt with the 'concrete' empirical data, the next stage in critical realist research is abstraction. Here Galt develops an explanatory framework based on political ecology and political economy, which identifies the structures and mechanisms (the 'real' in Bhaskar's triad) that operate to generate location-specific events. This framework encompasses the ecological relations of production, social relations of production and exchange, and global North–South dependency and regulatory relations, tracing the ways in which these can impact on farm-level decisions. It enables Galt to identify shortcomings in previously posed explanations based on the notion of the 'pesticide treadmill' (whereby the use of pesticide disrupts the beneficial insect populations that help to limit pest species abundance, resulting in higher pest populations, resulting in farmers using greater levels of pesticide). It also brings to light a contradiction in the relations of production. Farmers need to keep their production costs lower than the price they receive for their goods, to be able to make a living. They therefore use the most efficient means of pest control that they can, which may mean using the most powerful pesticides. The vegetables are then bought for export. If pesticide residues are higher than those permitted by the regulations, the export company will lose its shipment and hence lose money, so it is in the export companies' interests that farmers do not use pesticides excessively. However, competition between export companies means that these companies must also keep their costs to a minimum, by paying the lowest price they can to the farmers. This contradiction provides one explanation for persistently high rates of violation of the US import regulations associated with specific vegetables from particular countries.

We noted earlier that Roberts (2001) describes critical realist research as moving from concrete to abstract, and then abstract to còncrete. Galt's (2010) research follows this pattern, by next focusing on particular countries with record of high violation rates (intensive case study research). Examining four countries in turn – Guatemala, Spain, Jamaica and China – he uses his framework to develop tentative hypotheses which may explain the high violation rates in each case. Galt stresses that each of these would require field research to further confirm or refute these hypotheses. Overall, though, his work provides an example of critical realist research in practice, combining empirical evidence and abstraction to reveal the structures and mechanisms which result in events. In this case those events relate to the identification of high levels of pesticide residue on imported vegetables in the US.

Galt's paper (like Yeung, 1997) draws on a large project that resulted in a number of journal articles, each reporting different aspects. This perhaps indicates that critical realism lends itself to a research *programme* as much as to individual research projects. An intensive case study may offer a valuable dissertation-sized project in itself (as suggested by Richards et al., 2002), but could also contribute to a larger programme of critical realist research. This may make it harder to identify examples of critical realist research, as the characteristic pattern of 'concrete to abstract, abstract to concrete' may not be evident in a single journal article.

4.6 Marxism and critical realism at the beach

Galt's framework of structures, mechanisms and events demonstrates that critical realist research (and Marxist research) can be complicated. In full, such research combines empirical data analysis with abstraction, using both extensive and intensive modes of research. Critical realist beach research could draw on Marxian political economy or political ecology but, as the discussions of critical realism in geomorphology (Richards, 1990, 1999; Rhoads and Thorn, 1994, 1999; Harrison, 2001) illustrate, our focus could be elsewhere.

Prompted by political ecology's focus on relations, we could decide to study the environmental pressures associated with beach tourism. Mallorca, the Spanish Mediterranean island, is a well-known destination for holidaymakers seeking sun, surf and sand. Garcia and Servera (2003) provide some insight into the island's tourist economy and the problems that have arisen from it. The years 1955–1973 represent the island's first 'tourism boom', with a very rapid increase in tourism demand. In response to this, the growth in tourist infrastructure was somewhat chaotic and unplanned. This explosion in tourism significantly altered the economy and associated social structures, with growth in the industry continuing in subsequent years. By the 1990s, over three quarters of the population was working within the tourism sector, compared with 30 per cent in 1955. Equally, the growth in tourism has resulted in significant impact on Mallorca's beach environments (Figure 4.2).

Figure 4.2 The beach at Playa de Palma, Mallorca. Note that the beach consists of a relatively narrow strip of sand backed by a pedestrian walkway, road and hotels. The hotels extend to the right for around 300–500 metres, beyond which relics of the dune system are preserved in a municipal park. The tyre tracks in the sand are from the tractors used to clean the beach.

Massive development of hotels, restaurants and bars in some coastal locations now separates the beach from its associated dune system, preventing sediment transfers between the two. Meadows of the seagrass *Posidonia oceanica* growing on the submerged portion of the beach help to provide some stability, but these plants shed their leaves in the autumn. With the onset of storms, the leaves are washed onto the beaches and form a vegetal berm, which provides some protection from beach erosion (Roig-Munar et al., 2012). However, within the context of a tourist-dependent economy, seagrass leaves are considered unsightly and not conducive to tourist use of the beach. The beaches are thus regularly cleaned, as often as daily during the main tourist season. Using a form of plough across the surface of the beach, this cleaning inevitably removes some of the sand as well as the unwanted material. Roig et al. (2009) cite sediment losses of 4 per cent through beach cleaning. Combined with the loss of natural sediment transfers with the dune system, some beaches have become dependent upon artificial sand replenishment, becoming little more than 'sandy solariums'. Garcia and Servera (2003) go on to list additional impacts of tourist activity on Mallorca's beaches, identifying 13 in total. They provide a map of Mallorca's 37 tourism zones and 41 beaches, summarising the human activities associated with each of the beaches. Their research, then, provides an initial indication of the variations in pressures and management practices between Mallorca's beaches.

Garcia and Servera's research may provide sufficient basis to begin abstracting the relations associated with Mallorca's beach tourism. We would need to consider both the ecological relations and the social relations associated with the tourism industry. The social relations might include: the local and migrant workers' dependency on the tourist industry (including those whose employment directly relates to management of the beaches); the importance of local income from tourism and desire of decision-makers (such as local councils) to maintain this; access to knowledge about beaches and beach management practices; holiday companies' profits made from tourists; the place images that tourist companies promote to entice holidaymakers; and the systems of taxation by which these tourist companies contribute to the local infrastructure. The ecological relations may include physical changes to the beach associated with the construction of tourism infrastructure; sources and routes of sediment transfer; and the interactions between seagrass beds and beach, and management interventions in these. This provides a starting point, and much thought would be needed to develop this further. Note, though, that these suggestions focus on *relations* rather than *objects*. Once we had developed our abstraction fully, we could then identify specific locations for intensive case study research to examine how the necessary and contingent relations result in specific, local, events. Such 'events' might be decisions to implement specific management techniques, the ways those techniques are put into practice, and the associated biophysical effects on the beach.

4.7 Some criticisms

Critical realism is not without its critics. In human geography, Rose (1990) identified some dissatisfaction with the unobservable nature of 'real' causal mechanisms. Identifying such mechanisms on the basis of particular, empirical events also leaves it open to accusations of over-emphasising contingency, and hence unique circumstances. Yeung (1997) argues that many human geographers failed to appreciate critical realism as a philosophy, interpreting it instead as a methodology, though with little clarity around what that methodology actually should be. This seems to be echoed by Pratt (2011), who suggests that little critical realist research actually happened in human geography, despite considerable discussion of it.

As the **'cultural turn'** developed momentum through the 1990s, geographers working with **postmodernist, poststructuralist** (see Chapter 7) and **feminist** (Chapter 6) theories became more attuned to the messy realities of lived experience, and the multiple axes of difference that can impact on people's lives. Critical realism, in contrast, is founded on abstraction from such messy realities, which means that it can tend towards generalisation and normalisation (McCormack, 2012). In human geography, then, critical realism was overtaken by postmodern and poststructuralist critiques seemingly just as some physical geographers were developing interest in it.

More recently there have been some suggestions that critical realism still holds potential, for example in relation to migration research (Bakewell 2010) and economic geography (Jones and Murphy 2010). Overall though, it seems that critical realism's popularity may have had much to do with an alignment or compatibility with Marxian political economy approaches.

4.8 Marxism and critical realism in summary

Marxism and critical realism are both complex bodies of **theory**, neither of which prescribes particular *methods*, but both requiring careful attention to methodology. Their similarity rests on their underlying assumptions, in that both assume the existence of structures that cause, or can explain, events in the world. They are effectively structuralist with a small 's', and not to be confused with the Structuralist movement (addressed in Chapter 7), which is primarily concerned with linguistic structures. Marxism focuses on the material relations of production, while Bhaskar distinguishes between three ontological levels: 'real' causal structures and mechanisms; 'actual' events resulting from these; and 'empirical' observations by us.

The impact of Marxism on geographic thought should not be underestimated. The move to radical geography in the late 1960s and 1970s was explicitly Marxist, focusing on issues of justice, inequality and power in a variety of forms. These themes remain central to social geography today. Marxian political economy and political ecology are very much alive, despite the development or adoption of other approaches since the 1970s.

Critical realism's place in geography is perhaps more contested. Despite its popularity in the 1970s and '80s, some suggest that this was rarely followed through in the practices of geographical research. Significantly, though, critical realism can underpin the study of natural systems as well as social systems, and the interaction between the two. Moving from concrete to abstract, and abstract to concrete, the aim of such research is to provide explanation, and in this it represents a significant shift from the positivist and critical rationalist preoccupations with description and prediction.

FURTHER READING

For further explanations

Castree, N. (2008) 'The Limits to Capital (1982): David Harvey', in P. Hubbard, R. Kitchin and G. Valentine (eds), *Key Texts in Human Geography*. London: Sage. pp. 61–70.

Castree, N. (2011) 'David Harvey', in P. Hubbard and R. Kitchin (eds), *Key Thinkers on Space and Place*. London: Sage. pp. 234–41.

Castree, N. (2011) 'Neil Smith', in P. Hubbard and R. Kitchin (eds), *Key Thinkers on Space and Place*. London: Sage. pp. 374–9.

Cox, K.R. (2013) 'Notes on a brief encounter: critical realism, historical materialism, and human geography', *Dialogues in Human Geography* 3 (1): 3–21.
Forsyth, T. (2008) 'Political ecology and the epistemology of social justice', *Geoforum* 39: 756–64.
Harman, C. (2000) *How Marxism Works* (6th edition). London: Bookmarks Publications Ltd. http://users.comcen.com.au/~marcn/redflag/archive/harman/hmw/index.html [accessed 23/02/13].
Ollman, B. (2003) *Dance of the Dialectic: Steps in Marx's Method.* University of Illinois Press. http://www.nyu.edu/projects/ollman/books/dd.php [accessed 12/07/13].
Phillips, M. (2008) 'Uneven Development (1984): Neil Smith', in P. Hubbard, R. Kitchin and G. Valentine (eds), *Key Texts in Human Geography*. London: Sage. pp. 71–81.
Richards, K.S. (1990) 'Editorial: "Real" geomorphology', *Earth Surface Processes and Landforms* 15: 195–7. doi: 10.1002/esp.3290150302.
Rose, C. (1990) 'Toward pragmatic realism in human geography', *Cahiers de Géographie du Québec* 34 (92): 161–79. http://www.erudit.org/revue/cgq/1990/v34/n92/022102ar.pdf [accessed 12/07/13].
Samers, M. (2013) 'Stirrings in the attic: on the distinction between historical geographical materialism and critical realism', *Dialogues in Human Geography* 3 (1): 40–4.

Progress in Human Geography resources

Barnes, T.J. (1995) 'Political economy I: "the culture, stupid"', *Progress in Human Geography* 19 (3): 423–31. doi:10.1177/030913259501900309.
Birkenholtz, T. (2012) 'Network political ecology: method and theory in climate change vulnerability and adaptation research', *Progress in Human Geography* 36 (3): 295–315. doi: 10.1177/0309132511421532.
Glassman, J. (2011) 'Critical geography III: critical development geography', *Progress in Human Geography* 35 (5): 705–11. doi:10.1177/0309132510385615.
King, B. (2010) 'Political ecologies of health', *Progress in Human Geography* 34 (1): 38–55. doi:10.1177/0309132509338642.
Neumann, R.P. (2011) 'Political ecology III: theorizing landscape', *Progress in Human Geography* 35 (6): 843–50. doi: 10.1177/0309132510390870.
Pratt, A.C. (1995) 'Putting critical realism to work: the practical implications for geographical research', *Progress in Human Geography* 19 (1): 61–74. doi: 10.1177/030913259501900104.
Rangan, H. and Kull, C.A. (2009) 'What makes ecology "political"?: rethinking "scale" in political ecology', *Progress in Human Geography* 33 (1): 28–45. doi: 10.1177/0309132508090215.
Roberts, J.M. (2001) 'Realist spatial abstraction? Marxist observations of a claim within critical realist geography', *Progress in Human Geography* 25 (4): 545–67. doi: 10.1191/030913201682688931.
Walker, P.A. (2006) 'Political ecology: where is the policy?' *Progress in Human Geography* 30 (3): 382–95. doi:10.1191/0309132506ph613pr.
Yeung, H.W. (1997) 'Critical realism and realist research in human geography: a method, or a philosophy in search of a method?' *Progress in Human Geography* 21 (1): 51–74. doi: 10.1191/030913297668207944.

Examples

Fitzpatrick, S., Bramley, G. and Johnsen, S. (2013) 'Pathways into multiple exclusion homelessness in seven UK cities', *Urban Studies* 50 (1): 148–68. doi: 10.1177/0042098012452329.

Ioris, A.A.R. (2012) 'Applying the strategic-relational approach to urban political ecology: the water management problems of the Baixada Fluminense, Rio de Janeiro, Brazil', *Antipode* 44 (1): 122–50. doi: 10.1111/j.1467-8330.2011.00848.x.

Ojo, G.U. (2012) 'Economic diversification and second-tier political conflict: assessing bitumen political ecologies in southwestern Nigeria', *Singapore Journal of Tropical Geography* 33: 49–62. doi: 10.1111/j.1467-9493.2012.00447.x.

Watts, M. (2012) 'Sweet and sour: the oil curse in the Niger delta', in T. Butler, D. Lerch, and G. Wuerthner (eds), *The Energy Reader*. Post Carbon Institute, Santa Rosa, California. pp. 247–56. http://energy-reality.org/wp-content/uploads/2013/10/28_Sweet-and-Sour_R1_071413.pdf [accessed 15/02/14].

Phenomenology and Post-Phenomenology: The Essence of Experience, *Or*, Seeing a Shark is Different from Seeing a Dolphin

'Being' is the self-evident concept. 'Being' is used in all knowing...
(Heidegger, 1953, p. 4)

Geographers, generally speaking, are interested in the world around them. The key question is 'how do we know the world?' This whole book is about answers to that question, but phenomenology was philosopher Edmund Husserl's attempt to address it directly. Others took up his ideas and developed them in different ways, to understand the world as lived, experienced, enacted and always in-the-making. This chapter provides an introduction to phenomenology and then considers geography's two phases of engagement with it: the **'humanistic geography'** of the 1970s, and then a more recent re-engagement with phenomenological themes through **non-representational** geographies, sometimes drawing explicitly and intentionally on phenomenology, but also on other positions as well. This latter period is, some argue, 'post-phenomenological', although perhaps it is equally helpful to think of it as 'more-than-phenomenological'.

5.1 Introducing phenomenology

Before going any further, read the two accounts in Box 5.1. Both are descriptions of Live Aid, a fund-raising rock concert and huge media event held in the 1980s.

BOX 5.1   LIVE AID

Account 1

In 1983-4 Ethiopia experienced a drought which, combined with population growth, the agrarian economic policies of the time and years of war, resulted in the country's worst famine in a century (Tareke, 2009). Bob Geldof, singer-songwriter of the Boomtown Rats, wrote the hit single *Do They Know it's Christmas* to raise funds for famine relief, and then followed this with a huge music event. On July 13th, 1985, two stadium rock concerts were held 3500 miles (5700 km) apart, one at the Wembley Arena in London and the other at the JFK Stadium in Philadelphia. Over sixty acts performed on the two stages, timed so that live television coverage could switch between the two throughout the day for continuous music. The concert began in the UK at mid-day, finishing in the USA 16 hours later. Live audiences numbered 72,000 in London and 90,000 in Philadelphia, with an estimated 1.9 billion people in 150 countries watching on TV. This was Live Aid. Donations made on that one day amounted to between £40 and £50 million. Elavsky (2009, p. 384) describes Live Aid as 'the most ambitious media venture of its time'.

Account 2

And the lesson today is how to die

The words hung in the air. I stood stock still, my hand raised above my head, my fist clenched in unconscious salute. In front of me stood 80,000 people. Somewhere, invisible, behind them, another billion people all over the world had joined us. Together we held our breath. There are expressions we use all the time. When we are hungry we say, without thinking, that we are starving. When we are happy we declare, because the words come easy to us, that this must be the greatest moment of our lives. But there are times when the clichés are made flesh. Throughout Africa on this day people were starving. And, for me, at this particular moment, the threads of a lifetime were uniquely gathered, all there in that one uplifted hand.

...

I stopped *I Don't Like Mondays* in its tracks. It was an old song invested with new meaning. Something special was happening today; it seemed epitomized in this moment. I stood and looked, tracking my gaze from one side of the auditorium to the other as if to fix each individual with my eyes. I wanted to make contact with them all, and draw them in. Think about this thing today. Think about this thing we are doing for it may never happen in this way again.

...

The sun burned my knuckles. I opened my hand and the crowd quietened. I will remember this forever, I thought. The crowd was quite still now, the light breeze ruffled the stage. I had to move on. The moment had passed.
(Geldof, 1986, pp. 8–10).

The description in Account 1 is largely confined to the verifiable statements central to **positivism** (explained in Chapter 2). You understand what the sentences mean because you know what they say about the world. You know how each statement would be (or could have been) verified. These are, if you like, the 'facts' of the event, to use that word in a colloquial sense. The trouble is, having watched the concert as an impressionable not-quite-teenager, glued to the TV for as long as my parents would allow, this description captures nothing of the spirit of the event. It tells you nothing about the excitement of that hot summer's day, and how enormous it all seemed. Contrast this with Account 2, which is Bob Geldof's description of a single moment in the concert, when he paused mid-song.

The reason for including this here is not really to present Live Aid as something magical. The event has been criticised for depoliticising famine (Hague et al., 2008), and Geldof's account certainly falls into the trap of depicting Africa as a single, homogenous space, rather than a continent of over 50 countries and 1,000 languages. The point is that the contrast between the two descriptions provides a step towards understanding phenomenology.

5.1.1 Beginning with Husserl's phenomenology

It is useful to be clear at the start that phenomenology is not a single thing, even though it is sometimes referred to as 'a movement' within twentieth-century philosophy (Spiegelberg, 1994; Woodruff-Smith, 2008). Different forms of phenomenology have been promoted by different individuals at different times, but Edmund Husserl (1859–1938) is generally regarded as the starting point.

Husserl trained initially as a mathematician and physicist but in the early twentieth century he was becoming frustrated with science. There seemed to be no solution to the theoretical problems posed by relativity and quantum theory, and he was concerned that science was degenerating into 'an unphilosophical study of mere facts' (Spiegelberg, 1994, p. 74). It seemed incapable of dealing with issues of truth, value and meaning. He turned to philosophy and logic, wanting to understand the very beginnings of knowledge.

Science is based on observable phenomena, or sense data, and so Husserl initially focused on the 'things' (phenomena) that form the basis of our experience. Over time, though, he became convinced that he needed to look deeper than this. If our sense data provide the foundations of knowledge, science pays attention only to the 'objects' of those sense data. It completely misses part of the picture: us. The phenomena that form the objects of science are always perceived by us, but science, with its 'natural attitude' of **realism**, neglects that human component. Science pays no attention to consciousness, but without consciousness there are no sense data.

Husserl made two key points about consciousness. Firstly, the objects of science are things of which we are conscious. They are objects 'for us'. They have some kind of meaning for us, otherwise we would not recognise them as objects. A linear depression in an otherwise flat field may go unnoticed by most people, but a geomorphologist might identify it as a palaeochannel (Figure 5.1). The latter sees it as a distinct object because it has meaning. On a more mundane level, objects can be useful, useless, friendly, hostile or uncomfortable, but they are always useful, useless, friendly, hostile or uncomfortable *for us* (Scruton, 1995). Secondly, consciousness is always consciousness *of* something. As I type, I am conscious of the chair, the table, the laptop screen in front of me and the keyboard under my fingers. I am conscious of the television in the next room and the rain on the window. I am conscious of a

Figure 5.1   Palaeochannel beside the River Arrow, Warwickshire, UK. The curvilinear depression in the middle of the photograph is a palaeochannel, the remnant of a former river channel

kind of glowing feeling in my face, having been outside in the wind earlier. I am also conscious of the ideas I am writing about. 'Phenomena' are everything we are conscious of, including emotions, thoughts, memories, bodily awareness, embodied actions and social activities (Woodruff-Smith, 2008).

This characteristic of consciousness, that it is always directed towards something, Husserl called intentionality. Whether we begin by thinking about consciousness (which is always 'of' some phenomenon) or we begin by thinking about a phenomenon (which has a particular meaning for us), intentionality is present. Consciousness and phenomena are inseparable, as neither exists without the other. This is a significant shift from **Cartesian** thinking. The big problem with Descartes' conception of knowledge as internal to a person (subject) and reality as external (object) is that it leaves no means of validating knowledge. It gives us no way to compare the mental content of knowledge with external reality to check they match (Nakhnikian, 1964). In contrast, Husserl's phenomenology focuses on objects as phenomena of consciousness. He wanted to understand the structures underlying our conscious experience of phenomena, and the conditions that help to give conscious experience its intentionality.

By definition, conscious experience is awareness-of-experience. We live experience. It follows that conscious experience can only be understood from a first-person perspective. To return to the example of Live Aid in Box 5.1, Bob Geldof's account describes his conscious experience of the event, the meaning of that moment for him, and in doing so it conveys much more than the verifiable 'facts' of objective observation. If we break down the word 'phenomenology', we can see the component parts: phenomena, and 'ology', which comes from the Greek *logos,* to study. It makes sense that phenomenology is the study of phenomena. To put it in simpler words, it is the study of 'things as they present themselves to, and are perceived in consciousness' (Allen-Collinson, 2011, p. 300). Bob Geldof's description is not a phenomenological analysis, but it is the first step.

5.1.2 Variations in phenomenology: Husserl, Heidegger, Sartre and Merleau-Ponty

Husserl's focus on conscious experience and intentionality led him to declare that the 'real existence' of an object is irrelevant to phenomenological analysis. The significance of an object lies in its meaning in our experience, and this is separate from whether or not the object really exists. As a child you might have 'seen' a ghost, when actually it was a cloth fluttering in the wind (Scruton, 1995). Last summer I was lucky enough to see a basking shark in the sea off the Devon coast. The water was quite choppy and initially I just saw the tip of a dorsal fin break the surface. For a second I thought it was a dolphin. In that brief moment I had a 'dolphin experience' rather than a 'basking shark experience'. The two are different. To really understand meaning, Husserl argued that we need to 'bracket' belief in existence and focus solely on the experience. This is not to deny that the object of interest may exist. It is simply that the question of its existence does not help us in getting to the essence of meaning. This 'reduction', reducing our belief in the existence of phenomena to focus on meaning, is sometimes referred to as 'epoché' and is central to Husserl's phenomenology.

Examining one instance of a phenomenon may lead us to focus on the particularities of that one instance though, rather than the essence. What is it about the experience of seeing a dolphin that gives it 'dolphin-ness'? To answer a question like that, we need to perform a second reduction, reducing the particular facts to their general essences. The specific instance and circumstances of seeing a dolphin are irrelevant. We might see dolphins in movies (such as in Charles Martin Smith's *Dolphin Tale*, 2011), or in wildlife documentaries on television, or in photographs, or we might dream of dolphins. In all cases we 'see' a dolphin, and so a phenomenologist would seek to understand what is common to these experiences. This does not necessarily require studying examples of all these experiences, but distinguishing between the 'essence' and the particularities.

Once we understand our intentionality towards dolphins, the meaning that 'dolphins' have for us, then our attention can turn to trying to identify the conditions that shape that intentionality. Those conditions might relate to our physical make-up. The configuration of eyes, nose and mouth means dolphins have a recognisable face to us, but to humans (used to seeing human faces) the shape of dolphins' mouths look like they are smiling. This 'smiling' face and dolphins' seemingly playful nature are familiar through media images and so influence our perception of dolphins. Conditions for intentionality may also consist in our motor skills and physical habits (ability or non-ability to swim, perhaps), our social practices (the things that people do with dolphins – or the things people in movies do with dolphins) and our language. These things shape meaning.

In his last work, Husserl's attention had turned from the purely cognitive to recognise the social world (Scruton, 1995). He sketched out the notion of a 'lifeworld' (Lebenswelt, in German), described by Spiegelberg (1994, p. 747) as 'the encompassing world of our immediate experience'. The lifeworld refers to the shared meanings of a community of language-users, those meanings shaping or structuring the 'common sense' world for us. This idea was never fully realised in Husserl's work, and was published posthumously, but the theme was picked up again by Merleau-Ponty later.

While Husserl focused on cognition, Heidegger, Merleau-Ponty and Sartre were more interested in 'being', or existence, and so are often referred to as existential phenomenologists. Martin Heidegger (1889–1976) has been described as the most important thinker in existentialism, although his written works are so complex that Scruton (1995) suggests they may be unintelligible. The core concern for Heidegger was be*ing*; that is, being as a verb, the act of existing, rather than being as a noun (as in 'a human being'). For Heidegger, we are always already in the world, and so it makes no sense to 'bracket' the world as if it may not exist (Woodruff-Smith, 2008).

This emphasis on being-in-the-world is captured in Heidegger's (1953) notion of 'Dasein', which translates literally as 'being there'. We understand existence only through existence, and understand the world only through existing in it. All of our knowing is founded on our being-in-the-world. In a later essay Heidegger (1971) developed the concept of 'dwelling'. We do not just 'inhabit' or populate the world like so many LEGO figures. We live in and through the world. The contrast is something like having a home rather than just a house. Fundamentally, it involves care. Thinking, cultivating and constructing are all inter-related components of dwelling, being 'at peace within the free…sphere that safeguards each thing in its nature. *The fundamental character of dwelling is this sparing and preserving.*' (Heidegger, 1971, p. 147, emphasis in original). Heidegger's phenomenology, then, moves us from questions about knowledge to questions about what it is to be human (Entrikin, 1976).

The existential phenomenologies of Jean-Paul Sartre (1905–1980) and Maurice Merleau-Ponty (1908–1961) both emphasised the concrete instances of our being and acting in the world. The starting point for their phenomenology is description of 'ordinary human activities in the world' (Hammond et al., 1991, p. 96) rather than cognition, perception or reflections on activities. Sartre's work has largely been neglected in geography (Smith et al., 2012), and so the rest of this section will focus on Merleau-Ponty.

The key to Merleau-Ponty's phenomenology is embodiment. You are not just a free-floating 'consciousness'. Your being-in-the-world is an embodied being, and your body is central to your consciousness, knowledge, understanding and intentionality. You experience the world from and through your body. If a surface is soft or hard, it is because it feels soft or hard in relation to your body. Popular debates about chocolate bars (such as Wagon Wheels or Mars bars) getting smaller since childhood emphasise the point. In some cases the bars actually have changed size but, that aside, we judge objects relative to our own bodies.

Merleau-Ponty (1945) demonstrated the importance of embodiment by examining some exceptional examples. The first of these was 'phantom limb' phenomenon, in which amputees still feel sensations in, and try to use, a missing limb. He argued that this is not because the patients reject the fact that a limb is missing, but because they continue to act, physically, in the same way as they did before the amputation. Their whole experience of physically being in the world incorporates a limb that is now missing. His second case was a brain-damaged war veteran who could perform functional tasks such as blowing his nose, but not abstract movements such as touching his nose. Although the physical actions are similar, the meaning of these acts is different. Merleau-Ponty demonstrated that intentionality is embodied, lying in our capacity to act: 'I can', rather than 'I think'. When you learn a new skill (riding a bicycle, juggling, playing a musical instrument), you might watch someone else do it, and you might hear or read their explanations. At some point, though, you have to develop a bodily, rather than cognitive, understanding of the activity. You have to know how it feels to balance the bicycle, get the juggling balls into a rhythm, or make the notes on the instrument. This embodied knowing may take repeated bodily actions to learn, but it is not cognitive knowing, and can be pre-cognitive. You do not have to check that you have legs before you stand up.

To return to Husserl's lifeworld, the lifeworld is the world in which we act, and from which we are both inseparable and yet distinct. This leads to Merleau-Ponty's notion of reversibility. We see the world and, exactly because we are able to see the world, we know that we can be seen by the world. If I put my two hands together, they both touch and are touched by the other. I could say my left hand is touching my right (which is being touched by my left), or the other way round. Touching and being touched are not quite interchangeable, but not quite distinct either as they can be reversed. Extending this further, there is never quite separation between self and world, or subject and object. I am always an object to some other subject, and so subject and object both at once. This has ethical and political implications, in that 'alterity' (otherness) always involves and is involved in us, intertwined with subjectivity (Reynolds, 2005).

5.2 Phenomenology and humanistic geography of the 1970s

Geographers' first engagements with phenomenology heralded the advent of humanistic geography in the 1970s, although not all humanistic geography was necessarily phenomenological. This new approach was developed, at least in part, as a critique of positivism (Ley, 1981; Unwin, 1992; Creswell, 2013; see Chapter 2 for more on positivism). There is perhaps a kind of parallel with Husserl here. He developed his phenomenological philosophy out of frustration with science, and in the 1970s some human geographers were becoming frustrated with positivist 'spatial science' geography, arguing that the analyses it produced were too distant from social context. Detached, supposedly value-free positivist geography was considered to be both undesirable and unrealistic (Smith, 1979). Phenomenology's emphasis on everyday human experience led to a significant shift in the questions being asked within geography. Whereas the positivists sought patterns in the spatial distribution of 'objects' in the world, humanistic geography paid attention to how people relate to places, and to the question of what constitutes 'place' anyway.

Yi-Fu Tuan's 1974 and 1977 books were particularly significant, and are refreshingly readable texts. *Topophilia: A Study of Environmental Perception, Attitudes and Values* (1974) drew on a broad range of research (including anthropology and psychology, as well as geography) to examine the ways in which humans – as a species, in groups, and individually – relate to their surroundings. Tuan defined 'topophilia' as 'the affective bond between people and place or setting' (1974, p. 4). In other words, topophilia focused on experiences, feelings, emotions and values. His 1977 book, *Space and Place*, developed his ideas further to advance a distinction between 'space' and 'place'. Abstract 'space' is associated with an objective, 'scientific' conception of space, a kind of empty **Cartesian** grid on which any location can be pinpointed with a pair of coordinates. 'Place', in contrast, is location endowed with value and meaning, a bond that develops over time and with familiarity. As Dorothy said in *The Wizard of Oz* (1939), 'There's no place like home.'

Tuan does not actually identify his approach as phenomenological in either of the works referred to above but the influence is clear, for example in his urge that 'we should remember that feeling and its objects are often inseparable' (1974, p. 92). This is a reference to the classically phenomenological notion of intentionality. He had already explicitly advocated phenomenology for developing geographical knowledge in an earlier (1971) publication, and Rodaway (2011) identifies Tuan's work as being particularly influenced by Heidegger's notions of dwelling and being-in-the-world. Around the same time, Edward Relph's (1976) *Place and Placelessness* also focused on people's affective connections with places, particularly drawing a distinction between our experiences as either 'insiders' or 'outsiders' to places. Between them, Tuan and Relph highlighted that people *produce* places socially. Places become meaningful for us through thought and action (Hubbard et al., 2002), through our dwelling in them.

If thought, action and knowledge (of places, for example) are inseparable from experience, values and meaning, one implication is that geographical knowledge is also subject to such influences. Anne Buttimer's (1974) *Values in Geography* drew attention to the fact that all knowledge is produced by someone, somewhere, and so is underpinned by a particular set of values, experiences and meanings. Knowledge is 'situated', always developed within a particular context. This led Buttimer to question the values dominating the production of geographical knowledge (Ley, 1981), provoking geographers to develop an awareness of taken-for-granted assumptions and the spatial operation of power. By the mid-1990s such **reflexivity** had become part of the mainstream, human geographers' collective 'common sense', in rhetoric if not always in practice (Curry, 1996).

5.2.1 Methods in humanistic geography

Through the use of phenomenological ideas humanistic geography in the 1970s and 1980s reconsidered the ways in which people produce and experience places and environments in their everyday lives (Cloke et al., 1991). This substantive concern with lived experience clearly requires methods that will yield insights into that experience, and here it is useful to distinguish between two kinds of 'method' at work. As a particular philosophical movement, phenomenology is concerned to get at the 'essence' of human experience. It does so through methods of thinking like reduction, bracketing (in the case of Husserl) and examining exceptional cases to shed light on the unexceptional things we take for granted (as exemplified by Merleau-Ponty). Geographers and other social scientists conducting empirical research will also use methods of empirical data collection. Given that the focus is on personal experiences, phenomenological geography emphasises qualitative methods that produce intense descriptions of experience. It is not unusual for researchers to write about their own experiences, but it is also possible to obtain insight into the experiences of others. Indeed, Tuan's *Topophilia* was entirely based on the accounts of others. There are no rigid procedures for conducting phenomenology, Relph (1981, p. 113) suggesting that 'phenomenological topics and methods define each other'. Ethnography, participant observation, diaries, interviews, analysis of artistic and cultural artefacts all have potential. Allen-Collinson (2011, p. 305) describes phenomenology as requiring an 'encompassing attitude' rather than particular techniques; 'a certain attentive awareness to the things of the world as we *live* them rather than as we abstractly theorise them'.

Some of the geography of the 1970s was criticised for having interpreted phenomenology too vaguely. Creswell (2013) suggests that geographers of the era were selective in their use of phenomenology, and Wylie (2007) notes a tendency to simply equate phenomenology with subjectivity. As early as 1981, Relph had identified that some of the methodological papers on phenomenology were too reluctant to fully challenge positivist science, trying to reconcile the two instead of recognising the profound differences between them. Entrikin's (1976) account certainly seems to judge phenomenology using positivist criteria, in his concern for phenomenologists' ability to validate statements. Further criticisms of humanistic geography were that it failed to take sufficient account of the external social factors impinging on individuals' lives (Smith, 1979; Ley, 1981); that it was inherently **normative**, centred on a generic, universal (male) subject; and that its conception of 'place' was over-simplistic, ignoring power relations (Anderson and Harrison, 2010).

These latter concerns reflect the developing consciousness of the 'new cultural geography' that was beginning to emerge by the end of the 1980s. Inspired by postmodern and **poststructuralist** theories (Chapter 7), geographers turned their attention to the ways in which social and cultural processes produce and maintain dominant **discourses** and representations. The normativity of which humanistic geography was accused is one example; in assuming that phenomenological accounts are universal, the ways in which individuals' experiences are shaped by social categories such as gender, race, religion and sexuality are lost. Such differences are effectively erased, invisible and therefore unimportant. That then intersects with questions about power, who possesses it and who is affected by it. Extending such critical attention to society at large, geographers were able to treat all manner of things as 'text', from literature to film, music to museums, advertising to architecture. Representation became the central concern. Such work is still largely phenomenological in the broadest sense, in that its central focus is meaning, but the emphasis was on the 'collective symbolic order' (Anderson and Harrison, 2010) that projects meaning onto individuals and their actions, rather than on the individuals themselves. Poststructuralism, in particular, attempted to resolve the dichotomy between phenomenology's apparent individualism and **structuralism**'s emphasis on broader social context (Wylie, 2007). For the new cultural geography, the phenomenology of Husserl and Merleau-Ponty was old news.

5.3 A more recent return to experience

Since the mid-1990s human geography (along with other social sciences) has seen a re-emergence of ideas and themes that have some phenomenological orientation. Simonsen (2013) positions these as 'post-humanist', in contrast with the 'anti-humanism' of structuralism, poststructuralism and deconstruction. Relational, material, non-human and more-than-human geographies have come to the fore, paying renewed attention to questions of *being*, in multiple and complex ways. These non-representational geographies draw on a collection of theoretical approaches, among which Actor Network Theory (ANT) is prominent. Arguably, ANT is in the 'wrong' chapter here, as it is probably more poststructuralist (Chapter 7) than phenomenological. Bruno Latour, with whom ANT is primarily associated, was critical of phenomenology in his early work but Introna (2011) identifies his later publications as revealing a broadly phenomenological approach. Either way, ANT was significant in the 're-materialisation' of human geography. The new cultural geographies developed from the 1980s emphasised representation, but ANT led towards non-representational theories, focusing on everyday material relations and practices. It is thus included here as a step towards non-representational theories more broadly.

5.3.1 Actor Network Theory (ANT)

Latour's early work was in the multi-disciplinary field of science and technology studies. In the mid-1970s he undertook an ethnographic study in a laboratory at the Salk Institute for Biological Studies, California, observing the scientists' daily lives (Latour and Woolgar, 1979). Science and technology studies had tended to focus on the products of science, but Latour was more interested in the practices of science in-the-making. It became clear to him that the 'doing' of science is rather more complicated than the written products (journal articles) ever convey. The practices of science involve not just scientists, but a whole network of relations of human and non-human **actants**. Thinking through an example of physical geography research can provide some sense of such a network.

Shona is a (fictitious) geography student, who grew up in Herefordshire, where her parents still live. During the first two years of her degree Shona became interested in glacial geomorphology, particularly once she realised that the Herefordshire landscape contains lots of clues about its glacial past. There are some big, elongated mounds in the farmland not far from her parent's house. She thinks they may be **drumlins**, but the only written references to them she has found do not provide clear confirmation of this. Some mention drumlins, and others just refer vaguely to moraine and patches of till in the area. She decides to focus her undergraduate dissertation on these landforms. Already, Shona's own past and her **affective** ties to Herefordshire have influenced her project, forming part of the network of her research practice.

Shona spends time reading about glacial geomorphology and drumlins, their formation, shapes and sedimentary characteristics. This reading provides her background knowledge for the study, shaping her ideas about what counts as 'evidence' and what fieldwork she should do. Her dissertation tutor, being much more experienced in glacial geomorphology, guides her on what is feasible and what is not, and how big her study should be. She then consults the department's technician on what equipment she can use for her fieldwork. The texts written by previous researchers, Shona's tutor, and the technician are all components of the network.

Shona had to get permission from the landowner to do her fieldwork (another part of the network). She starts by mapping the features, surveying breaks of slope and changes of slope to create a morphological map using a GPS. Here her practices are shaped by the technical capabilities of the instrument, such as its accuracy and the definition of features as points, lines or polygons. Once she has done the mapping, she uses a soil augur to take soil samples at various depths and places on three of the landforms. Shona struggles a bit here, as the soil has quite a high silt–clay content as well as some larger stones in it. In some places she is unable to get as deep as she would have liked, finding that either the soil is too stiff for her to turn the augur or she just hits stones. Three more elements of the network are apparent here, in the technology she uses for fieldwork, the soil and stones that disrupt her plans, and Shona's own body as she uses this technology.

So even before Shona analyses any data, the network of relations we have identified includes her past and affective ties with place, previously published research that forms her 'background knowledge', her tutor and the departmental technician, the landowner, the technology used for fieldwork, the soil and stones of the field site, and her body.

The network of relations involved in the practices of doing research, then, involves not just humans and the decisions they make, but also equipment, ideas, journal articles and books, and the space of the field site or laboratory itself: a multitude of human and non-human actants. A key characteristic of Actor Network Theory is that all actants are considered to be equally important in the network (Crawford, 2004). This means that humans are not privileged above the non-human components. Shona is just one actant among many in her dissertation research. Anything that makes a difference to the practice is an actant in the network (Creswell, 2013).

Networks are produced and reproduced, becoming more or less extended and more or less stable, only through the concrete, 'on the ground', activities of the constituent actants. Shona's research practice would not exist without each of the actants in the network but, equally, those actants are defined and given meaning by their place in the network (in her research). Her dissertation tutor is a person with multiple and fluid identities of his own (academic, father, son, brother, footballer, trumpet player), but those other identities are meaningless within the network of interest here. Network and actants are mutually constitutive. As in phenomenology, ANT bypasses binaries such as context/content, structure/agency, global/local, and even society/nature, as each term is inherently part of the other. Rather than seek 'deep' explanations (as in critical realism, described in Chapter 4), an ANT understanding of any practice requires only that we trace the connections of the network and 'make the list... of those who do the work' (Latour, 1987, p. 258). Even global activities such as international air travel or the workings of the United Nations function through specific actants (human and non-human) performing specific tasks in specific places. This means that networks are inherently spatial.

Jöns' (2006) analysis of the practices of high-energy physics research demonstrates just how complex such spatial networks can be. She argues that much ANT research has uncritically relied on a proclaimed 'symmetry' between human and non-human actants, overlooking an important portion of networks as a result. ANT emphasises materiality, yet Jöns' work revealed that high-energy physics research is influenced as much by the scientists' social connections with each other as by the physical facilities of laboratories. These two dimensions – the material and immaterial (mental, emotional) – have different geographies, different spatial networks, with humans as the connection between them. Jöns thus proposes that, instead of 'human' and 'non-human' actants, we should be considering three kinds: material, immaterial, and 'dynamic hybrids' (such as humans) in which those two are connected.

In the example of Shona's dissertation research, we used ANT to understand the practice of physical geography research: Shona was not using ANT herself. Barratt's (2012) study of rock and ice climbing provides an example of ANT used in geography, setting out to examine how technology extends a climber's bodily capacities to climb. From clothing and footwear to ice axe, crampons, rope and harness, his study was about the 'climber as the archetypal "cyborg" or "more-than-human" climber' (p. 47). Barratt used a combination of participant observation and semi-structured interviews for his research. He gained access to climbers by advertising through climbing clubs, Internet forums and at indoor climbing walls, interviewing 40 climbers. Being a climber himself, he took his own rack of climbing kit to interviews, so his participants were able to explain actions and body movements without relying only on words. He then used participant observation to link the climbers' accounts with their practices on the rock face, gaining further insight into the relations between climber, kit and environment in a non-representational manner.

A **grounded theory** approach to data analysis led Barratt to identify themes arising from the data, of which his (2012) paper discusses three. Without repeating the detail, the data took him in a slightly different direction from that he had originally envisaged, and one which echoes Jöns' (2006) concern for the immaterial actants in the network. Rather than focusing on the intended functionality of the kit – in other words, the purposes for which the kit was designed – Barratt's research revealed a more subtle, but equally important network. This is a network of 'less obvious enabling relations built on familiarity, superstition, traditions, risk, security, comfort, safety, personal ethics and desired relations with the environment' (p. 47).

Climbers have favourite pieces of kit that give them confidence, for example, or they have physical rituals (chalking their hands, slipping the heels of their boots off and on) that prepare them psychologically for the climb ahead. These parts of the network are just as important as the physical equipment. Barratt thus illustrates that people, technologies, environments and practices are co-constitutive, each influencing the other in unpredictable ways, such that 'during the practice the competencies of the climber are negotiated as an assemblage' (p. 52). The focus on the everyday experience of 'being' (a climber) is clearly evident.

5.3.2 Non-representational theories

Non-representational theories developed from the mid-1990s onwards, led by Nigel Thrift (2008). Whereas the 'new cultural geographies' had emphasised representation and meaning, treating the world as 'text', non-representational geographies recognise that the world is experienced before it is represented. Our lives comprise a myriad of embodied, **affective** and emotional actions and interactions with everything (living and non-living) around us. Daya (2011) illustrates the distinction in a discussion of theatrical plays, explaining that rather than focusing on the script of the play, non-representational theory requires attention to the moment of performance. Places and identities are *experienced* first and foremost, from being both 'in' and 'up against' the landscape when walking a long-distance path (Wylie, 2005) to being stared at on a train for looking different (Simonsen, 2013). Being-in-the-world is how we know the world.

Like phenomenology, the label 'non-representational' refers to a plurality of approaches (Colls, 2011) rather than a single entity. However, Cadman (2009) identifies five core themes, and these can be summarised as:

1. An attention to practice, emphasising non-cognitive or pre-cognitive practices; in other words, the practices that you do not need to think about before doing;

2. Engagement with everyday life, from the mundane to the sacred and special, and particularly with the emotional and affective dimensions of this;

3. A concern with performance and performativity, understanding performance in a similar manner to Judith Butler, as a 'bringing forth' of being;

4. Embodiment and the body as our means of being-in-the-world;

5. Virtuality and multiplicity, in terms of an openness to the potential for multiple time-spaces to co-exist.

A very simple illustration of these is provided in Box 5.2. Ultimately, non-representational geographies are relational, understanding our being-in-the-world through our relations (physical, emotional, affective) with those around us.

BOX 5.2 A NON-REPRESENTATIONAL UNDERSTANDING OF FIELDWORK

In some exploratory work of my own, I conducted some fieldwork with a colleague, Louise Ansell, whose expertise is in outdoor learning and outdoor leadership. The fieldwork was on part of the River Plym on Dartmoor, Devon, and began with us each drawing the field site in an exercise to understand the different perspectives we were bringing to the research. We spent the rest of the day surveying the river channel and measuring flow depth and velocities, but the nature of the work led us to discuss the embodied experiences of fieldwork (Couper and Ansell, 2012). The following description cross-refers to Cadman's (2009) five themes of non-representational geographies summarised in the main text.

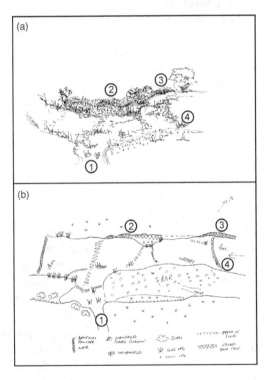

Figure 5.2 Field sketches of a pilot research site: a) by Louise Ansell; b) by Pauline Couper. The numbers identify common elements: 1 is the tributary inlet; 2 and 3 are sections of vertical bank face, bare of vegetation; 4 is a boulder weir (Couper and Ansell, 2012, p. 18).

(Continued)

(Continued)

In Couper and Ansell (2012) we consider the way in which the field 'site' was created through the drawing (mapping, in my case) of it, defining it on paper. Our attention here is on a practice (theme 1), and one that, for geographers, forms part of the taken-for-granted, everyday life (theme 2) of fieldwork. Our approaches to drawing the field site were very different. Louise stood in one place and drew an oblique sketch (see previous page), focusing her attention on the aspects that would be important if she were crossing the river. As an outdoor practitioner, to her the river was something she might encounter in a journey in the hills. In contrast, I roamed across the field site to draw a map, focusing on the geomorphological features of the river. Here we see both performance, in that we were each performing our disciplinary identities, and performativity, in that our doing so brought the field 'site' into being (theme 3). The drawings illustrate, though, that our field sites were not the same. In effect two field sites were co-existing (theme 5); two task-scapes (Dewsbury and Naylor, 2002) were enacted on the river bank. Throughout our discussion of the mapping and the rest of the day's fieldwork we drew attention to corporeal practices and embodied experience (theme 4), highlighting that 'in a multitude of...tiny interactions, a constant interplay between field, researcher and equipment, the field site itself shapes the data collected' (Couper and Ansell, p. 19). This last point also hints at Actor Network Theory.

Non-representational geographies (sometimes referred to as more-than-representational, to emphasise that they are not *against* representation) draw on and share sensibilities with a range of positions, of which phenomenology, and particularly Merleau–Ponty's phenomenology, is just one. Alongside ANT, Gilles Deleuze's work has a strong influence, not least in his conception of events as 'leading to', or opening up multiple potentialities, possibilities that are always in the process of becoming. The Deleuzian notion of **assemblage** is also important, emphasising the coming together of actors, objects and discourses in more or less stable formations (Davies, 2013).

Theoretical discussion of non-representational theory can be quite dense, and arguably the best way to get to grips with this kind of approach to geographical research is to look at some specific examples. One of the immediate challenges is that the non-representational, pre-cognitive or non-cognitive dimensions of experience are, by definition, difficult if not impossible to fully capture (represent) in words. There are effectively two dimensions to this. Firstly, to understand experience researchers may draw on their own experiences and/or try to investigate the experiences of others, but the latter is dependent upon those others being able to articulate feelings, meanings, emotions and affective encounters (Hubbard et al., 2002). Secondly, the researcher then needs to find an effective

way of communicating such experiences, and communication is inherently representational. Different geographers have approached these challenges in different
ways, adopting qualitative methods such as participant observation, diaries and
interviews, and adapting them into observant participation, participant 'sensing'
as opposed to just observation (see Wood's 2012 account of music festivals) and
performative ethnographies. As in the earlier (humanistic) phenomenological
geographies, the emphasis is on describing rather than analysing, but the balance
between description and analysis varies between studies. Waitt and Cook's (2007)
study of ecotourism, and Vannini and Taggart's (2013) work on 'islandness' provide two examples, which will be discussed next.

Researching ecotourism, Waitt and Cook (2007) aimed to investigate embodied relations with non-human entities. They focused on two kayaking ecotours
in Thailand, using a combination of participant observation and photograph-
interviews. One of the researchers joined the ecotours daily over a two-week
period, recording observations in a diary. Ecotour participants were given dispos-
able cameras at the start of their tour, and asked to take photographs of places,
objects or events that they found interesting or memorable. The photographs
were then used as prompts in semi-structured interviews two or three days after
their tour.

Waitt and Cook recognise the time lag between experience and interview as
problematic, in that the 'situatedness of the embodied knowledge' (p. 540) being
explored was partially lost. In addition, some of the photographs were lost because
of the conditions in which the cameras were stored, so the researchers had to rely
more on observations and verbal interview data than originally planned.
Nonetheless, they identify that participants privileged sight above their other
senses, with little acknowledgement of the role of touch, smell and hearing in their
experiences. Indeed, an anxiety about 'touching nature' was apparent. The researchers highlight the dominance of Western dualist notions of nature as separate from
humans, noting the ways in which the ecotour guides reinforce a sense that
'authentic' nature requires an absence of humans. They also point out, though, that
their research was dependent upon language. The English language has a rich
vocabulary for expressing the visual elements of tourism: sightseeing, views, landscape, panorama, postcards – all prioritise the visual. There are no equivalents to
describe knowledge based on smell or hearing. While this is a methodological issue,
in the context of ecotourism and human relations with nature it is also a substantive point, as it highlights that embodied practices are culturally scripted. The close
connection between topics and methods that we noted earlier as characteristic of
phenomenology remains valid for non-representational geographies.

Waitt and Cook's (2007) research draws on non-representational theory, but
their paper 'analyses' as much as 'describes' the experiences of their research participants. In contrast, description is central to Vannini and Taggart's (2013) account
of 'islandness'. Much of their paper presents an account of Phillip Vannini's lived
experience of one island, aiming to 'reveal, enliven and animate' (p. 228) rather than

analyse and explain. They describe their approach to the research as 'arts-informed'. Links to moving images and sounds are embedded in the paper, making it a multi-dimensional and multi-sensory experience, but the text itself is also literary and evocative in style. It begins:

> Visualize a billboard ad along the side of the highway, as you zoom by. Perhaps visualize the very last one you saw, on your way to the office. Can you tell me what it said? Did you slow down to read it, to take it all in?

> Visualize a bulletin board now. Its cork-like texture. Its multiple colourful thumbtacks. The panoply of old signs posted weeks and months ago, now buried beneath newer ones with less rugged edges, with more hope of catching your attention. Visualize it hung up on the paint-yearning wall of a small island ferry terminal. Well, 'terminal', hardly. More like a garage of sorts: stuffy and unkempt inside, full of old cheesy furniture and bad plumbing, and surrounded by dusty cars and old bikes on the outside.

> Visualize your attention not needing large letters or flashing neon lights. You're close enough to read, you live near enough to care. And the ferry's unhurried pace has gifted you time to read.

Reading the full account goes some way to developing a sense of the embodied, non-cognitive, and non-linguistic ways that we encounter places. The authors then theorise 'islandness', drawing on the phenomenological notion of dwelling. In essence, Vannini and Taggart argue that the starting point for understanding island-ness is not what an island is, but what islanders do, their everyday practices and being-in-the-world. 'Sense of place' lies in kinaesthetic, embodied performance.

Phenomenological themes associated with experience and meaning are thus present in non-representational geographies and Actor Network Theory. Both of these have been described as poststructuralist, or even post-poststructuralist, and post-phenomenological as well. Inspired in part by Don Ihde's work in science and technology studies, post-phenomenology draws on phenomenology and **pragmatism**, emphasising empirical experiences and rejecting the **transcendental** tendencies of Husserl's phenomenology. Some post-phenomenology is also anti-essentialist, against the Husserlian search for essences in recognition that phenomena can be multi-stable (Ihde, 2008), having multiple possible uses and hence multiple meanings. In comparison with the new cultural geography's focus on representation, non-representational geographies recognise that embodied gestures, actions and movements do not just express cultural meanings but enact, perform or (re)produce them. This 'radically constructivist' position (as opposed to social constructivist, addressed in Chapter 6) introduces an inherently political and ethical dimension, opening up possibilities for change (Anderson and Harrison, 2010). If we act differently, we change the world.

EXERCISE 5.1

Researching the materialities of sugar-cane fields

Richardson-Ngwenya (2014) recounts her attempt to develop 'vitalist material' geographies in fieldwork during her doctoral research. Read her account and try to answer the following questions:

1) What was the focus of her research?

2) Richardson-Ngwenya's research took a 'vital materialist' stance:

   a) What is vital materialism?

   b) How does it connect with phenomenology and post-phenomenology?

3) What methods did use she use in her fieldwork?

4) In Richardson-Ngwenya's experience, what were the benefits and shortcomings of these methods?

5) Look at the online videos linked to the paper. Do these make any difference to your understanding of her research?

Richardson-Ngwenya's paper is available on the companion website, along with some answers to these questions. The full reference for the paper is:

Richardson-Ngwenya, P. (2014) 'Performing a more-than-human material imagination during fieldwork: muddy boots, diarizing and putting vitalism on video', *Cultural Geographies* 21 (2): 293–9. doi: 10.1177/1474474012469004.

5.4 Phenomenology, or post-phenomenology, at the beach

The recent work on materiality, embodiment, non-representational theory, Actor Network Theory, non-human and relational geographies offers much potential for research at the beach. The beach is, after all, a place where embodied experience is paramount. Obrador Pons developed **haptic** geographies of the beach, focusing on touch and the production of feeling in relation to nudity (2007), sunbathing and building sandcastles (2009). The rituals of preparing to surf are noted by Ford and Brown (2006), involving waxing surfboards, donning wetsuits and paddling out through the spaces between waves. Evers (2009) identifies the ways in which male Australian surfers perform masculinity through their surfing practices, while Anderson (2012) focuses on the experience of surfing. He describes the coming together of surfer, board and wave to create the surfed wave as a place in its own right, an assemblage and convergence of human and non-human.

For inspiration, we could consider the many practices associated with the beach: the swimming, running, dog-walking, paddling, barbecuing or beach-combing. We might examine the ways in which the beach is delineated into territories, whether through formally designated and regulated swimming zones or through the practices of groups of beach-goers laying out towels and erecting sun- or wind-screens. Our experiences of, and negotiated movements through, such territories would lend itself to participant observation or observant participation. Performances of gender, health, youth and parenthood could be observed on a busy beach. For more overtly political engagement we might focus on the practices, performances and experiences of campaigning and activism, with groups like Surfers Against Sewage or Save the Waves, in much the way that Lee (2013) considers climate change activism.

Whatever people are doing at the beach, there is potential for non-representational research. An essential step in this, though, is to clearly establish a theoretical framing for the study. Relational geographies are many and varied, and so it is important to set out the assumptions and parameters of the research.

5.5 Phenomenology and post-phenomenology in summary

Phenomenology developed in explicit recognition that the phenomena we experience through our senses, phenomena which form the basis of positivist science, are all perceived by *us*. The ways in which we know, experience and live (through) the world are central, in a non-**idealist** and non-**realist** manner. If we were to identify key characteristics of phenomenology, then the attempts to overcome Cartesian binaries, understanding humans as being-in-the-world, would have to be contenders.

Geographers' engagement with phenomenology has largely happened in two waves. Humanistic geography of the 1970s led to a shift in the questions being asked in geography, focusing on how people experience and produce places. Since the 1990s, phenomenology has been one influence in a heady mix of philosophical and theoretical positions that together form non-representational geographies, paying attention to our embodied, relational, material everyday practices, and the constant in-the-making of the world.

FURTHER READING

For further explanations

Anderson, B. and Harrison, P. (2010) 'The promise of non-representational theories', in B. Anderson and P. Harrison (eds), *Taking Place: Non-Representational Theories and Geography*. Farnham: Ashgate. pp. 1–34.

Larsen, S.C. and Johnson, J.T. (2012) 'Toward an open sense of place: phenomenology, affinity, and the question of being', *Annals of the Association of American Geographers* 102 (3): 632–46. [Recommended reading for explanation of Husserl and particularly Heidegger, pp. 636–40, but especially 636–8].

Seamon, D. and Sowers, S. (2008) 'Place and Placelessness: Edward Relph', in P. Hubbard, R. Kitchin and G. Valentine (eds), *Key Texts in Human Geography*. London: Sage. pp. 43–51.

Whatmore, S. (2006) 'Materialist returns: practising cultural geography in and for a more-than-human world', *Cultural Geographies* 13: 600–9.

Wylie, J. (2007) *Landscape*. Abingdon: Routledge. (See Chapter 5, 'Landscape and Phenomenology').

Progress in Human Geography resources

Butcher, S. (2012) 'Embodied cognitive geographies', *Progress in Human Geography* 36 (1): 90–110. doi: 10.1177/0309132511412997.

Daniels, S., Guelke, L. and Buttimer, A. (1994) 'Classics in Human Geography revisited: Buttimer, A. (1976) Grasping the dynamism of the lifeworld. *Annals of the Association of American Geographers* 66, 277–92', *Progress in Human Geography* 18 (4): 501–6.

Gold, J.R., Stock, M. and Relph, E (2000) 'Classics in Human Geography revisited: Relph, E. (1976) *Place and Placelessness*. London: Pion', *Progress in Human Geography* 24 (4): 613–19. doi: 10.1191/030913200100189139.

Lorimer, H. (2005) 'Cultural geography: the busyness of being "more-than-representational"', *Progress in Human Geography* 29 (1): 83-94. doi: 10.1191/0309132505ph531pr.

Paterson, M. (2009) 'Haptic geographies: ethnography, haptic knowledges and sensuous dispositions', *Progress in Human Geography* 33 (6): 766–88. doi: 10.1177/0309132509910355.

Robert, E. (2013) 'Geography and the visual image: a hauntological approach', *Progress in Human Geography* 37 (3): 386–402. doi: 10.1177/0309132512460902.

Simonsen, K. (2013) 'In quest of a new humanism: embodiment, experience and phenomenology as critical geography', *Progress in Human Geography* 37 (1): 10–26. doi: 10.1177/03091325467573.

Examples

Barratt, P. (2012) '"My magic cam": a more-than-representational account of the climbing assemblage', *Area* 44 (1): 46–53.

Brown, K. (2012) 'Sharing public space across difference: attunement and the contested burdens of choreographing encounter', *Social & Cultural Geography* 13 (7): 801–20.

Daya, S. (2011) 'Performing place, mobility and identity in South Africa', *Area* 43 (4): 488–94.

Maddrell, A. (2013) 'Living with the deceased: absence, presence and absence-presence', *Cultural Geographies* 20 (4): 501–22.

Vannini, P. and Taggart, J. (2013) 'Doing islandness: a non-representational approach to an island's sense of place', *Cultural Geographies* 20 (2): 225–42.

6

Social Constructionism and Feminism: It's All Down to Us

Figure 6.1   The Lyd Valley, Devon, UK (Photograph by Tony Atkin)

Take a look at the photograph in Figure 6.1. You can probably pick out the stream meandering across the valley floor (centre foreground), although it is visible only as a line of shadows and vegetation changes. If you were asked to delineate the valley sides and the floodplain, you would probably be able to. You might also identify several small debris cones on the left side of the valley, covered by vegetation, but suggesting there has been some downslope movement of materials at some time. The question is: do these landforms really exist, or are they just our invention, a way of ordering and making sense of the landscape around us? This may seem like an odd question: of course they exist, we can see them! But the processes of water and sediment transfer operate across multiple landforms, the physical landscape functioning more as a continuum of surfaces, materials and forces than as a patchwork of discrete forms. The question of whether landforms really constitute 'natural kinds' (groups of real, distinguishable entities) has long been debated in geomorphology (Rhoads and Thorn, 1999; Bishop and Shroder, 2004; Berthling, 2011).

What is your ethnic group? This question is often used in social surveys, as well as in equality monitoring associated with recruitment to jobs or entry into universities. In the UK, government surveys such as the census use standard lists of ethnic groups, one of which is reproduced in Table 6.1. The question is: do these groups represent real similarities and differences between people, or are they just our invention, a set of expectations about people that then shape our behaviour to make those differences 'real'?

Table 6.1   The ethnic groups that feature in the UK Government's 'recommended country specific ethnic group question for use in England'

White

1. English / Welsh / Scottish / Northern Irish / British
2. Irish
3. Gypsy or Irish Traveller
4. Any other White background, please describe

Mixed / Multiple ethnic groups

5. White and Black Caribbean
6. White and Black African
7. White and Asian
8. Any other Mixed / Multiple ethnic background, please describe

Asian / Asian British

9. Indian
10. Pakistani
11. Bangladeshi
12. Chinese
13. Any other Asian background, please describe

Black / African / Caribbean / Black British

14. African
15. Caribbean
16. Any other Black / African / Caribbean background, please describe

Other ethnic group

17. Arab
18. Any other ethnic group, please describe

Social constructionism provides a particular kind of response to questions like these, holding that our knowledge, concepts and sometimes even phenomena themselves are artefacts (constructs) of our language and actions. Since the 'cultural turn' of the 1980s, much human geography has been broadly social constructionist: I would include here feminist, **postmodern** and **poststructuralist** geographies, although other authors provide conflicting accounts of the relations between these. This chapter offers a basic introduction to social constructionism, considers geography (and academic disciplines more broadly) as socially constructed, and then focuses on feminist geographies. Postmodern and poststructuralist geographies are addressed in Chapter 7.

6.1 Introducing social constructionism

Social constructionism is popular in many fields, including geography, sociology, anthropology, history and psychology. Given the number of researchers and diversity of interests across these, there is plenty of scope for variation. A particular point of confusion arises around the related terms 'constructionism' and 'constructivism'. The latter is used in psychology and education to refer to a particular theory of how individuals learn. Geographers seem to use the two terms more or less interchangeably though, the emphasis being on social processes that shape our knowledge or understanding of the world. For the sake of clarity, I will stick to 'social constructionism'.

Probably the most wide-ranging account of social constructionism (wide ranging in disciplinary coverage) is Ian Hacking's (1999) book, *The Social Construction of What?* Hacking points out that the objects to which social constructionism has been applied are many and varied, from 'authorship' to 'Zulu nationalism', with emotions, gender, mental illness, nature, quarks, sexuality and youth homelessness in between (Hacking, 1999; Mallon, 2013). He thus suggests that it is helpful to look at the purpose of social constructionist arguments, rather than trying to define social construction. Put simply, such arguments tend to adopt a format of, firstly, pointing out how 'X' (the object of study) is taken for granted, and seems inevitable; then, secondly, demonstrating that 'X' is not inevitable, determined by the nature of things, but is an artefact of social life. 'X' could be different. The common purpose of such arguments is consciousness-raising, challenging the status quo.

6.1.1 How are things socially constructed?

The term 'social construction' was popularised in the social sciences by Berger and Luckmann (1966). Arguing that studies of the sociology of knowledge had focused too much on theoretical, 'academic' knowledge, they turned their attention to the kind of common-sense knowledge that we all rely on, beginning with a phenomenological analysis of everyday life. **Phenomenology** is described in Chapter 5, but at its core is a notion that our only knowledge of the material world is through perception, or mental acts. Every mental act involves intentionality, being directed towards some object or concept. Intentional objects might be objects of belief (propositions), objects of thought (ideas), objects of love or hate or fear (such as individuals, pets or spiders). These intentional objects have no existence independently of the mental state that 'refers' to them. This is not to say that the spider you are frightened of does not exist, but you cannot separate the feared spider (intentional object) from the 'real' spider. The feared spider is your only consciousness of the spider. Phenomenology seeks to understand these mental acts that provide our consciousness of the world (Scruton, 1995).

Berger and Luckman sought to reconcile two dominant understandings of society. On the one hand, Weber thought that all human actions express subjective meaning. To understand society we must therefore understand individuals' choices and actions (agency). On the other, Durkheim considered society to have 'objective facticity'. The facts of society exist independently of individuals and provide the everyday reality in which we live, thereby shaping our actions. The café, the library, the night club, breakfast, computers, footballs, mobile phones, banks, rent and student loans all exist to each of us, providing a shared, ordered reality (Durkheim), and yet all of these things are the products of human thoughts and actions (Weber). This raises questions about how our thoughts and actions can produce an objective reality external to us as individuals. Berger and Luckman identified a number of processes by which this happens.

When we do something regularly, we tend to develop a habitual way of doing it. Think of the way you brush your teeth, the order in which you put clothes on in the morning, or make a cup of tea. It is quite likely that you have some habitual way of doing these everyday tasks. Without these kinds of routines we would have to think our way through a myriad of decisions in everything we do throughout the day. Habitualisation saves us that effort.

Habits can also become collective. I used to take the bus to work. For over two years I got on the same bus each day, joining other people who used that bus route at that time of day for their daily commute. I soon realised that each passenger sat in the same place each day, although there was no verbalised 'rule' or instruction for us to do so. It may have started with one person. Perhaps the first person on the bus each day always sat in the same place, and others then reciprocated the habit. When types of actors (in this case, bus passengers) share types of habitualised actions (such as sitting in the same seat each day), the habit becomes institutionalised.

In becoming institutionalised a habit also becomes objectivated. The habit of passengers sitting in the same seat every day was clearly established before I started using the bus. It therefore formed part of the objective reality of bus travel for me and I quickly conformed to type, identifying a seat that was unused and sitting there each day, thereby claiming it as 'my' seat. I had become 'socialised' into the institution of regular bus travel.

This very simple example of everyday life has highlighted some of the processes Berger and Luckmann identified as central to social construction: habitualisation leading to institutionalisation; objectivation; and socialisation. Crucially, there is nothing about regular bus travel that necessitates sitting in the same seat each day. This objective reality was entirely the result of individual and collective human actions. You can find a more extended account, introducing other, related processes, on the companion website.

Language is the most pervasive means of objectivation. As children learn the words used by those around them, they learn (shared) meanings about things, and these meanings enable us to make (common) sense of the world. The same is true for students learning the various branches of geography; certain words are used in certain ways, and you learn the shared use of language at the same time as learning the concepts. Language thus has a role in shaping our understanding of 'reality'.

Ultimately, social constructionism maintains that the objective reality of our everyday lives is being constantly constructed and reproduced socially. The way we think, communicate and act affects the world around us (Elder-Vass, 2012).

6.1.2 Social constructionism in geography

Within geography, social constructionist ideas have become particularly prevalent since the cultural turn of the 1980s. Peter Jackson is often cited as a leading proponent in this. Drawing on the work of cultural theorist Stuart Hall, Jackson and Smith (1981) developed an understanding of race and ethnicity as socially constructed. Jackson's 1989 book, *Maps of Meaning*, then urged geographers to look beyond a notion of culture as simply 'material artefacts', the products of the intellectual or artistic elite. He demonstrated that social and cultural theory from outside the discipline offered geographers a means of understanding culture as the on-going process of meaning-making through which identities are socially constructed, imposed and contested in our everyday lives. The unequal relations of power that underpin social and cultural categorisation (class, race, gender and sexuality) were a particular concern. **Discourse** and cultural politics became central to the 'new cultural geographies' (Jackson and Taylor, 1996; Lorimer, 2005; Mitchell, 2011), paving the way for postmodern and poststructuralist geographies. A key theme in this work is 'representation', and the ways in which social categories, groups and identities are constructed through social and cultural processes.

The adoption of a social constructionist perspective thus drew attention to identities and the social and spatial practices associated with them. Who we are, and who we consider others to be in relation to ourselves, becomes manifest in space. From women's fear of particular places in the city (Pain, 1991) to the role of planning and architecture in attempts to construct national identity in Israel (Yacobi, 2008); from depictions of Eastern Europe through novels and films such as Bram Stoker's *Dracula* (Dittmer, 2006) to risk-taking in the 'death zone' by

Himalayan climbers (Wilson, 2012), or vulnerability to climate change resulting from political discourses and policies (Shearer, 2012); places and identities are socially constructed in tandem.

6.1.3 The social construction of academic knowledge

Not only have geographers used social constructionist ideas to understand the world around us, but geography itself, and the popularity of particular philosophies and theories within it at any one time, can be understood as socially constructed. The ideas of Thomas Kuhn (1922–96) are central here.

Kuhn began his academic career as a physicist but became a particularly influential philosopher of science. His 1962 book, *The Structure of Scientific Revolutions*, is one of the most cited academic books of all time (Bird, 2013). When he wrote it, the development of science was commonly seen as a continuous accumulation of facts and theories, progressing ever closer to the 'truth'. Kuhn directly challenged this understanding. By examining historic developments in science he found evidence of a cyclical pattern of development, rather than a continuous, linear progression.

The early stages of any science (such as physics, chemistry or biology) are dominated by the collection of 'facts', with any number of competing approaches to making sense of those facts. Gradually, one view becomes dominant, and so provides the frame of reference by which legitimate problems and methods for the science are determined. In the Earth sciences, the evolutionary perspective of landscape development promoted by Hutton and Lyell in the late eighteenth and early nineteenth centuries could be seen as an example of this. Kuhn used the term '**paradigm**' to describe this frame of reference, a point that we shall come back to later.

Once a dominant paradigm is established, the science enters a period that Kuhn termed 'normal science'. He described this as being what the majority of scientists do throughout their careers, essentially solving puzzles within the frame of reference provided by the paradigm, further articulating and specifying its implications. My own doctoral research on river bank erosion provides an example. Examining the ways in which soil particle size distribution influences bank erosion processes, I was working firmly within the framing of deterministic systems geomorphology, drawing on physical and chemical theories of soil properties and river bank stability. The research did not challenge these theories, but added in a small way to the stock of knowledge developed within this framing (such as in Couper and Maddock, 2001).

Kuhn found that, over time, members of a scientific community come across anomalies, or problems that cannot be solved within the paradigm. These anomalies accumulate to a point of crisis, when it is clear that the paradigm is inadequate, and this opens the door to revolution. New approaches to resolving these problems are sought, and new theories developed, eventually leading the subject community to a new paradigm, and commitment to a new frame of reference. Kuhn's structure of scientific revolutions thus runs as in Figure 6.2.

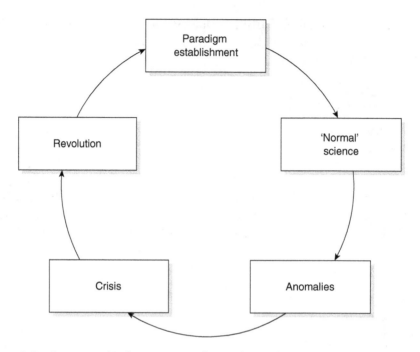

Figure 6.2 Summary of Kuhn's structure of scientific revolutions

On the surface of it this may not sound much like social constructionism. However, Kuhn (1962) describes a number of social processes operating in science. Perhaps the most challenging aspect of his work at the time that it was published was the assertion that there is always a degree of arbitrariness in science. What a researcher makes of a problem, or of a set of data, will be influenced by his or her prior educa-tion and experience, and the expectations these lead to. Different researchers will interpret data in different, but quite possibly equally valid, ways. Similarly, for a com-munity of scientists, there is nothing that particularly necessitates the emergence of one paradigm and not another. Once established, though, a paradigm determines what entities are considered to be worth studying, what questions can legitimately be asked, and what methods can be used to establish answers. It provides a collective, *habitual* way for members of the subject community to approach research problems. The next generation of researchers is then *socialised* into these institutionalised prac-tices and assumptions through their education.

A paradigm also affects the social structure of the scientific community. Other schools of thought become sidelined, ignored or disappear altogether, much as Davisian geomorphology did in the second half of the twentieth century. Specialisation occurs, with specialist journals established and individuals concentrat-ing on specific topics. Communication becomes more restricted, confined to this specialist community (think how difficult some journal articles are to read!). The paradigm has become *institutionalised*. Except for student textbooks, there is no need for every communication to articulate and justify its underlying principles, as the paradigm does this. The paradigm thus legitimates these foundations, providing both explanation of and prescription for the ways in which research is carried out.

In Kuhn's work, then, we can see the characteristic processes of social constructionism: habitualisation, institutionalisation and socialisation. Objectivation is there too. The ideas and practices of the paradigm have begun with the ideas and practices of individuals, yet they form the objective reality of the subject for those working within the paradigm, and particularly for new entrants to the community. Box 6.1 provides an example of paradigm shift within the Earth sciences.

BOX 6.1 THE PARADIGM OF PLATE TECTONICS

A classic example of a paradigm shift is provided by the Earth sciences, in the transition from a 'fixed Earth' paradigm to that of plate tectonics. Marx and Bornmann (2012) provide a very readable account of this shift, based on an analysis of citation networks (whose work was cited by whom). The early Earth sciences were based on the assumption that the Earth's crust is fixed. Marx and Bornmann trace the gradual accumulation of anomalies that could not be explained in this framework of thought: the match between fossil plants and animals in North America and Europe, identified in the mid-1800s; the similarity in geology between Africa and Brazil noted in the late 1800s. In the early 1900s, Alfred Wegener first published the idea that the continents originated from a single land mass, split apart. The problem was that Wegener could offer no convincing explanation for this. A gradual accumulation of further anomalies throughout the next 30–40 years meant that, by the end of the 1950s, serious doubts had been raised about the idea of the Earth's crust being fixed. With the growth of seismology after the Second World War (when seismology was seen as important for monitoring nuclear test ban treaties), the evidence that earthquakes were concentrated along the plate boundaries enabled connection to be made between seismology and tectonics in the late 1960s. This, according to Marx and Bornmann (2012), provided convincing evidence to ensure the paradigm shift. Their summary of this whole process emphasises both the logical and sociological elements involved in the scientific community's acceptance of an idea:

> The initial starts (forerunners) were not taken up by the scientific community at first, since, for one, the consequences for the foundations of the geosciences were far-reaching and revolutionary, and, for another, the indications stood on shaky ground. It took the courage of unbiased,

(Continued)

> *(Continued)*
>
> young researchers and support from some older leading figures in the geo-sciences ... to get broad discussion of the existing and the new paradigms going. The fragmentation of fields in the geosciences made it difficult to be aware of all of the relevant factors that spoke for the new paradigm. There were too few researchers working across the sub-disciplines or having overarching interests. It took a critical mass of convincing data in combination with the synthesis of the pieces in a satisfactory overall picture, which was finally accepted by the scientific community in the geosciences. (p. 611)

Kuhn's work presented a direct challenge to the commonly held view of scientific progress and so, unsurprisingly, it was subject to criticism. There has been much confusion over the term 'paradigm'. His original text used the word in over 20 different ways. Kuhn acknowledged this and tried to rectify it in a postscript (1969), but by this time the word had become so popular that it had effectively acquired a life of its own. His 1969 clarification (in the postscript to the second edition) identifies two usages of the term that were central to the 1962 book. The first of these is a 'global' sense, referring to the shared theories, generalisations, models, beliefs about the world, and values of a scientific community. Kuhn (1969) is clear that he considers this usage of the term to be erroneous, suggesting that 'disciplinary matrix' would be better. The second use is rather more specific (or 'local'), referring to a paradigm as an exemplar. Here Kuhn was thinking of the kinds of problems found in science textbooks. By working through these problems, students learn to 'think like' a physicist, or chemist, or whatever their discipline is. The problems model the practices of the discipline, and so are 'paradigmatic' examples. Within geography, Holt-Jensen (2009) suggests that the regional monographs written by Vidal de la Blache provided the paradigm for regional geography.

The second major criticism of Kuhn is one of **relativism**. In the transition between paradigms, proponents of different paradigms find themselves 'arguing past each other', their views so different that even the meaning of common words can be different, resulting in miscommunication. Some have interpreted this as a form of relativism, implying that both groups could in some sense be 'right', and so there is no such thing as scientific 'progress'. Kuhn (1974) argues against this criticism. Seeing science as essentially a problem-solving activity, he points out that more recent theories are generally better at solving problems than earlier theories, hence progress is made. Kuhn does quite clearly explain, though, that he is against the view of scientific progress as moving 'closer to the truth', as there is no basis for assuming that the things postulated in our theories have a 'real' match in nature. It would seem, then, that Kuhn allows for realism in the assumption that a mind–independent world exists, but he rejects the semantic commitment of scientific realism (see Chapter 1). With this in mind, he could be said to be a 'weak' social constructionist.

He is not necessarily claiming that things-in-themselves (such as trees or rocks) are socially constructed, but that our understanding of them is.

Kuhn's notion of paradigms reached geography quite quickly, being introduced by Chorley and Haggett in 1967 (Gregory, 2000). A number of contenders for 'paradigm' status have since been proposed. Hubbard et al. (2002) list: exploration; environmental determinism; regionalism; spatial science; **humanistic** and behavioural geography; and radical and structural geography. We could add **postmodern**, **poststructuralist** and **feminist** geographies. In geomorphology, the Davisian geomorphology of the early twentieth century and the systems geomorphology that developed from the middle of that century are often seen as different paradigms (Rhoads and Thorn, 1994). There seems to be little real agreement on paradigms in geography, though. The lack of clarity noted above may offer one reason for this. Holt-Jensen (2009) suggests that the 'disciplinary matrix' version of the term has been the most often used within geography, and this is exemplified by Inkpen (2005). Alternatively, Kuhn focused on the 'basic' sciences (physics, chemistry, biology), and it may be that his ideas do not apply quite so well to 'composite' sciences such as ecology and geography (Gregory, 2000). Geographers have long been eclectic in their influences, and competing schools of thought continue to co-exist.

Unwin (1992) suggests that perhaps Kuhn's work has been popular within geography because 'its concentration on the replacement of ideas could also be extended to apply to the replacement of practitioners' (p. 81). Those who advocated the notion of paradigms and revolution saw themselves as 'heroically' replacing an older generation whose ideas were outmoded. What is interesting here is the implicit suggestion that a social constructionist theory of academic knowledge was popular for social (rather than 'scientific') reasons. This is exactly the argument that Kuhn was making.

From a social constructionist perspective, then, academic disciplines such as geography and its sub-fields (social and cultural geography, historical geography, economic geography, geomorphology, hydrology, glaciology, etc.) are social phenomena, spatially and temporally situated as much as any other geographic phenomena.

6.2 Feminism

6.2.1 Some starting points

As a 10-year-old I went to a small, rural primary school, which found itself without enough boys in the junior class to form two teams for football practice. The head teacher asked for two girls to volunteer to stand in, and I jumped at the chance. I was in the netball team, but at home my football was one of my favourite possessions. I joined the boys in PE lessons for the rest of that term, scoring two goals. At the end of term the head teacher confessed to my parents that the only reason he would not pick me for the school football team was that he thought the other schools, against which matches were played, would object.

I bought my first guitar shortly before turning 17. When I got to university, several times I was told by other students who heard me playing, 'You're really good... for a girl.' The compliment was always accompanied by the caveat. By the time I finished my doctorate I had been playing gigs in local pubs and clubs for a couple of years, and on more than one occasion had people tell me 'You're really good. You play like a bloke.' The guitar, it seems, is a very gendered instrument. In fact, the live music scene in that town during the 1990s consisted almost entirely of males.

These two short anecdotes recount minor events, but we can draw three points from them. First, they illustrate the kinds of – largely unconscious – expectations about males and females that permeate everyday life. Second, individuals who challenge these expectations, however unwittingly, encounter resistance. I was not allowed to play in the school football team, and the idea that a female could be a 'good' guitarist (whatever we mean by that) was clearly problematic. Third, both examples have spatial implications, in that the football pitch and the live music stage are dominated by men. Taken together they seem to suggest that the space for women is not at the centre of attention, but around the edges, in the audience, as spectators and supporters. Undoubtedly some things have changed since these events. England now has an international women's football team, whose matches are – at least sometimes – shown on television. But perhaps things have not changed a great deal. As recently as 2006, I heard from a music industry 'insider' that he had promoted a female rock band to a record company, but the band was not signed. The feedback from the company was that the young women were 'not pretty enough'. It was not their music that was criticised.

Women constitute roughly half of the global population but account for the majority of the world's poor (Browne et al., 2013). Globally just 21 per cent of seats in national parliaments were held by women in 2012 (World Bank Development Indicators, 2012). In 2006 the World Economics Forum devised the 'gender gap index', measuring national gender differences relating to economic, political, educational and health criteria for over a hundred countries. Having repeated the assessment annually since then, the *Global Gender Gap Report 2012* concluded that 'no country in the world has achieved gender equality' (Hausman et al., 2012, p. 33). Men's and women's lives differ, and this is the starting point for feminism.

Biologically, of course, there are differences between male and female sexes. But in 1949 French writer and philosopher Simone de Beauvoir undertook a phenomenological analysis of lived, embodied experience (see Chapter 5 for phenomenology). This led her to argue that biological sex and gender are two different things. Gender is socially constructed. Collectively we have particular ideas about masculine and feminine behaviours and characteristics, and we are socialised into these ideas from an early age. To take the obvious stereotype: pink baby clothes are for girls, blue for boys. A parent can dress a girl in blue, of course, but the child is sure to be mistaken for a boy. Boys have toy cars and guns, girls have dolls. 'Pirates and Princesses' parties may be fun for small children, but reinforce the stereotypes. Through school, friends, television programmes, books, comics, advertising hoardings and more, children learn what it is to be female or male. To not conform is to risk being ostracised, teased and bullied.

Social constructions of gender persist into adulthood. Miller and Sassler (2012) studied cohabiting couples in the US who both work, and found that women still do the majority of household chores. In British universities, employment statistics for 2011–12 reveal that over 90 per cent of 'secretaries, typists, receptionists and telephonists' are female whereas almost 84 per cent of 'drivers, maintenance supervisors and plant operatives' are male (Higher Education Statistics Agency Ltd, 2013). In our home and work lives, socially constructed expectations about men and women still shape what we do.

Recognising gender as socially constructed, however, tells us little about *why* women's and men's lives differ in the ways they do. Beauvoir's work also highlighted that gender identity is relational. 'Woman' is constructed in relation to – and in opposition to – 'Man'. As with other binaries in Western thinking, the two are not equally valued. In both French and English, for example, the word designating male humans ('homme' or 'man') is also used to refer to humans in general. Man is the norm, the archetypal human, against which Woman is defined as 'Other'. Beauvoir illustrates this by describing how annoyed she used to get in discussions when men told her, 'You only think such and such a thing because you're a woman' (Beauvoir, 1949, p. 5). The implication is that 'woman' is a particularity, an exception from normal human being. She goes on to highlight how long-held this unequal conception of the sexes is, traceable in the writings of ancient Greek philosopher Aristotle, as well as in the Adam and Eve story of the Bible. Woman is 'the second sex', always inferior to dominant Man. Gender relations are thus inherently hierarchical, and this patriarchy (the dominance of men) operates on many levels.

6.2.2 Feminism and geography

The development of geographical societies in the early 1800s formalised geography as an academic discipline (Unwin, 1992), and established it as the preserve of men. Closely intertwined with exploration and **imperialism**, geography's practitioners heroically conquered mountains and continents, subjecting the globe to the disciplining gaze of objective science. The Royal Geographical Society (established in 1830) was a male-only club, just one among many men's clubs situated in the heart of London. It was not that women never travelled. On large expeditions they carried out essential, if informal, roles: cooking food, cutting hair, generally ensuring that the men were physically up to the task at hand (Evans, 2013). Some undertook expeditions of their own. But, for those who did write of their travels, their accounts were often dismissed as subjective and unscientific. Women's lack of access to geographical institutions meant they had no access to training in surveying or other measurement techniques required for the production of valid 'geographical' knowledge (Maddrell, 2009). As a result, the knowledge they did develop was not deemed geographical. Only objective, male accounts counted as scientific knowledge.

In the late nineteenth and early twentieth centuries, movements for social reform developed across Europe, the United States, Canada, Australia and New Zealand. Women campaigned for suffrage, eventually achieving the right for all women to vote in New Zealand in 1896, with Australia, Britain, the USA and Canada following suit by 1920. More locally, women in the US were actively campaigning to change the cities in which they lived, participating in public life and gaining influential positions (Parker, 2011). Gender possibilities were changing, and geography was not isolated from this first wave of feminism. In Britain women began to gain admission to geographical societies from the 1880s. Having then proven their ability to produce scientifically credible work, women were admitted as Fellows (members) of the Royal Geographical Society in 1913, although this was only after considerable debate.

The second wave of feminism developed through the late 1960s and 1970s, the foundations having been laid by Beauvoir's 1949 book (Bergoffen, 2010). Increasingly, women in Western societies were challenging gender inequalities, campaigning on issues ranging from pay to violence against women. In the 1970s women held just 2.9 per cent of full professorships in geography in US universities. Criticisms of such under-representation began to appear in academic journals in the early 1970s, but it was not until the 1980s that feminism in geography began to gain real momentum. In 1982, Jan Monk and Susan Hanson provided a turning point with their paper, 'On not excluding half of the human in human geography'.

Monk and Hanson explained that geography was riddled with passive, inadvertent, sexism. Given that knowledge is socially constructed, the kind of knowledge produced is determined by who produces it and the methods they use. With such a small number of women geographers in universities, geographical knowledge production was dominated by men, and hence by men's interests. They argued that, as a result, geography was sexist in content, method and purpose.

In content, geographers were focusing on arenas traditionally dominated by men: farmsteads, housing exteriors and gas stations, for example. They were defining research problems in ways that neglected women's lives. Studies of family migration or urbanisation analysed only the experiences of men, yet the different family roles of men and women can lead to very different experiences and needs. Where women were explicitly addressed, Monk and Hanson found that they were assumed to play the traditional gender roles of home and childcare, exactly the kinds of activities that research did not focus on.

In methods, women were often rendered invisible. Households were defined in terms of a man's occupation. Women were difficult to trace in secondary data sources such as the census, their surnames changing between records through marriage. Knowledge was thus being formulated in ways that excluded women, and

Monk and Hanson argued that this meant geographers' results would only ever reinforce the power dynamics already existing in society. The lives of women, or of any other oppressed group, could never be changed by such research.

Since Monk and Hanson's analysis, geographers have drawn on feminist philosophy to more explicitly identify masculinist epistemologies dominating the discipline. Rose (1993) provided a particularly comprehensive and influential analysis. Since the Enlightenment of the seventeenth century, Western cultures have prioritised 'science': rational, universal, compartmentalised, and objective. These characteristics are associated with the male faculties of reason. Their opposites – irrationality, particularity, relationality, and subjectivity – are 'the domain of unreasoning, female faculties driven by mere sensibility' (Dixon and Jones, 2006, p. 45). In particular, fieldwork – often considered to be so central to the discipline – was highlighted by Rose (1993) as 'an example of geographical masculinities in action' (p. 65).

Feminist geography, then, began with the politics of the discipline. This led to the development of feminist approaches to studying geographical phenomena, exploring gender roles and relations, the operation of patriarchy in society, and the ways in which these intersect with space and place. That feminism has a place within geography is now without question. Gender is widely accepted as a valid analytical category (Browne et al., 2013), and feminism has had a significant impact on the way (human) geography research and, in some cases, teaching is practised. Whether it can be said to be part of the disciplinary mainstream is less certain. In terms of disciplinary politics, the practice of feminist geographies is still difficult in some countries. Geography – and physical geography in particular – remains a male-dominated discipline globally. Inequalities still exist.

EXERCISE 6.1

Gender in your local context

Use the following questions to think about how gender plays out in the department in which you are studying:

1) Among the academic staff, are there more males than females?

2) What is the gender balance of staff among human geographers and among physical geographers? If there is any difference, why do you think this is?

3) What gender are the administrative staff you come into contact with?

4) Think back to your own experiences of field trips. Have you noticed any differences in behaviour between male and female students?

6.2.3 Feminist geographies

The term 'feminism' has been used rather unquestioningly in the account above, but feminism is not a single entity. There are different forms of feminism, and different feminist geographies. A convenient way to make sense of the differences is to take a broadly chronological approach, outlining different emphases in feminist geography at different times. This risks over-simplification, giving the impression of a linear progression in ideas when the reality has been somewhat messier (McDowell, 1993a). With that caveat, I follow the lead of McDowell (1993a; 1993b) and Aitchison (2005) in highlighting three broad perspectives: empirical feminism; feminist standpoint theory; and poststructuralist feminism.

Empirical feminism

In the 1970s and early 1980s, geographers were increasingly recognising the exclusion of women from disciplinary life and public life (such as waged work and politics) more generally. In this context, much early feminist geography focused on illustrating such inequalities and advocating policies that would change them. Empirical feminist geography, in effect, represents a continuation of the kinds of methods that geographers were already using, but with a focus on women: the 'add women and stir' approach (McDowell, 1993a, p. 161). Spatial analyses highlighted the differences in living standards of women compared with that of men. In urban geography, feminist insights revealed that geographers' conceptions of urban life were male-centric, focused on 'public' activities (as was common across all kinds of geography). Domestic life and the domestic restructuring that accompanied industrial change and urbanisation were entirely neglected. More than that, feminist geographers revealed that gender divisions and power relations were embedded in the city itself, in land use patterns and architecture. Harman (1983, p. 104) explained:

> The city has been shaped to keep women confined to their traditional roles as wives and mothers. Suburbs are built expressly for the family; job opportunities are few for many; the public transport system is geared for the movement of commuters in peak periods and it is difficult for women to cross between suburbs; public places equipped with revolving doors or turnstiles render the woman with a pram or pushchair a 'handicapped person'.

Gender shapes experiences of the city, but also perceptions. Gill Valentine (1989; 1990) highlighted the ways in which women's fear of crime affects their interactions with, and movements through, urban spaces, offering an early example of a now significant strand of work (recent examples including Sandberg and Tollefsen, 2010 and Paul, 2011).

Empirical feminism achieved much, but was not without limitations (McDowell 1993a; 1993b). Its emphasis lay in identifying gendered social relations in the material world and challenging inequalities. This was underpinned by a rationalist, modernist mode of thinking, rather than challenging the status quo at the level of epistemology and theory. In effect, feminist empiricism acts for reform rather than wholesale change (Aitchison, 2005).

Feminist standpoint theory

To begin with an example: Harriet Jacobs arrived in the world in 1813, born into slavery in the southern states of the USA. Having lived in slavery for 27 years she managed to escape, hiding in a small space above a store room for the next seven years before travelling north and eventually securing her freedom. Harriet then wrote her autobiography, *Incidents in the Life of a Slave Girl* (1861). Through telling her story she hoped to help Americans in the northern (free) states to understand the lives of slaves. 'Only [by] experience can anyone realize how deep, and dark, and foul is that pit of abominations', she wrote (p. 6). Her account of the exploitation, the physical, emotional and sexual abuse she had suffered as a slave, did indeed reach out to the women in the northern states, who added their voices to the growing anti-slavery movement. Hesse-Biber and Leavy (2006, p. 53) explain: 'Speaking from a position of direct experience, Jacob's words filled the widespread silence and ignorance about the condition of female slaves and challenged many of the misconceptions about slave women that were predominant at the time.'

Harriet Jacobs' knowledge of slavery was not based on a distant, objective observation and analysis, but on her own experience. This gave her a kind of knowledge that was not available to others who did not share her position. Her account of the abusive power relations between master and slave shone a different light on slavery for people who had no direct experience of it. This illustrates three principal claims of feminist standpoint theory (Bowell, 2011):

1. Knowledge is socially situated. In other words, knowledge is developed from a particular position, and within a particular context, in society. Knowledge is shaped by this context and positionality. Harriet knew slavery as a (former) slave.

2. Marginalised groups are socially situated in ways that give them particular insights into society, enabling them to ask more, or different, questions from non-marginalised groups. A situation (in this example, slavery) may look very different from the 'inside' than from the 'outside'.

3. Research should begin with the lives of the marginalised, particularly research focusing on power relations.

The term 'standpoint' should not be taken to imply this is simply about 'women's views'. A standpoint is a collective identity or consciousness, achieved through shared political struggle. A feminist standpoint, then, designates a women's perspective with a consciousness of women as an oppressed and marginalised group in society. In writing her account of slavery, Harriet Jacobs was conscious of her position as a member of an oppressed group and used that position to ask questions of society more broadly.

A fundamental difference between feminist standpoint theory and empirical feminism lies in understandings of equality. Empirical feminism views equality as 'sameness' (McDowell, 1993b). The implication is that 'difference' is unequal and hence unfair. From a feminist standpoint, this conception of equality is itself a masculinist position: it negates difference, arguing that we all deserve equal opportunities because we are really all the same. In contrast, feminist standpoint theory celebrates difference. This means seeking out 'female' knowledge specifically because it is different from male knowledge, seeking the voices of the marginalised because they will have a better understanding of their marginalisation than an 'outsider' would. Donna Haraway thus argued that researchers should recognise the knowledge they produce as 'situated', positioned in a certain way and in a particular context (McDowell, 1993b).

Second-wave feminism thus signalled a more significant shift in geography, challenging epistemological assumptions. Empirical feminism had continued the tradition of seeking objective, disinterested knowledge. Standpoint theory introduced different assumptions about what counts as valid knowledge and who has access to such knowledge, such that experiential knowledge became key (Feminist Pedagogy Working Group, 2002). This required different kinds of research questions, in an attempt to understand women's experiences and perspectives rather than just describe their lives from a distance. This, in turn, presented methodological challenges. If the kinds of data sources previously used in geography left women hidden, then new sources of data and new kinds of data needed to be found. Feminist geographers found themselves using diaries, letters, oral histories, folklore, artwork, songs and photographs, broadening ideas about what might constitute valid 'evidence' and analysis in geography (Baschlind, 2002; Cope, 2002).

Beth Bee's (2013) study of rural Mexican women's environmental knowledge and capacity to adapt to climate change provides a recent example of the use of feminist standpoint theory. Her research focused on two 'ejido' communities in Guanajuato state, ejidos being agrarian communities in which individuals are allocated the right to use plots of land, with decisions made collectively by an ejido assembly. In Guanajuato at large, just 17.8 per cent of the ejido assembly members are female. Bee's research set out to examine women's knowledge and decision-making, and how these influence their capacity to adapt to uncertainties associated with climate change.

Bee used a combination of four qualitative methods. She conducted 70 household interviews, with women being the main respondent in these, and undertook participant observation, visiting the two communities daily for four months each (Bee, 2011). She then worked with participants to construct 'gender resource maps'.

These involved drawing a participant's house and the resources on which it depended, and then labelling each resource according to the gender of who controlled it, whose labour went into it, and who was responsible for it. Finally, groups of eight women were gathered together for collaborative mental modelling activities, sharing and constructing knowledge of climate change and associated vulnerabilities.

Bee's research revealed that the women provided much labour in the fields, sowing, weeding, helping with harvest and often shepherding. Their knowledge of edible wild plants growing alongside the crops contributed to ensuring food security. Many of the women had little influence on decision-making in the fields, but were conscious to pass on their agro-environmental knowledge to their children – an act that Bee (2013) describes as representing the women's ability to act within the socio-political constraints of their labour responsibilities. In contrast to the fields, the home was where women provided the majority of labour, and had responsibility and decision-making control. Their day-to-day running of the home meant they had expert knowledge of increasing food prices, as well as costs of resources such as electricity and water. The small proportion of women who had decision-making control in the fields utilised this knowledge to inform their decisions about which crops to plant, in order to minimise vulnerability to uncertain climatic conditions (such as the risk of drought).

Bee's research, then, demonstrated that women in the ejido communities have significant knowledge, but the degree to which this knowledge can be transferred into actions and strategies for adapting to climate change is constrained by social and political structures. She concludes that, 'as feminist standpoint theory posits, there is often a gap between what women know and what they are able to do, and this difference has something to do with the relations of power in their families and communities' (Bee, 2013, p. 146).

Postmodern/poststructural feminism

In the summer of 2008, Canadian geographer Caroline Desbiens took her first trip to Salluit, Nunavik, in the Canadian Arctic. Not unlike Bee (2013) above, Desbiens aimed to study the local Sallumiut (Inuit) women's knowledge of the land in the context of climate change. From the outset this was a feminist project. Inuit men, who hunt large animals such as caribou, bear and whale, roam wide areas of land and develop an understanding of weather patterns and sea ice in order to hunt successfully. Studies of their knowledge and the large-animal resources it focuses on attract funds for researchers. The women's knowledge of resources is much closer to home and smaller scale. Berries, plants and fish are less impressive than bears and whales, less likely to attract research funding. Desbiens was starting with the marginalised, the overlooked.

Desbiens' (2010) paper recounts the process of her research with the women of Salluit, and the way her preconceptions about their environmental knowledge were dismantled. Having prepared questions to focus on changing resources, she found herself setting these aside in order to listen to the women's narratives about themselves; their histories, their families, their lives. Knowledge of the environment was inseparable from these identities. Desbiens had to risk being distracted from her research, risk not achieving anything at all, to develop any kind of understanding. She comments (p. 414) that, 'at times building meaningful human connections during fieldwork is more important than "the project".' In taking that risk, she achieved some insight into how 'climate change' is framed within Western, developed world agendas in ways that may never address the issues faced by Northern Aboriginal (or 'First Nations') communities.

A not dissimilar story is found in sociologist Janet Hinson Shope's (2006) account of her research, as a White North American researcher among rural Black women in South Africa. Having planned interviews, Shope found that focus groups were more appropriate in a culture that emphasises groups or collectivities. After conducting some interviews with married couples, she realised that she was then interpreting these encounters through a Western feminist framing that emphasises individualism. As she puts it, 'Too often feminist frameworks have presented a view of women and their subjectivities as universally homogeneous. Without cultural and historical specificity, women become an already constituted, homogeneous group with similar needs and interests regardless of their class and racial location, and despite the particular historic contexts that form the backdrop to their lives' (p. 171). Shope, like Desbiens, had to allow her own preconceptions to be dismantled.

The point is that, with somewhere in the region of 3½ billion women on the planet, of different ages, cultures, colours, shapes, sizes, life experiences and histories, there may be no such thing as a women's standpoint. In the 1970–80s the dominant feminist discourse had been one of solidarity, an urge to women to unite in 'universal sisterhood' against discrimination (Maddrell, 2009). By the middle of 1990s critiques of this position were well established.

These critiques stemmed particularly from postcolonial feminists. In the nineteenth century Europe's empires covered 90 per cent of the globe, and this has left a legacy of power relations. Globally, Western culture is dominant. Edward Said's (1979) book *Orientalism* used Foucauldian discourse analysis (see Chapter 7) to reveal the ways in which non-European peoples were – and still are – constructed as 'Other'. Identity, knowledge and power are interrelated.

Postcolonial feminists therefore questioned the use of gender as the most important social category. Gregson et al. (1993) identify three particular critiques:

1. Taking gender as the most important social category homogenises the experiences of 'men' and of 'women', ignoring other differences. But social hierarchy is not based on gender alone. Race and class are just as important, and a Black working-class woman's experiences will be very different from a White middle-class woman's experiences. If we ignore social categories other than gender, we are left with no way of understanding how the social relations associated with those

other differences may intersect with, and shape, the gendered nature of experiences and identities. 'Intersectionality', recognising the intersections of different
facets of identity that shape individuals' experiences, is thus a key theme.

2. Focusing on gender as the primary social category assumes that it is possible
    to separate out the different components of our identity, to tell which experi-
    ences derive from gender differences, which from differences in sexuality, or
    age, for example.

3. Assuming gender is the most important social category also normalises par-
    ticular identities. To base arguments on 'women's experiences' implies that
    all women's experiences are the same; other social categories such as race
    only needed to be identified when they meant that a woman experienced
    something other than 'normal'. In practice, this meant that these social cat-
    egories were only identified when they were not White, middle-class, and
    heterosexual.

Such critiques coincided with the increasing influence of postmodernism and poststructuralism on geography, leading to an emphasis on meaning, representation and
power relations. Together, postcolonial, postmodern and poststructural feminist
geographies sought to destabilise and decentre gender; to dismantle gender as a
stable construct, reposition it as one of many identity producers, and to examine the
ways that gender categories themselves are socially constructed.

Meaning, representations and power relations come together in Gökarıksel's
(2012) study of women's headscarves in the everyday spaces of Istanbul, Turkey.
Muslim women's dress, in particular the headscarf, has become increasingly intertwined with geopolitical discourse (including debates about immigration,
Muslim minority populations and Islamic extremism) and with religious/secular
tensions. In the 1980s the Turkish government banned headscarves from universities, schools and courtrooms. In the intervening years, the development of a
veiling-fashion has increased the popularity of a particular kind of scarf. The
headscarf, then, is a means by which women's bodies are inscribed with, and
produce, geopolitical discourses and practices. Gökarıksel's paper analyses the
ways in which the 'intimate politics' (p. 2) of the headscarf play out in different
spaces within the city.

Her research includes some analysis of a popular Turkish film, but is largely based
on many years of fieldwork (including observation and interviews) in Istanbul. She
provides 'analytical snapshots' of three very different parts of the city:

• Akmerkez shopping mall. A product of global capitalism, the mall symbolises and
  contributes to the growth of consumerism. This privately owned space is managed to explicitly align with secularism, evident in the images and advertisements
  displayed, and in the absence of veiling-fashion in its stores. Women in headscarves do not feel welcome in Akmerkez.

- The main street of Fatih district, a religiously and socially conservative area characterised by public spaces and 'rooted in history' (p. 9). On the streets of Fatih women of all ages can be seen in a multitude of dress styles, from head-to-toe coverings to headscarf-free.

- Beyazıt Square, the site of many political protests including over the headscarf ban.

Gokarıksel's work demonstrates the ways in which women's bodies, through headscarf-wearing, become part of the gendered spatial constructions of the secular and the religious across Istanbul. At the same time, veiling-fashion and the variety of headscarves and scarf-less heads on the streets of Fatih mean that women's everyday headscarf wearing serves to disrupt the simple binary distinction between secular and Islamic. Gokarıksel argues that women 'create the dissident and discontinuous spaces that can be described as post-secular and post-Islamic' (2012, p. 15). Her research thus offers an example of the poststructuralist interests of examining the intersection of social categories (gender and religion) to understand how meaning and power are co-constituted with place.

6.2.4 Feminist geographies in practice

There is, then, a longstanding tension in feminist research. On the one hand, some feminist work seeks to build the identity 'woman' and develop its political significance. On the other hand, feminist research may operate to dismantle social categories (including the category 'woman'), celebrating difference and the legitimacy of multiple claims to 'truth' (Rose, 1993; Feminist Pedagogy Working Group, 2002). The two need not be seen as mutually exclusive. Rather, Rose (1993) suggests each may be useful in different contexts, each revealing dominations and possibilities the other may not.

The examples described above illustrate that if there are different kinds of feminism, it follows that there is no single way of doing feminist geography research. Rather, feminism presents an epistemological challenge (Aitchison, 2005) that demands careful attention to the whole research process, from defining research questions, to choosing methods for data collection and analysis, to representing the stories or lives of others in the presentation of the research.

Feminist research entails a commitment to research *for* and *with*, rather than *on*, women or other marginalised groups. A principle of feminist standpoint theory is that research should begin with the lives of the marginalised. Given the lack of women's presence in public life, this has opened geography up to studying the quotidian: the seemingly mundane experiences of everyday life. For researchers working in universities, by definition part of the educationally and economically privileged, an emphasis on the marginalised means that power differentials between researcher and participants will always be present.

Feminism rejects the notion that knowledge can ever be objective, value-free, independent of the 'knower'. Recognition that knowledge is not only cognitive, but embodied, has its own implications for methods. A rigorous and critical approach to research involves acknowledgement of the researcher's positionality, a reflexive awareness of their multiple identities and the ways in which this may impact on the research. As Desbiens (2010) and Shope (2006) demonstrate, this is not easy to achieve and can be uncomfortable. It requires an openness and honesty to confront your own prejudices and preconceptions.

The power relations between researcher and research participants then have implications for methods. An emphasis on research *participants*, rather than research *subjects*, is often central, allowing participants some say in how the research is shaped. Analysis then requires interpretation, reflection and re-evaluation, considering implications and meanings (Cope, 2002). It is all too easy for a researcher to impose a framing on the basis of their prior experience, education and expectations. Often feminist geographers seek to confirm interpretation of the data with participants, giving them some say in the analysis and representation of the research. In some cases this extends to co-authorship of resulting publications.

These feminist approaches to research, emphasising collaboration, **reflexivity** and attention to power, have been taken up in geography beyond those studies directly concerned with gender. Work through Exercise 6.2 for an example of this.

EXERCISE 6.2

Where is the 'global city'?

Datta's (2012) research examines how male migrants from Eastern Europe experience London. Her research does not focus on women, representations of women or gender inequalities, yet is arguably feminist in approach. Read Datta's paper and try to answer the following questions:

1) In what way(s) are the migrants who participated in the research a marginalised or invisible group?

2) Feminist research often acts to destabilise categories. What categories are brought into question through this research?

3) In what way(s) was Datta doing research 'with' rather than 'on' her participants?

4) How was 'embodied' experience important in the research?

Datta's paper is available via the companion website, along with answers to the questions. The full reference for the paper is:

Datta, A. (2012) '"Where is the global city?" Visual narratives of London among east European migrants', *Urban Studies* 49 (8): 1725–40. doi: 10.1177/0042098011417906.

6.3 Feminism at the beach

In British culture the idea of the beach as a place to visit and 'play', a site for recreation and relaxation, has developed since the industrial revolution. Increasing leisure time, combined with an increase in mobility provided by an expanding rail network, made the beach a popular destination for day or weekend visits. 'The beach', in terms of the popular imagination, is itself a social construct. Variants on the Western construction of beaches as leisure sites exist in different places and at different times, from the British deckchairs, sandcastles and donkey rides depicted in the 'saucy postcards' of the early twentieth century to the 'sun, sand and skin' sensual economy of the Australian beach (Khamis, 2010, p. 384). Indeed, Nagakawa and Payne (2011, pp. 97–8) describe Australian lifeguards as 'a caricature of national heroes who colonise the beach as the natural frontier into the human domain'.

The dominant Western construction of the beach, then, offers potential for feminist research just as it does for poststructuralist research (Chapter 7). An obvious avenue for study would be the ways in which gender is represented and performed within these constructions; from the masculinities of surfing and women's negotiation of this culture (McMahon, 2005), to women's bikini-clad beach volleyball as a spectator sport, or the idealised female 'beach body' promoted by women's magazines as summer approaches each year.

Equally interesting would be a focus on women's beach experiences. An analysis of surf lifeguarding underpinned by feminist standpoint theory might involve interviews with female lifeguards and beach users, along with observations of the roles and spatialities of male and female lifeguards. Questions of who drives the vehicles, who performs rescues from which parts of the beach, who takes on responsibility for lost children and who occupies the first aid station, for example, might be worthy of consideration. Lifeguards, though, are in the minority on the beach. The popularity of the beach for family outings offers opportunities for the study of domestic gender roles and relations, and the ways in which decisions and responsibilities are divided or shared between parents. Is a day at the beach equally relaxing for all?

6.4 Social constructionism and feminism in summary

Social constructionism has its roots in phenomenology, in that we know the world only through our perceptions. Geographers tend to associate phenomenology primarily with the humanistic geography of the 1970s, with acknowledgement of some influence in the more recent **non–representational** geographies (see Chapter 5). Where humanistic geography emphasised the individual, social constructionism emphasises the collective, social processes that shape our perception of the world.

Social constructionists are often divided into two camps: 'strong' and 'weak' constructionists. Strong social constructionism posits that the entities we perceive – even physical, material entities – are socially constructed. This is an anti-realist position that many physical geographers would find problematic. Weak social constructionism takes our concepts to be socially constructed, but does not deny the possibility of a reality independent of us. It is only that we can never know this reality directly, outside of our concepts.

Social constructionism is prevalent throughout much human geography, in that postmodernism and poststructuralism understand knowledge as socially constructed, albeit with different emphases. Feminism is founded on an understanding of gender as socially constructed. Geographers' first engagements with feminism were focused on disciplinary politics, exposing the gender inequalities within the discipline. This then led to feminist challenges to masculinist epistemologies dominating the discipline. Through feminist standpoint theory and poststructuralist feminism, geographers have come to understand knowledge as always partial, situated and political. Feminists have highlighted the power relations always inherent in knowledge production, and sought ways to conduct research 'with participants' rather than 'on subjects'. The feminist urge to give voice to the marginalised has expanded geographers' repertoire of research methods and data sources, to encompass diaries, letters, music, art, literature, auto-photography, participatory and collaborative mapping, modelling and storytelling, among others. The impact of these developments has, at least to some degree, spread throughout human geography.

A century after women achieved the right to Fellowship of the Royal Geographical Society (with the Institute of British Geographers), inequalities within the discipline still remain – more so in some parts of the world, and some parts of the discipline, than others. Geography, after all, is a social construct and is part of the societies in which it is found. It is no less susceptible to social influences than any other aspect of society.

FURTHER READING

For further explanations

Brickell, K., Maddrell, A., Marting, A. and Price, L. (2012) 'By any other name? The Women and Geography Study Group', *Area* 45 (1): 11–12.

Evans, S.L., Keighran, I.M. and Maddrell, A. (2013) 'Coming of age? Reflections on the centenary of women's admission to the Royal Geographical Society', *The Geographical Journal* 179 (4): 372–6. doi: 10.1111/geoj.12051.

Monk, J. (1994) 'Place matters: comparative international perspectives on feminist geography', *Professional Geographer* 46 (3): 277–88.

Sultana, F. (2007) 'Reflexivity, positionality and participatory ethics: negotiating fieldwork dilemmas in international research', *ACME: An International E-Journal for Critical Geographies* 6 (3): 374–85.

Progress in Human/Physical Geography resources

Crampton, J.W. (2001) 'Maps as social constructions: power, communication and visualiza-tion', *Progress in Human Geography* 25 (2): 235–52. doi:10.1191/030913201678580494.

Demeritt, D. (2002) 'What is the "social construction of nature"? A typology and sympathetic critique', *Progress in Human Geography* 26 (6): 767–90. doi: 10.1191/10309132502ph402oa.

Grainger, A. (2010) 'Uncertainty in the construction of global knowledge of tropical forests', *Progress in Physical Geography* 34 (6): 811–44. doi: 10.1177/0309133310387326.

McDowell, L. (1993a) 'Space, place and gender relations: Part I. Feminist empiricism and the geography of social relations', *Progress in Human Geography* 17 (2): 157–79. doi: 10.1177/030913259301700202.

McDowell, L. (1993b) 'Space, place and gender relations: Part II. Identity, difference, fem-inist geometries and geographies', *Progress in Human Geography* 17 (3): 305–18. doi: 0.1177/030913259301700301.

Pedynowski, D. (2003) 'Science(s) – which, when and whose? Probing the metanarrative of scientific knowledge in the social construction of nature', *Progress in Human Geography* 27 (6): 735–52. doi: 10.1191/0309132503ph459oa.

Silvey, R. (2004) 'Power, difference and mobility: feminist advances in migration studies', *Progress in Human Geography* 28 (4): 490–506. doi: 10.1191/0309132504ph490oa.

Wainwright, S.P. (2012) 'Science studies in physical geography: an idea whose time has come?' *Progress in Physical Geography* 36 (6): 786–812. doi: 10.1177/0309133312450997.

Wright, M.W. (2010) 'Gender and geography II: bridging the gap – feminist, queer, and the geographical imaginary', *Progress in Human Geography* 34 (1): 56–66. doi: 10.1177/0309132509008.

Examples

Pain, R. (2001) 'Gender, race, age and fear in the city', *Urban Studies* 38 (5–6): 899–913.

Parker, B. (2011) 'Material matters: gender and the city', *Geography Compass* 5/6: 433–47.

Structuralism, Poststructuralism, and Postmodernism: Life at the Surface

One morning in January 2011, residents of Biscayne Bay, Miami, Florida, awoke to find a grand piano sitting on a sand bar roughly 200 yards offshore in the bay. Local photographer Suzanne Beard and her husband took their boat out for a closer look, and Suzanne later posted one of her pictures on the National Geographic website. When this was spotted by Yahoo News the 'piano bar' went global, reported all across the US and beyond. Responses were mixed, some delighting in the oddity while others disapproved (Kruse, 2012, p. 133). How did the piano get there? Why would a piano be sitting on a sand bar? On the other hand, why *shouldn't* a piano be on a sand bar?

Kruse (2012) explains that the media coverage of the piano resulted in the sand bar achieving a certain notoriety, becoming *that* bar rather than just an anonymous sand bar. Once the piano was removed, this newfound notoriety led to other events: first a book signing was held on the bar, and then a café table temporarily appeared, complete with two chairs, place settings and a bottle of wine. At this, the Florida Fish and Wildlife Conservation Commission made it clear that leaving objects on the bar was considered an infringement of the law, effectively preventing any subsequent installations.

The fascination of the piano bar, Kruse suggests, resulted from the cultural **discourses** around beaches, islands, nature and pianos being brought together. We all have ideas about what is 'normal' for beaches, islands, nature and pianos, and 'piano' normally bears no relation to those other categories. The result was 'the impression that neither the piano nor the sandbar was behaving themselves, so to speak' (p. 142).

If you try to articulate such ideas about what is normal, it is really quite difficult. It is almost as if we cannot see what is normal, because it is just 'how the world is'. Our understanding of what is normal for beaches, islands and pianos is entwined with our understanding of what these things *are* and what we can do with them. We are often not aware of such norms until something challenges them. The piano on the sand bar, in seeming 'wrong', highlights our assumptions about what is 'right'. The story illustrates that the meanings we ascribe to places and spaces are not just a product of the places themselves, but also of our categories, values and practices, all of which are bound up with our language. The ideas introduced in this chapter provide greater insight into this.

Three modes of thought are addressed here: **structuralism, poststructuralism** and **postmodernism**. A fourth and fifth could easily have been added: **social constructionism** (sometimes referred to as social constructivism) and **feminism**, which are discussed in Chapter 6. There is no clear-cut division between social constructionism, poststructuralism and postmodernism, with conflicting accounts of their relation to (or difference from) each other in the literature. As Agger (1999, p. 111) explains, it is possible to 'cut the theoretical pie in any number of ways'. Similarly, feminism draws on social constructionism and sometimes poststructuralism, but not all feminist research is necessarily poststructuralist. By the end of this chapter it should be evident that the slippery nature of these terms, never quite offering us discrete categories, is entirely in keeping with the modes of thought themselves. The common thread running through them is the theme that what we know, in both our 'common sense' knowledge of everyday life and our academic knowledge, is inseparable from language, social institutions and culture (Kellner, 2013).

We begin with structuralism here, which provides a departure point for poststructuralism and postmodernism.

7.1 Structuralism: A useful departure point

The term 'structuralism', according to Sperber (1979, p. 46) 'has been used in many different senses and sometimes with no sense at all'. Marxism and critical realism (see Chapter 4) could both be described as structuralist, as they aim to analyse the structures underlying events in the world. In the case of Marx, the basis of these structures is **materialist**, in that the origins of political and economic structures in society lay in the means of material production of goods or wealth. There is some sense in which our practical interactions with the world shape society. Bhaskar's **critical realism** seeks to identify 'real structures' of the world that provide the causal mechanisms which generate events. The assumption is that such structures are real phenomena, independent of our knowledge of them. Unlike both of these, the Structuralism discussed here assumes that the structures in the world have their origins in human minds and societies. The capital 's' is probably unusual, but is used here to distinguish this mode of thought from Marxist and critical realist forms of structuralism.

Structuralism traces back to the work of Swiss linguist Ferdinand de Saussure (1857–1913). Interested in understanding how language works, he developed a particular system of 'semiotics', or means of studying signs and their use. To Saussure (1916), every word is a sign, and every sign consists of two elements. These are:

1. the 'signifier', which is the oral component, the sound made (or in written language, the marks on the page or screen);

2. the 'signified', which is the object or concept that the word 'points to'.

When you say the sound (signifier) 'river', the signified is a moving body of water (along with sediment and nutrients) normally confined within a channel.

Saussure pointed out that both the signifier and the signified are arbitrary. There is no inherent property to a moving body of water in a channel that compels us to use the signifier 'river'. We do so simply through convention. Moreover, the sound only has that meaning in a particular system of signs (the English language). We could consider other sounds that have no meaning within English: afon, fiume, река, sông. These have meaning within Welsh, Italian, Russian and Vietnamese respectively (they all translate as 'river'), but to anyone not familiar with those languages, they would just be sounds.

The signified is also arbitrary, as it is a function of the way we perceive the world. Humans divide the world up into convenient 'bits' and classes of things. When you look at a rainbow, the colour spectrum is a continuum of varying light input (wavelength and luminosity), but you 'see' distinct colours of red, yellow, green, blue. Your brain has split the continuum into segments and imposed some kind of order on it (Leach, 1970). Different cultures divide the world up in different ways. The popular (although debated) example of this is the idea that the Inuit have tens, or even hundreds, of words for snow. There are words in other cultures that have no direct English equivalent: 'mana' in Maori, or 'Schadenfreude' in German, for example. (You can look them up to find out what they mean.) These concepts do not exist in the English language, so we can only refer directly to them by using the Maori or German words respectively. This also demonstrates that signifier and signified are inter-dependent. A sound is only a signifier if it relates to some concept/object (the signified), but that concept or object can only be signified if it has a signifier, otherwise we have no means of referring to it.

Given that a sign only has meaning within a system of signs, Saussure focused on the relations between words and their place within language. In spoken language, each word occupies a 'space' determined by its phonetic (sound) and semantic (meaning) aspects. The word 'book' is phonetically close to, but distinct from, 'cook' and 'look', and semantically close to 'magazine', 'journal' and 'newspaper'. Its sound and meaning are defined through relation to the sounds and meanings of those words which occupy the spaces around it. Saussure argued that studying these kinds of relations would reveal the underlying structures of language, which he took to be indicative of the structure of the human mind.

It was French anthropologist Claude Lévi-Strauss who first applied Saussure's Structuralism within the social sciences (Murdoch, 2005). Lévi-Strauss worked on the assumption that culture could be studied as a system of signs in the same way that Saussure had studied language. Every act, such as giving a gift, or marrying, is an expression (signifier) of some signified meaning, and that meaning is provided by the place of the act within the total system of culture. By studying many instances of something (such as kinship, and myths) among different cultures, he sought to identify the conceptual system underpinning culture. Structuralism thus assumes that:

1. the systems of representation constituting society are 'a privileged order of reality' (Clarke, 1981, p. 108), in that they are real and have explanatory power, and;

2. social scientists can objectively discover their meaning.

A group of other French theorists are sometimes associated with Structuralism. Sturrock (1979) lists Roland Barthes, Michel Foucault, Jaques Lacan and Jacques Derrida, but stresses that there were variations between them, and that only Lévi-Strauss identified himself as Structuralist. The others are probably more known for the transition to **poststructuralism** than for Structuralism. Within geography, Saussure's Structuralism makes some kind of appearance in many of the 'geographic thought' textbooks (Hubbard et al., 2002; Holt-Jensen, 2009; Creswell, 2013), but there are suggestions that it has been little used in geography (Johnston, 1986; Unwin, 1992; Calberac, 2011). However, it does provide us with a reference point against which to position the more prominent poststructuralist movement.

7.2 Poststructuralism

Poststructuralism emerged from the French philosophers and theorists of the 1960s, being particularly associated with the names of Derrida, Foucault, Lyotard and Baudrillard (among others). Boundaries and distinctions between poststructuralism and postmodernism are anything but clear. The individuals listed here are variously assigned either label by different authors, and the labels are interpreted differently anyway. But then both poststructuralism and postmodernism emphasise that meaning is not fixed, but fluid and contested. This does mean that the organisation of the rest of this chapter deserves some explanation though. For the sake of drawing the line somewhere, this section (on poststructuralism) highlights the work of Derrida and Foucault, while the ideas of Baudrillard and Lyotard are introduced in the section on postmodernism. Lyotard specifically identified his work as postmodernist. Baudrillard resisted the label, but some consider him to have had the greatest influence on post-modern thought. Postmodernism and poststructuralism are then treated together to consider their influence on geography and geographical research practices.

7.2.1 Derrida: Difference and deconstruction

It is not unusual for geographers to categorise space, or places. It is convenient for us to do so. We cannot study everything at once so we have to draw boundaries somewhere. In the early twentieth century it was common to use the idea of a region as a means of delimiting a focus. Geographers specialised in their chosen region. With the move to 'systematic' geography (discussed in Chapter 2), it made sense to draw boundaries by defining types of things (including spaces). One such category is 'urban'. Curiously, when we identify somewhere as urban, we are also identifying it as *not* rural, and the existence of other, rural places is actually part of our definition of *this* place as urban. If rural places did not exist we would have no use for the category 'urban', as we would have nothing to distinguish it from. This kind of idea is central to the work of Jacques Derrida (1930–2004).

Derrida was critical of Saussure's linguistics, and particularly the idea that a stable structure underlies language and provides a simple connection between signifier and signified. We saw earlier in the chapter that a signifier derives meaning from its position in relation to, and distinct from, those signifiers 'around it' in the sign system ('book' as semantically related to, but different from, 'journal', 'magazine' or 'newspaper'). This rests on the notion of 'difference', and so 'difference' has some prior value outside of the sign system. So how are we to understand 'difference', if the meaning of a sign is always determined by its position within the sign system? 'Difference' cannot be both outside of the sign system and yet have its meaning determined within the sign system at the same time. Derrida argued there is no direct connection between signifier and signified. Instead, meaning is *always* relational, dependent upon relation to (or difference from) other signs, other meanings, which in turn are dependent upon relations to others. The meaning of any sign is as much 'not signifying' something as it is signifying something else. So just as 'urban' is 'not rural', the title of Cosgrove and della Dora's (2008) fasci-nating book, *High Places*, tells of the existence of other, low, places.

Derrida (1976) pointed out that these kinds of binaries exist throughout much of Western philosophy (and hence throughout academic subjects such as geogra-phy), and that there is always an asymmetry of value in them. 'High places' sound much more exciting than 'low places'. If we consider the binaries of fact/value, man/woman, true/false, nature/culture, mind/matter, good/evil, these oppositions are defined hierarchically, the first being valued more than the second, the second being a corruption of the first. Derrida's method of 'deconstruction' involved a critical and close examination of texts to reveal these underlying binaries and the value positions inherent to them. He insisted that anything could be 'read' as a text, including works of art, film, popular culture or political scenarios (Butler, 2004).

However, 'reading' is dependent on interpretation of signs. Given that meaning is relational (the meaning of a sign is dependent on its relation to other signs), different people may interpret texts in different ways, and so the author of a text is never entirely in control of what that text says. Equally, there is no single interpretation of a text, only multiple possible interpretations.

7.2.2 Foucault: Connecting knowledge with power

The Baekdu-Daegan (sometimes written Paektudaegan) mountain ridge extends roughly 700km from Jirisan, a mountain close to the southern coast of South Korea, to Baekdu (or Paektu) Mountain, on the border between North Korea and China. Stretching from one end of the peninsula to the other (Figure 7.1), the mountain ridge has long been considered the backbone of Korea. Or has it? Jong-Heon Jin

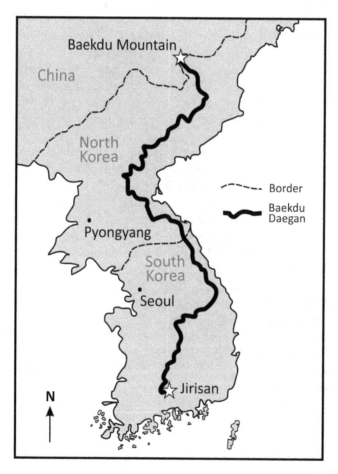

Figure 7.1   The Baekdu-Daegan ridge, Korean peninsula

(2008) explains that the existence of Baekdu-Daegan is not simple. Between 1900 and 1902 a Japanese geologist, Koto Bunjiro, undertook the first modern geomorphological survey of the Korean peninsula. Having trained in Western science, Koto identified that what had been understood as a single mountain ridge was actually two distinct geological structures. Baekdu-Daegan was broken in two.

At the time of Koto's work, Korea was under Japanese occupation (eventually being annexed to Japan in 1910). His scientific assessment replaced a singular Korea with two halves, the colonised territory deconstructed and superseded by 'the image of a modern landscape' (p. 201). Koto's geological map, reinforced by his identification of historical and cultural distinctions between North and South, became part of the official understanding of Korea, reproduced through national maps and geographical education. Koreans were taught to think of Korea in two halves. Although North and South were not formally divided as separate countries until the middle of the twentieth century, under Japanese control Korea's Baekdu-Daegan was 'banished from the realm of public discourse' (p. 197). The single mountain ridge no longer existed.

Jin (2008) goes on to explain that, since the late 1980s, the practice of *jongju* ('traversing') mountaineering has challenged the official, scientific discourse. Through *jongju,* mountaineers have trekked the entire length of the mountain ridge. This popular practice has reignited interest in Baekdu-Daegan among Korean people, enabling the re-imagination of a single national landscape, and an associated desire for re-unification of Korea.

While this is a very simplified version of Jin's account of Baekdu-Daegan, it points us in the right direction for understanding some of Foucault's work, hinting at the connections between knowledge, power, and actions or practices, and how they intersect with geographical themes of space and place. As Japan colonised Korea, indigenous knowledge of the way the world is was replaced with new, 'scientific' knowledge. In the twenty-first century, when the formal structures of national territory divide Korea in two, resistance is found through the physical acts and associated imagination of *jongju.*

Like Derrida, Michel Foucault (1926–1984) was interested in the role of language in knowledge. He undertook historical studies that sought to 'excavate' the knowledge underpinning intellectual orthodoxy and practices through European history (Philo, 2011). For geographers, probably the most influential of these was *Discipline and Punish: The Birth of the Prison* (1979), which examined the changing ways that European societies dealt with miscreants through the eighteenth and nineteenth centuries. Early in this period, 'sovereign power' was exerted through the public spectacle of torture and execution, instilling fear of such punishment in the population. The development of prisons was accompanied by a shift in emphasis from punishing convicts to reforming them. Foucault identified that this focus on reformation leads to a much more diffuse operation of power, more subtle yet pervasive throughout society. This is 'disciplinary power', and it functions through three mechanisms:

1. Hierarchical observation. This is simply the observation of people of low status (in whatever context status is defined) by those of higher status.

2. Normalising judgement. The reform of criminals is concerned with the correction of 'deviant' behaviour, which is predicated on assumptions about how people *should* behave (in other words, ideas about what behaviour is normal).

3. Examination. This involves a combination of hierarchical observation and normalising judgement. A medical examination to determine whether someone has an illness involves a doctor (in a position of power) observing the patient to ascertain whether they are ill against criteria that define a healthy (normal) person. A driving test similarly involves someone in a position of power observing you driving to determine whether you perform to a required (normal) standard. Such judgements then control subsequent behaviour, prescribing that a patient should take a particular course of treatment, and allowing or not allowing you to drive.

EXERCISE 7.1

The model prison

Foucault illustrated the operation of power in society through reference to a particular kind of prison building. Using the Internet, find images of:

i)   The Presidio Modelo, Cuba

ii) Stateville Penitentiary, Illinois

What are the similarities?

The prisons identified in Exercise 7.1 are versions of a 'Panopticon' prison, a design developed by Jeremy Bentham in the mid-nineteenth century. In essence, the Panopticon consists of a circle of prison cells with a watch tower in the middle. The Presidio Modelo in Cuba (which is now a museum) is probably the closest to Bentham's original design, in that the outside wall of every cell is a window, and the inner wall just bars. This means that from the central watch tower every prisoner is visible against the back-light of their cell window. The observer in the watchtower can watch any prisoner at any time. Crucially, the prisoners have no way of knowing whether, or when, they are being watched, only that they can always be watched. There is no escape from visibility, and so the prisoners self-regulate their behaviour at all times *in case* they are being watched. This self-regulation is a much more effective and efficient way of exerting power over a large number of people than trying to impose force on them.

The important point, for Foucault, was not that the Panopticon provided a design for a building. He saw it as a model for the functioning of disciplinary power in its ideal form. It illustrates the principle, and he explained that it was applicable to any social context:

> ...it serves to reform prisoners, but also to treat patients, to instruct schoolchildren, to confine the insane, to supervise workers, to put beggars and idlers to work. It is a type of location of bodies in space, of distribution of individuals in relation to one another, of hierarchical organisation, of disposition of centres and channels of power, of definition of the instruments and modes of intervention of power, which can be implemented in hospitals, workshops, schools, prisons. Whenever one is dealing with a multiplicity of individuals on whom a task or a particular form of behaviour must be imposed, the panoptic schema may be used. (Foucault, 1977, p. 205)

From those three sentences alone, we begin to get a hint that Foucault's work connects power with space.

EXERCISE 7.2

Self-regulation according to norms

The most obvious situations in which we self-regulate our behaviour are those involving formal rules and regulations. Most car drivers in the UK will avoid parking on double-yellow lines (denoting 'no parking' zones). If you do park you may well not get caught, but there is no way of knowing whether a traffic warden is likely to appear, resulting in a fine. Like in the panopticon prison, drivers do not know when they (their car) might be seen parked in the wrong place, only that it might be seen at any time. That is enough for most to self-regulate their behaviour. We also regulate our own behaviour according to social norms, often without being conscious of it. Examples in the UK include waiting patiently in a queue for something, or answering 'fine', or 'not too bad', when someone has asked how you are.

Try to list some other examples of the ways you self-regulate your behaviour in certain places or spaces. Who is 'watching' you in these spaces?

Throughout this and his other works, Foucault demonstrates the ways that truth, knowledge and power are interrelated through **discourse**. A basic definition of discourse is 'conversation', but Foucault's use of the term is not just about language.

Think back to Saussure's semiotics, introduced earlier in the chapter: something is only signified if it has a signifier, and so our language is closely connected to how we understand the world. Our understanding of the world, our concepts and ideas, shape how we act and our possibilities for action, and so discourse extends beyond just words into actions and practices.

Meaning is created and constrained through discourse. The kinds of discourses associated with the development of prisons and penal reform criminalised particular activities, designating them as 'deviant' and thereby creating particular kinds of criminals and prisoners, which had not previously existed. So the kinds of things we say, and the associated actions and practices of the discourse, produce identities. All social categories, such as age, gender, sexuality, ethnicity or (dis)ability are constructed discursively. This means that identities are complex and fluid, changing as discourse changes (Hubbard et al., 2005). Similarly, places – such as Korea and Baektu-Degan – are constructed discursively.

In his 1969 book, *Archaeology of Knowledge* (trans. 2002), Foucault emphasised that his analysis of discourse was not concerned to identify underlying structures (as in Saussure's Structuralism). What Foucault saw as important was 'that field in which questions of the human being, consciousness, origin, and the subject emerge, intersect, mingle, and separate off' (1969, p. 18). Foucault's emphasis was on the discursive practices at the 'surface' of our everyday lives.

Some key ideas emerge from this brief discussion of Foucault's work: firstly, that knowledge and meaning (including identity) are discursively produced; secondly, that knowledge, meaning and power are intertwined; and thirdly, that space is central to the distribution and exercise of power.

While Derrida and Foucault are by no means all there is to poststructuralism, some characteristics are apparent here. There are clear influences of structuralism, in a focus on meaning and emphasis on context – that is, on social systems rather than individuals. However, poststructuralism rejects the notion of a single structure underlying everything. Instead it moves attention to the surface; to the practices, actions, texts and utterances through which meanings and identities are created, and the distribution and role of power within these.

Poststructuralism also takes up Saussure's understanding that meaning is relational, defined in relation to other meanings. But where Saussure assumed that meaning was fixed within (and by) relations in a single sign system, poststructuralism emphasises the multiple relations that act to produce particular meanings in particular places at particular times. Meanings, and hence identities, are not stable and fixed. They are historically and geographically produced (Creswell, 2013) and contested, intertwined with power, its operation and negotiation. This emphasis on relations acts to 'decentre' subjectivity (Murdoch, 2005). Your identity is more about your relations to others and place within a system of meanings than it is about you as an individual. Power, similarly, is a fluid and constantly (re)negotiated 'amalgam of *forces, practices, processes* and *relations*' (Sharp et al., 2000, p. 20, emphasis in original).

Finally, we should recognise that poststructuralism represents a distinctly different understanding of, and approach to, society than that adopted by 'science'. The focus of science is on an external, observable world, making sense of an objective reality. Poststructuralism challenges the very idea that it is possible to know an objective reality. We cannot know the world independently of our concepts, independently of the words and ideas with which we make sense of the world (Braun and Wainwright, 2001). Much science (whether **positivist, critical rationalist**, or **structuralist**) involves the examination of **contingent** events to identify the necessary components of them. Poststructuralism, particularly after Foucault, is more concerned to examine the things that seem necessary or stable (and taken-for-granted) and identify what is really contingent, being socially constructed.

EXERCISE 7.3

National identity on the Fourth Plinth

Trafalgar Square in London has four plinths, one at each corner, with permanent statues on three of them. The fourth was left empty. Since 1999, the Fourth Plinth Prize has seen a series of temporary displays of contemporary artworks, most of them commissioned specifically for the empty plinth. Sumartojo (2013) analyses the responses to four of these artworks in terms of what they reveal about national identity. Read Sumartojo's paper and try to answer the following questions:

1) Why are urban public places described as 'important for the life of nations'?

2) Through pages 68–9, Sumartojo contrasts structuralist perspectives on) nation and national identity with alternative (poststructuralist) perspectives. Try to summarise key features of each.

3) Why is 'place' particularly relevant to the study of national identity and national narratives?

4) What method and data sources form the basis for Sumartojo's research?

5) Sumartojo argues that being in Trafalgar Square was central to the ways in which each of the four artworks was understood by the various commentators. Outline the connections made between each artwork and the Square.

Sumartojo's paper is available via the companion website, along with answers to the questions. You can also find latitude and longitude coordinates to paste into Google Earth, if you want to have a look at Trafalgar Square and its statues. The full reference for the paper is:
    Sumartojo, S. (2013) 'The Fourth Plinth: creating and contesting national identity in Trafalgar Square, 2005–2010', *Cultural Geographies* 20 (1): 67–81. doi: 10.1177/1474474012448304.

7.3 Postmodernism

Postmodernism, say Dear and Wassmansdorf (1993, p. 321), 'hit geography like a tidal wave'. In the development of ideas among French theorists, poststructuralism was a precursor to postmodernism, but within geography they seem to have arrived the other way round. The 'new cultural geographies' of the 1980s were influenced by the critical attitude of Marxist geographies (Chapter 4), but rapidly drew on other theories. Central to these was postmodernism.

   Not only is the distinction of postmodernism from poststructuralism not clear, but postmodernism is also notoriously difficult to define. 'It' is not just one thing. Rather, most commentators seem to agree that there are generally three forms of postmodernism: style; epoch; and theory or method. Each will be considered in turn here.

7.3.1 Postmodernism as style

Postmodern style emerged in literature and literary criticism in the 1960s and 1970s, spreading to art, photography, design, architecture, film and other areas. Architecture is often used to explain the distinctions between modern and postmodern style, perhaps because the difference is relatively clear here. Modernist architecture was functional and machine-like, based on a deterministic notion that if the design was right, social improvement would follow. Box-like structures, homogeneous high-rise tower blocks for working and living in that were designed to cater for our every need, were inserted into the city. They were built to realise a utopian ideal, yet resulted only in alienation and disaffection: the architecture failed to deliver.

   Postmodern buildings, in contrast, are highly individualised, mixing up styles, drawing together multiple influences and turning them inside out – quite literally, in the case of the Pompidou centre in Paris (opened in 1977), where all the plumbing and conduits for wiring surround the outside of the building. Place matters, and these buildings are inspired by and make reference to their localities, at the same time as being distinctively individual. In London, Vauxhall Cross (Figure 7.2a) is one of several prominent postmodern buildings. Constructed in the first half of the 1990s, it references 1930s architecture and particularly the power stations of Battersea and Bankside in London, but also Mayan and Aztec temples (www.sis.gov. uk). Compare this with the Sydney Opera House (Figure 7.2b), whose curves echo the shapes in the waters surrounding it.

   In music postmodernism came to the fore in the 1980s. Identity categories such as race and gender were blurred by artists like Michael Jackson, Grace Jones and David Bowie, the latter being particularly adept at reinvention. Cloke et al. (1991) highlight Prince as an exemplar of postmodernism, his music bringing together multiple influences and genres to defy categorisation. More recently, hip hop is perhaps the ultimate postmodern musical form, epitomising a 'remix culture' (Rennett, 2012, p. 392).

Figure 7.2   Two examples of postmodern architecture. a) Vauxhall Cross in London. Vauxhall Cross is headquarters of the British Secret Intelligence Service and so has featured in several James Bond films, with a central role in *Skyfall* (2012). b) Sydney Opera House (photograph by Kevin Couper). Probably one of the most famous buildings in the world, construction of the Sydney Opera House began in 1957. It was anticipated that it would take 18 months, but the opera house finally opened in 1973. While some describe this as 'late modern' architecture, others describe it as postmodern. It is certainly highly individual and cleverly references its location (particularly when seen from the water).

For examples of postmodern film we can turn to Quentin Tarantino, who often uses non-linear narratives (*Reservoir Dogs*, *Pulp Fiction*, *Kill Bill*) and tells stories from multiple perspectives (*Pulp Fiction*). His films are also highly referential, drawing on other films, television programmes and music from multiple genres and decades such that Rennett (2012) refers to him as a 'director as DJ', making a direct connection with the musical sampling of hip hop. *Pulp Fiction* is also self-referential, being marketed as a film about a film (Booker, 2007). Tarantino's works are by no means the only instances of postmodernism in film though. In *Life of Pi* (2012) we follow a single narrative line of shipwreck, struggle and survival, only to be presented with an alternative version of the story at the end. The possibility of multiple interpretations, multiple meanings coexisting, is emphasised by the character Pi asking not which story we think is 'true', but which story we prefer.

While postmodern style can be difficult to pin down, some characteristics should be evident from these examples. A multiplicity of ideas and references are borrowed, appropriated and brought together in the creation of something new, in what Derrida (following Lévi-Strauss) termed *bricolage*. A rejection of singular, linear ('totalising') narratives is apparent, with homogeneity and difference celebrated. Categories become blurred. According to Adamson and Pavitt (2011, p. 13), 'For postmodernism, style was everything. Instead of authenticity, postmodernism celebrated hybridity. In place of truth, postmodernism had attitude.'

7.3.2 Postmodernism as epoch

If hip hop is the ultimate postmodern musical form then will.i.am, one of hip hop's practitioners (albeit at the 'pop' end), is illustrative of the postmodern epoch. Characteristically for hip hop, his songs can be both referential (a single line in *This is Love* hinting at Lionel Ritchie's *Dancing on the Ceiling* and *All Night Long*) and self-referential (*Scream and Shout*'s opening lines referring to the song being played in night clubs). However, turning attention to will.i.am himself, he is variously described as songwriter, musician, producer, recording artist, rapper, actor, entrepreneur, philanthropist, designer, television talent show coach/judge, self-confessed 'geek' and advocate of education, science and technology. He is not one thing or another but all at the same time. The moniker (will.i.am) signals a consciously constructed persona, and this is a powerful media image with a distinctive style, packaged with a logo and marketed globally. Variations on the theme, including i.am. clothing and i.am.auto, extend the brand. Image is everything for this global commodity. Yet will.i.am is local at the same time as global, individually present and accessible to over 12 million followers on Twitter, vocal about his childhood in the Boyle Heights district of East Los Angeles and retaining an active presence there through philanthropy. And here, perhaps, is the crux: will.i.am is not *just* a media image, clearly separable from the 'real' William Adams. He has a story, foregrounded through his philanthropic and advocacy activities. It is not clear where the person ends and the persona, the media image, begins. will.i.am is not a 'real person' pretending to be someone else, nor a false media image pretending to be a real person (unlike Dame Edna Everage and Barry Humphries, who are clearly separable). There is no deception here; distinction between 'real' (the person) and 'image' (the global media brand) is undecidable. This is captured in 'will.*i.am*', which simultaneously tells us it is a stage name and more than a stage name. Arguably, will.i.am is a phenomenon of a postmodern world: a multi-faceted media brand that pulls together a multitude of influences, never just one thing or another, both global and local, 'image' (simulation) yet more than image.

The postmodern epoch is configured as a new era following the modern. Where modernism was dominated by industrial capital production, the postmodern epoch is dominated by cultural production and characterised by 'new types of consumption; planned obsolescence; an ever more rapid rhythm of fashion and styling changes; the penetration of advertising, television and the media generally to a hitherto unparalleled degree throughout society' (Jameson, 1988/1998, p. 19). To this we could add the huge technological advances and development of social media that have occurred since Jameson's words were published, and which have enabled different kinds of participation in social, cultural and political life. In the twenty-first century, news can spread faster via social media than via the big news agencies. Everything is instant. We are all more connected to everyone everywhere in myriad ways, resulting in both homogenisation and differentiation simultaneously. Distinctions between local and global, real and virtual, have become blurred. Jameson (1988/1998: 19) notes a variety of descriptions for such a society: 'post-industrial society, multinational capitalism, consumer society, media society'. To this we could add more recent descriptors of the knowledge society or knowledge economy.

The conception of postmodernism as epoch entails the idea of a radical shift in society. Modernism embraced reason and rationality in a search for truth and progress. Postmodernism is characterised by complexity, ambiguity and a lack of any single direction or goal. The question of whether such a shift has actually happened is contested (Dear and Wassmansdorf, 1993). Some Marxist thinkers (including Fredric Jameson and geographer David Harvey) consider the postmodern era to be a late stage of capitalism, subsuming it under a totalising narrative of shifts in modes of production (see Box 7.1 for more on this). Notwithstanding such debates, for geographers the postmodern epoch and postmodern style together may form a postmodern object of enquiry (Cloke et al., 1991; Berg, 1993; Hubbard et al., 2002). Postmodern theory or method, in contrast, provides an approach to study.

BOX 7.1   THE PROBLEM WITH REJECTING METANARRATIVES

One of the central characteristics of postmodernism (and common to postmodernism as style, epoch and theory) is a rejection of metanarratives, grand narratives or totalisations. In other words, postmodernism rejects the idea of comprehensive, overarching explanations or ideas. Two problems arise from this:

(Continued)

(Continued)

1. Rejecting grand narratives or totalising ideas entails an assertion that claims to 'truth' are groundless (Berg, 1993). There can only be multiple truths. So if a postmodernist says there is no such thing as 'truth', can this be true? Postmodernism is itself a kind of metanarrative, and so turns against itself. It might be tempting to see this as grounds for dismissal but, before taking such a position, we perhaps also need to ask ourselves a further question: is postmodernism useful?

2. Some authors, Fredric Jameson and David Harvey among them, interpret postmodernism as a late form of capitalism. By this reading, the development of more flexible systems of production and consumption (and hence capital accumulation) have resulted in the emergence of a new cultural condition. This squeezes postmodernism into the metanarrative of Marxist modes of production, essentially offering a 'modern' interpretation of postmodernism (Unwin, 1992; Müller, 2006). Jameson (1989/1998) was clearly aware of such criticism and countered that there is a distinction between object and concept. The concept 'dog' does not bark, and the concept 'sugar' does not taste sweet, so there is no reason to expect the concepts with which we analyse or understand the condition of postmodernity (postmodernism as epoch) to share the characteristics of postmodernism.

7.3.3 Postmodernist theory and method

As theory or method, postmodernism offers us a way of understanding the world around us. Two key thinkers here are Baudrillard and Lyotard.

Do you prefer McDonald's or KFC? Costa Coffee or Starbucks? Is your mobile phone an iPhone or Android? What ring tone do you have? Do you prefer Cadbury's or Nestlé chocolate? Life is full of such choices. According to Baudrillard, the clothes we wear, the music we listen to and the headphones we use to listen to it, the pens we write with, the leisure activities we participate in, the food we buy, are all decisions that help to distinguish us from each other, defining who we are and how others see us.

Jean Baudrillard (1929–2007) was a French theorist who rejected the label of 'postmodernist' himself, but is arguably one of the key postmodern theorists (Ritzer, 2009). His early work was on consumer society. Marx (see Chapter 4 on Marxism) had recognised that every product has a use value and an exchange value, but Baudrillard argued that every product also has a sign value. A Fiat saloon car and a Jaguar have the same use value, but very different exchange values. This difference is because of sign value. The Jaguar has higher status in the sign system of cars. In this way the meaning of any commodity is determined by its relation to, and differentiation from, other similar commodities in the 'code', or system of signs.

Sign value is about style, status, luxury, power and prestige. When we choose the goods we purchase, we are consumers of signs more than of objects. Baudrillard argued that our consumption is not about 'needs' or 'reality', but is driven by a desire to differentiate ourselves from each other. This is a lifelong desire, never satisfied, and so it only results in an endless proliferation of consumption, fuelled by constant advertising and the generation of new products for us to consume (Ritzer, 2009). As Porter (1993: 2) depicts it:

> Desire itself is manufactured, and nothing any longer possesses intrinsic value, in and for itself. Meaning is produced by endless, symbolic exchanges within a dominant code, whose rhetoric is entirely self-referential; a sexy woman is used to sell a car; a car sells cigarettes; cigarettes sell machismo; machismo is used to sell jeans; and so the symbolic magic circle is sealed. Sex, youth, health, speed, style, power, money, mobility – all transvalue and interpenetrate in the mesmerizing dreamworld of 'floating signifiers' that typifies the ephemeral, destabilized vortex of late capitalism.

The code, then, is all-encompassing, and consumption is about communication within the sign system of the code. This pervasiveness of signs means that we now live in a world dominated by simulations. Everywhere we look there are simulations of reality, from TV programmes to video games to virtual worlds and more. The dominant mode of cultural production is simulation, such that simulations now exceed reality. In the desert environment of the United Arab Emirates, the indoor ski facility of Ski Dubai simulates a mountain resort, complete with chairlifts and restaurants. But this is no ordinary Alpine resort. Snow conditions are perfect all year round. 'Real' snow is generated by machines, with snow texture, coverage and temperature controlled to maintain ideal skiing conditions at all times (The Playmania/Ski Dubai, undated). Skiers here are not hampered by the weather. Igloos, ice sculptures and 'Frostbite the friendly polar bear' add to the atmosphere, and a colony of live penguins is marched through daily (Ski Dubai Penguins, 2012). No real ski resort offers a close encounter with penguins; Ski Dubai is better than the real thing. Baudrillard (1981) described Disneyland as an example of such **'hyperreality'**, a simulation of a perfect world for which there is no original. Ski Dubai is only a more recent incarnation of hyperreality. In having no original, such imagery is neither true or false, the distinction between true and false left undecidable.

While Baudrillard gave us notions of simulacra and hyperreality, Jean-François Lyotard (1924–1998) provided the clearest articulation of the postmodern rejection of metanarratives. Like Derrida, Foucault and Baudrillard, Lyotard was a French thinker, but unlike those others he specifically identified himself as postmodernist. Lyotard's best known work is a report commissioned by the government of Quebec, which was published in book form in 1979 (the English version appearing in 1984): *The Postmodern Condition: A Report on Knowledge*. This work examines the condition of knowledge in highly developed, technological societies.

Lyotard identifies that there are essentially two forms of knowledge, narrative ('traditional') knowledge and scientific knowledge. Narrative knowledge consists in the myths, legends and stories of a society. These narratives tell us about the world and also provide their own legitimation, defining what knowledge is and why it is important, who can know, and who has authority to repeat the narrative. Narrative knowledge encompasses many different kinds of statements (see Box 7.2 for examples). Scientific knowledge, in contrast, rests solely on denotative utterances, statements referring to verifiable or falsifiable 'facts'. The people with authority to say something in science are those who have the competence to utter denotative statements that are verifiably true.

BOX 7.2   DIFFERENT KINDS OF STATEMENTS

Speech encompasses many different kinds of utterances. Examples include (but are not limited to):

Denotative utterances: these are verifiable or falsifiable statements about things, such as 'the river is in flood' or 'global population is increasing'. Positivism (Chapter 2) and critical rationalism (Chapter 3) prioritise denotative statements.

Performative utterances: these are statements that perform an act simply by being spoken. For example, 'You're fired', 'thank you', 'I apologise', or 'I declare the graduation ceremony open'.

Prescriptive utterances: these tell people what to do, for example: 'Go away', 'keep left', 'put the kettle on' or 'donate £1 a month'.

Because it consists entirely of denotative utterances, scientific knowledge cannot legitimate itself. For legitimation, it has to turn to an over-arching narrative – a metanarrative – to justify the pursuit of scientific knowledge. Lyotard identified that two metanarratives have been used through history. These are the ideas that:

1. Knowledge leads to human emancipation and liberty, and so everyone should have access to knowledge (for the good of the individual and society).

2. The pursuit of scientific knowledge will one day lead us to the unity of all knowledge.

As science has become the dominant form of knowledge, we have become suspicious of metanarratives. After all, only denotative utterances count in science. At the same time, the rapid development of computer sciences means that the only legitimate knowledge is that which can be translated into computer language. Knowledge has become simply an informational commodity, detached from individual people as 'knowers'. Lyotard pointed out that what matters for computers is quantities of information. The combined effect is an emphasis on the ever-increasing production of scientific knowledge, rather than an overarching purpose for developing such knowledge. We produce knowledge for the sake of producing more knowledge, more of the commodity. In Lyotard's view, knowledge was becoming so important economically, that he predicted that control of information would one day be the focus of war.

Postmodern theory, then, is characterised by the rejection of metanarratives, acknowledgement of differences, blurring of categories and proliferation of meanings. Methodologically, this weighs against seeking 'essences' or 'foundations' for phenomena, and against seeking to impose or identify all-encompassing theories to explain phenomena. It requires an attention to the problems of representation, the ways that language acts to produce reality, and the possibility of multiple readings being equally 'true'.

7.4 Poststructuralism and postmodernism in geography

We noted earlier that postmodernism impacted on geography before poststructuralism, and it was urban geographers who led the way, extending the idea of postmodern architecture to understand whole cities as postmodern. Los Angeles (LA) was promoted as the paradigmatic example, with both Edward Soja and Michael Dear focusing much of their attention on LA. Models of 'modern' cities, largely based on Chicago, envisioned the city with a Central Business District surrounded by concentric rings or segments, each a homogeneous functional zone. Modern cities were planned and rational. Los Angeles, in contrast, is 'a polycentric, polycultural, polyglot metropolis' (Dear, 2000, p. 3) for which models based on assumptions of centre and periphery were meaningless. Chaotic, multimodal and incoherent, LA required a different understanding. Soja and Dear, alongside others such as David Ley, sought to develop an understanding of cities as postmodern, advocating the use of postmodern theory. Soja's (1989) *Postmodern Geographies* is regarded as a seminal text of the period, arguing for a spatially oriented, postmodern social theory. Dear, too, made links between geography and social theory, and specifically urged human geographers to take up the 'postmodern challenge' (Dear, 1988).

Creswell (2013) observes that postmodernism provided two related opportunities for geography. Firstly, in social theory more broadly, postmodernism meant that 'space' re-emerged to prominence. Particularity and difference are inherently spatial. Secondly, postmodernism offered the possibility of a re-invigorated engagement with place, more theoretically orientated than the descriptive regional geographies of the early twentieth century. Soja and Dear have thus both been credited with opening up geography's theoretical horizons and encouraging dialogue across traditional disciplinary boundaries (Strohmayer, 2007; Latham, 2011).

Beyond the 1980s human geographers drew on rapidly multiplying theoretical inspirations. The term 'poststructuralism' has far greater presence than 'postmodernism' in recent human geography literature, but this is little reason to assume that postmodernism has been left behind. To the contrary: in revisiting Dear's (1988) 'postmodern challenge', both Doel (2007) and Strohmayer (2007) suggest that postmodernism has become subsumed into the discipline to the point of invisibility. This leaves us with the question of what postmodern and poststructuralist geographies look like.

Where Marxist and other structuralist geographies seek to understand the underlying order of the (social) world, poststructuralist and postmodernist geographies, being against metanarratives, are more likely to emphasise disorder, multiplicity and difference. The significance of social categories such as race, gender, religion and sexuality in social processes is often foregrounded, along with sensitivity to the ways in which such categories are (re)produced, and to the power relations in social processes. The productive nature of language and discourse is explicitly acknowledged and often provides a focus for investigation, attention being paid to the ways in which categories, identities and places are discursively produced. Poststructuralist and postmodern geographies understand spaces and places as open and emerging, connected with other spaces and places through multiple processes, practices, identities and forms of belonging (Murdoch, 2005). Recognition of the partial and situated nature of knowledge requires **reflexivity** on the part of the researcher, acknowledging their own role in the creation of knowledge and the power relations inherent in producing geographical knowledge, shaping discourse, 'about' others.

The new cultural geographies thus called for new ways of defining both what geographers study and how they practise the discipline. Geographers no longer need to go 'out' to do fieldwork (an argument that was particularly promoted by feminist geographers). With an emphasis on representation, anything could be analysed as text, from cities to policy documents, popular culture (such as film or music) to personal diaries. Geographical research can be undertaken in the cinema, lounge or café as much as in more traditional 'field' sites, using a host of (predominantly qualitative) approaches perhaps limited only by our imagination.

7.4.1 Rapa Nui/Easter Island: a postmodern analysis of a postmodern place?

While little geographical research is specifically portrayed as postmodern these days, Young's (2012) study of Rapa Nui (or Easter Island) provides an example of postmodern research in practice as well as demonstrating the blurred boundaries between geography and other disciplines. Neither the research nor the journal it is published in are identified as specifically 'geographical', but the work could easily have fitted a geographical journal.

Rapa Nui is a small island in the Pacific Ocean, approximately 3,500km to the west of the South American continental land mass. The island has been governed as part of Chile since 1888. Young (2012) identifies Rapa Nui as a place in which and through which multiple groups encounter each other daily, identifying these principally as Chileans, indigenous Rapa Nui people, international archaeologists and international tourists. His analysis focuses on these groups, and the multiple discourses about the island that are variously promoted, ignored or resisted by each. These discourses are inherently connected to space and place, and to conflicts over space and place.

Young's primary research method, then, is critical discourse analysis (influenced by Foucault). His project is ethnographic, involving a lengthy stay on the island and drawing on multiple sources: government documents, tourist guidebooks, observations, overheard conversations, and meetings (interviews) with Rapa Nui people. Each group constructs Rapa Nui island and particular places on the island in different ways: 'What Rapa Nui considered a sacred and storied place on the island was alternatively imagined by an archaeologist as a rich archaeological site, by a tourist as a nice context for a photo, and by the Chilean government as a convenient location for a new military base' (p. 3). The dominant Chilean discourses configure the island (and its people) either simply as Chilean, or as a particular bi-cultural Chilean/Polynesian hybrid. These two discourses dominate in different places and institutions on the island, but both depict Rapa Nui island as postcolonial (a former colony). The discourse of Rapa Nui people, in contrast, positions the island in colonial terms (currently colonised), with the Chilean presence viewed quite differently.

Young's conclusion discusses the idea that Rapa Nui could be characterised as a postmodern place, situated within a 'deterritorialised global ethnoscape' in which everyone lives hybrid lives and places are imagined in many different ways. However, he points out that characterising the island in this way involves imposing a particular narrative which is itself positioned and empowered (the academic researcher having considerable discursive power). The postmodern rejection of metanarratives, concern for difference, and recognition that knowledge is always situated and partial are thus exemplified and followed through in a self-reflexive manner.

7.4.2 Discipline and control in the classroom

Gallagher's (2011) examination of the exercise of power in primary schools presents an overt application of Foucault's ideas on power. This ethnographic study involved observation of a single classroom in a suburban primary school in Scotland for almost a year. Gallagher noticed early in his fieldwork that quietness was highly valued in the school's culture, and this drew his attention to the role of sound within the school setting. To analyse his observations he makes use of the idea of the panopticon, emphasising this as a model of the operation of surveillance.

Surveillance in school is, of course, predominantly about children's behaviour, and the key person enacting the surveillance is the class teacher. Gallagher notes that she not only uses visual surveillance (observation) in her classroom, but combines this with aural surveillance, listening to the children. When sitting at a table with a small reading group, the teacher was observed to reprimand children behind her in the classroom for chatting loudly. This reinforces the impression of omnipresent surveillance (the idea of the panopticon being that any prisoner may be observed at any time), as it emphasises that the teacher knows what is going on behind her. Gallagher suggests that aural surveillance creates 'a more diffuse and uncertain space of surveillance' (p. 51) than visual observation. The children could see whether the teacher was looking at them but were less sure about whether she could hear them.

Classroom activities entail different spatial arrangements, including positioning of the teacher, for different lessons. If the teacher is at the front she can see and hear much of the room. In one corner at reading time, her visual surveillance of the children is restricted but her aural surveillance extends across the room. For art lessons, space is used more fluidly and the general classroom atmosphere is noisier. The teacher interacts with small groups at a time, and this limits the space of her visual surveillance, while the background noise level also limits the extent of her aural surveillance. The spatialities of classroom surveillance therefore change throughout the week.

Gallagher also discusses the children's cooperation and participation in the surveillance themselves (individuals telling others to be quiet, for example), as well as noting the ways in which they resist or evade surveillance. On one occasion, he noticed two boys quietly talking to each other only because he saw one of them turn around in his chair to the other. These two were evading the aural surveillance of the teacher, their voices inaudible from only a couple of metres away.

Sound is used more overtly in controlling the children as well, with the teacher raising her voice or clapping her hands to quieten them. The school bell was a sonic marker in the exercise of power, regulating the school day and its spatialities. The bell signalling the end of break time was also a cue for the children to line up near the entrance, moving back into the space of the teacher's (closer) surveillance.

Gallagher's research thus draws out the multi-sensory, multi-participant nature of surveillance in the school and its spatial dimensions, and he uses this to argue for greater attention to be paid to sound, space and power.

These two examples illustrate the ways in which postmodernist and poststructuralist research may be carried out, but offer little sense of the diversity of such geographies. From the representation of bodies and city spaces in zombie films (May, 2010) to the discursive negotiation of individual identities by children on family farms (Riley, 2009), or the moral geographies of graffiti in an Australian city (McAuliffe, 2012), postmodernist and poststructuralist geographies tackle the myriad ways in which people encounter, construct and represent places and identities.

7.4.3 Beyond poststructuralism and postmodernism

Returning to the idea that postmodernism has sunk into geography's 'disciplinary unconsciousness', Doel (2007, p. 675) puts it thus: 'Who, today, does not aspire to be sensitive to difference, otherness and alterity? Who, today, is not suspicious of grand narratives, totalizing claims, and unsituated knowledge? And who, today, truly believes that we were ever rational, edified, and modern? Only fools and despots lack the good grace to be modest in their theoretical, explanatory, and normative ambitions.'

Since the mid-1990s, criticisms that poststructuralism and postmodernism led to an over-emphasis on representation have prompted a return to the materialities of the world, and to the ways in which places and spaces are experienced. Embodied, **affective** and emotional geographies have emerged in response. While a poststructuralist sensibility is retained (as indicated in Doel's comment above), such geographies draw as much on **phenomenology** and pragmatism as they do on postmodernism and poststructuralism. These developments are discussed further in Chapter 5, although some of them (particularly Latour's Actor Network Theory) would equally fit here. Again, boundaries can be difficult to define.

7.5 Postmodernism and poststructuralism at the beach

The beach has considerable potential for social research, with notions of 'sun, sea, sand and surf' occupying a particular place in Western culture. Normal self- and social controls are relaxed at particular times and places, the beach being one of them (Powell, 2010). Notions of '**liminality**' have been applied to the beach (Gale, 2009; Powell, 2010), identifying this as a space where the normal constraints of everyday life are relaxed. Dress codes and behaviours are different at the beach. This can result in tensions when beachgoers temporarily leave the beach, for example entering local shops in minimal clothing. The negotiation of such boundaries between 'beach' and 'not beach' might offer potential for research.

Gale's (2009) examination of the 'Paris Plage' emphasises this difference in beach behaviour in a particularly postmodern setting: 'Paris Plage' translates as 'Paris Beach', an artificial beach in an inland urban setting. Gale notes how the beach is performed by those who use it: whether sunbathing on the too-fine sand or jogging, cycling or roller-blading along the waterfront, they 'behave as they would if visiting the seaside for real, but are all too aware that they are not' (p. 126). We have a particular conception of what the beach is for.

Despite the associations of liminality, the beach is not a place where 'anything goes'. The dominant beach discourse prioritises bodies that are young, slim, fit, able and tanned. The production and reproduction of beach discourses, their operation to exclude or include those who do not match the 'beach body', and the ways in which such discourses may be resisted are avenues that could be explored.

Methodologically, there are many possibilities. We could interrogate the representation of beaches through popular culture, such as television programmes and films, tourist promotions or news media. Durrheim and Dixon (2001) undertook a textual analysis of newspaper articles to identify the ways in which South African beaches were constructed as 'white' spaces during the Apartheid era. Even without the exclusionary practices formalised by such politics, representations of beaches may tell us much. Farid (2009) also examines the racialised nature of beach spaces, drawing on two particularly violent incidents on beaches in Australia and Palestine/ Israel, in which beaches appear to be understood as 'white' spaces.

Ethnographic studies might enable examination of what constitutes 'normal' or accepted behaviour at the beach, and how this is socially determined, regulated and resisted. Schoemaker Holmes' (2006) ethnographic research on a Canadian nude beach revealed the ways in which the dominant heteronormative construction of sexuality is continually contested by alternative discourses. Waitt and Warren (2008) used a combination of diaries, sketches, photo-diaries and video-narratives to explore masculinity among a small group of Australian surfers. Equally, it is important to recognise the limitations of autoethnography and participant observation, in that these approaches would only access beachgoers. We might therefore wish to consider how best to reach individuals who feel most excluded from, or by, 'beach culture', to develop a fuller understanding.

These ideas are restricted to a particular notion of 'the beach'. We could explore different kinds of beaches, beachgoers and beach activities all together. Not all beaches fit the 'sun, sea, surf, sand' ideal. Alternative discourses may exist around rocky beaches, for example. Places, like people, are constructed by what they are *not* as much as what they *are*. Looking further afield, beaches can be even more distant from the dominant Western notions. Since 2009, over 2,600 commercial ships have been sent to the beaches of India, Bangladesh and Pakistan for dismantling (Reuter, 2013). Workers are exposed to the toxic contents of the defunct vessels (contents including asbestos, heavy metals and organic waste), as well as the likelihood of explosions, falls from great heights or being crushed by falling metal (Heidegger and Jenssen, 2013). The soft sands limit the use of heavy lifting equipment. Beaches here might mean a wage for the day, with a high risk attached.

7.6 Structuralism, poststructuralism and postmodernism in summary

Structuralism focused attention on meaning, Saussure highlighting that the words (signs) we use are not simply correlated with the things they signify. Rather, the combination of signifier and signified is one of convention, and the meaning of any sign is established through its relations to other signs within the sign system. Methodologically, a Structuralist approach to society follows the pattern of 'science', seeking generalisable regularities (structures) to explain phenomena. Structuralism appears to have had little direct impact on geography, but provides a starting point for understanding the much more significant (to geographers) modes of thought that followed.

Poststructuralism and postmodernism retain this emphasis on meaning, and an understanding of meaning as dependent upon context. However, the notion of a singular system or structure providing that context is rejected. This opens the door for an appreciation of meaning as relational, and hence geographically, historically and socially situated. The discursive construction of identities, spaces and places is revealed, along with the ways in which such meanings are reproduced and resisted. Foucault's work, in particular, connected this to the distribution and operation of power in society. Sensitivity to difference, and to the power inherent in knowledge production, characterises poststructuralist geographies.

If we understand knowledge and meaning as being dependent upon discourse, then our possibilities for knowledge of the world are always shaped by the discourses with which we are familiar – and, indeed, in which we participate. Postructuralism, in effect, challenges a simple binary understanding of **ontology** and **epistemology** as distinct. Theory and reality are inseparable. This is not necessarily to assume that there is no 'real world' independent of us, but only that we can never know the world outside of our theoretical or discursive framings. We see what we are taught to see, and this applies to physical geographers as much as to human geographers. Trudgill (2003) provides a nice example of this, describing how students faced with unfamiliar geomorphology in the Mediterranean attempted to offer explanations based on mechanical weathering or volcanic processes of which they had some knowledge. In fact the landforms were the result of chemical weathering. In effect, then, poststructuralism can be interpreted as being silent on matters of ontology, as we can never know what may be in the world beyond our access to it.

Poststructuralism and postmodernism had an enormous influence on human geography from the 1980s onwards. As the 'new cultural geographies' reflected the cultural turn of the social sciences more broadly, geographers began to pay attention to the ways in which we represent the world, and to the ways in which places, spaces, groups and identities are socially produced. This was accompanied by a diversification in the methods available for geographical research and the 'sites' at which such research could be conducted. While poststructuralist geographies have been criticised for over-emphasising representation, the more materially oriented geographies that have followed have not rejected poststructuralism as much as built on it, fusing it with influences from phenomenology, pragmatism and elsewhere.

FURTHER READING

For further explanations

Crampton, J.W. and Elden, S. (eds) (2007) *Space, Knowledge and Power: Foucault and Geography*. Aldershot: Ashgate.

Dear, M. and Wassmansdorf, G. (1993) 'Postmodern consequences', *Geographical Review* 83 (3): 321–6.

Doel, M. (2010) 'Analysing cultural texts', in N. Clifford, S. French and G. Valentine (eds), *Key Methods in Geography*. London: Sage. pp. 485–96.

Hubbard, P. and Kitchin, R. (eds) (2011) *Key Thinkers on Space and Place* (2nd edition). London: Sage. See chapters on: Jean Baudrillard (Clarke and Doel, pp. 40–6); Michael Dear (McNeill and Tewdwr-Jones, pp. 134–40); Michel Foucault (Philo, pp. 162–70); Edward W. Soja (Latham, pp. 380–86).

Murdoch, J. (2005) *Post-structuralist Geography: A Guide to Relational Space*. London: Sage. Online at http://www.univpgri-palembang.ac.id/perpus-fkip/Perpustakaan/Geography/Geografi%20manusia/Geografi%20Post-Struturalis.pdf.

Ritzer, G. (1997) *Postmodern Social Theory*. London: McGraw-Hill.

Progress in Human Geography resources

Berg, L.D. (1993) 'Between modernism and postmodernism', *Progress in Human Geography* 17 (4): 490–507. doi: 10.1177/030913259301700403.

Dear, M. (2007) 'Classics in human geography revisited: Dear, M. 1988: The postmodern challenge: reconstructing human geography. Transactions of the Institute of British Geographers NS 13, 262–74: Author's response – postmodern evils; postmodern lives', *Progress in Human Geography* 31 (5): 680–3. doi: 10.1177/030913250703100050903.

Doel, M.A. (2007) 'Classics in human geography revisited: Dear, M. 1988: The postmodern challenge: reconstructing human geography. Transactions of the Institute of British Geographers NS 13, 262–74: Commentary 1', *Progress in Human Geography* 31 (5): 675–8. doi: 10.1177/0309132507081497.

Gandy, M. (1996) 'Crumbling the land: the postmodernity debate and the analysis of environmental problems', *Progress in Human Geography* 20 (1): 23–40. doi: 10.1177/030913259602000102.

Mackinnon, D. (2011) 'Reconstructing scale: towards a new scalar politics', *Progress in Human Geography* 35 (1): 21–36. doi: 10.1177/0309132510367841.

Marden, P. (1992) 'The deconstructionist tendencies of postmodern geographies: a compelling logic?' *Progress in Human Geography* 16 (1): 41–57. doi: 10.1177/030913259201600103.

Martin, R. (2001) 'Geography and public policy: the case of the missing agenda', *Progress in Human Geography* 25 (2): 189–210. doi: 10.1191/0309132201678580476.

Mayhew, R.J. (2009) 'Historical geography 2007–8: Foucault's avatars – still in (the) Driver's seat', *Progress in Human Geography* 33 (3): 387–97. doi: 10.1177/0309132508096354.

Newman, D. and Paasi, A. (1998) 'Fences and neighbours in the postmodern world: boundary narratives in political geography', *Progress in Human Geography* 22 (2): 186–207. doi: 10.1191/030913298666039113.

Strohmayer, U. (2007) 'Classics in human geography revisited: Dear, M. 1988: The postmodern challenge: reconstructing human geography. Transactions of the Institute of British Geographers NS 13, 262–74: Commentary 2', *Progress in Human Geography* 31 (5): 678–80. doi: 10.1177/0309132507031 0050902.

Examples

Longhurst, R. (2012) 'Becoming smaller: autobiographical spaces of weight loss', *Antipode* 44 (3): 871–88.

May, J. (2011) 'Zombie geographies and the undead city', *Social & Cultural Geography* 11 (3): 285–98.

Morrison, C.-A. (2012) 'Solicited diaries and the everyday geographies of heterosexual love and home: reflections on methodological process and practice', *Area* 44 (1): 68–75 [an example of feminist poststructuralist research, specifically discussing methods].

Ott, B.L. (2003) "'I'm Bart Simpson, who the hell are you?" A study in postmodern identity (re)construction', *Journal of Popular Culture* 37 (1): 56–82.

Yarwood, R. and Charlton, C. (2009) "'Country life"? Rurality, folk music and "Show of Hands"', *Journal of Rural Studies* 25: 194–206.

Young, F.W. (2012) "'I Hē Koe?" Placing Rapa Nui', *The Contemporary Pacific* 24 (1): 1–30.

8

Complexity Theory: From Butterfly Wings to Fairy Rings

At the estuary of the River Erme in south Devon (UK), low tide reveals the expanses of sand each side of the river known as Coastguard's Beach (Mothecombe) and Wonwell Beach. Venture onto the sand and you are quite likely to find yourself stepping among an expanse of ripples (Figure 8.1). Each runs roughly parallel to the next, individual ripples occasionally breaking into two, or two merging back into one. The resulting pattern is not dissimilar from the stripes on a zebra. We may know much about the mechanics of entrainment, transport and deposition of an individual sand grain, but such understanding would never lead us to predict the pattern of ripples that emerges from thousands of such movements. The sand ripples arise from complex system dynamics.

Complexity theory comprises a collection of inter-related ideas that are often interpreted in different ways by different authors, so it can be difficult to define precisely. This chapter first looks a bit more closely at what 'complexity' means. It then provides an introduction to some key ideas, before considering how complex systems research is undertaken.

8.1 Introducing complexity: Emergence and interdependence

Since the seventeenth century, the dominant approach of science has been to develop understanding by breaking large things down into their component parts.

Figure 8.1   Sand ripples in the inter-tidal zone at Coastguard's Beach, Mothecombe, south Devon, UK. These lie across the estuary, normal to the dominant direction of river/ sea flow. The ridges are spaced approximately 0.75m apart, but much smaller ripples (the smallest with ridge spacing of around 0.07m) can be found elsewhere in the estuary. In some places, the slopes of large ripples are patterned with a sequence of small ripples lying at right angles to the ridge of the large ripple. (Photograph by Kevin Couper)

This **reductionist** tendency was recognised by Auguste Comte when he developed his ideas on **positivism** in the 1820s (Chapter 2). In describing how science works, Comte established a hierarchy of disciplines (Figure 2.1 in Chapter 2). To explain biological phenomena we often look to chemistry; to explain chemical phenomena we look to physics; to explain terrestrial physics we look to celestial (universal) physics. In each case, scientists turn to simpler, more generally applicable phenomena for explanation. As we can see from the sand ripples, the problem of such an approach is that breaking something down into its component parts means that we overlook any interactions between the parts.

In the second half of the twentieth century, researchers across a number of disciplines (though perhaps predominantly physics, computer science and cybernetics) began to turn their attention to these kinds of interactions. The result is complexity theory, sometimes referred to as 'complex systems', 'complexity science' or just 'complexity'. This is an approach to science that focuses on the relationships between parts of a system, on how these relationships generate collective behaviours, and on how the system interacts with its environment. Ideas from complexity science have been used across many fields of study, from physics to anthropology.

Crucially, 'complex' is not the same as 'complicated', although we tend to use those words interchangeably in everyday speech. Something that is complicated may be a challenge to understand, but ultimately can be broken down into its component parts, the interactions between these parts being predictable. Clocks and cars are complicated. Complex systems consist of multiple component parts whose interactions create something less predictable. They are, in effect, more than the sum of their parts – a notion that dates back to Aristotle (Favis-Mortlock and de Boer, 2003). Bar-Yam (2004) identifies two key concepts as integral to complexity science: **emergence** and interdependence.

Emergence and interdependence are both illustrated by the example of a starling murmuration. This spectacular phenomenon occurs in the winter months across much of Europe (including the UK), perhaps most famously in Rome. It involves thousands of Common Starlings (latin name *Sturnus vulgaris*) gathering together as the day draws to a close, forming a swooping, swirling, rippling cloud that moves as if it was a single entity. No individual is in control. The seemingly singular movement of the flock is generated by the relations between the individual birds in flight: each stays close to its nearest seven neighbours, though without actually touching, and each matches its velocity to these neighbours (Cavagna and Giardina, 2008). As one bird turns, its seven neighbours respond in kind, and each of their neighbours then does the same, the movement rippling through the flock. The resulting behaviour of the flock is an emergent phenomenon, arising from the many smaller-scale interactions between individual birds. If we were to focus on the flight of a single bird, we would miss the higher-level behaviour of the whole flock. If we stand back and view the movement of the whole flock, we lose sight of individual birds. Emergence is about the relationship between the details of a system and the bigger picture. The sand ripples in Figure 8.1 are also emergent phenomena.

Within a starling murmuration, a sudden change of direction by one bird – perhaps triggered by an incoming predator such as a hawk or peregrine falcon – will result in change throughout the whole flock. This is interdependence. As Bar-Yam (2004, p. 27) puts it, 'Pushing on a complex system "here" often has effects "over there"…', effects that are usually difficult to predict. Each part of the system is dependent upon multiple other parts, in a complex network of interactions.

EXERCISE 8.1

Emergence and interdependence in action

On the companion website you will find some links to short videos of starling murmurations in action. Watch one (or more) of these to get a sense of emergence and interdependence.

8.2 Key ideas

The notions of emergence and interdependence are central to complexity theory. Some of the other ideas that make up complexity theory are **chaos, path dependence, attractors, self-organisation**, and **fractals**. Each of these will be addressed in turn, before looking at examples of complexity research later in the chapter.

8.2.1 Chaos

Edward Lorenz (1917–2008) was a mathematician and meteorologist working at the Massachusetts Institute of Technology in the early 1960s. He made a seemingly chance discovery that had significant impact on science.

According to Gleick's (1988) popular account, in 1960 Lorenz had developed a computer model to simulate weather patterns. Twelve equations represented the relations between atmospheric pressure, temperature and wind speed. Repeatedly working through its calculations, the computer printed a line of digits every minute, each line characterising the weather for a day; roughly two months of weather processed in every hour. Lorenz's twelve equations, repeated again and again and again, produced weather patterns that looked recognisably familiar to the scientists working around him.

In the winter of 1961, Lorenz wanted to re-run a particular sequence of his computer weather in order to study it more closely. Rather than begin the whole thing again, he took numbers from the print-out half way through the sequence and programmed them into the computer, providing it with initial conditions to begin its simulation. He then left the computer to its processing. When he returned an hour later, something strange had happened. The first stages of the new print-out matched the earlier sequence, but the two rapidly diverged. A completely different weather pattern had been produced. Lorenz first thought that perhaps there was something wrong with the machine, as the two print-outs should have been exactly the same. Eventually he realised what had happened. The computer's calculations worked with six decimal places, but the print-outs recorded only three. Lorenz had typed in numbers to three decimal places, assuming that the tiny difference between 0.506127 and 0.506 (which the computer interpreted as 0.506000) would be irrelevant. It was not.

Edward Lorenz had stumbled across what became known as the 'butterfly effect', captured in the analogy that a butterfly flapping its wings in Brazil might lead to a tornado in Texas. More technically, this is known as 'sensitivity to initial conditions' or 'deterministic chaos'. What seems an insignificantly small difference in the initial conditions of the system can make a big difference to its trajectory. Lorenz's twelve equations were deterministic; given an input, the equations define the output. There are no random elements at work. But from the repeated iteration of these relatively simple equations, the long-term results are impossible to predict. This later came to be known as chaotic behaviour.

Although Lorenz is widely credited with being the 'founder' of chaos theory, the mathematical foundations had been established by Henri Poincaré in the late nineteenth century (Murzi, 2005), and Keller (2009) claims that the term 'chaos' was not actually used until 1975. Nevertheless, recognition of the butterfly effect challenged some widely held assumptions about the natural world. Many scientists had worked on the basis that change in natural systems was linear, with small forces producing small responses, larger forces producing proportionally larger responses (Thornes, 2009). Any disturbance would be minimised by negative feedback, a 'dampening' effect that would eventually return the system to an equilibrium state (see Box 8.1 for an example). Grabbatin and Rossi (2012) describe this as a 'balance of nature' conception, common to both religious and secular world views, and which imagines nature as predictable and controllable. Chaos challenges those assumptions. **Nonlinear** change means that a small force can have a disproportionately large effect. Nonlinearity itself does not necessarily lead to chaotic behaviour (nonlinear systems can be simple), but chaos is always underpinned by nonlinearity.

BOX 8.1   BASAL ENDPOINT CONTROL – AN EXAMPLE OF NEGATIVE FEEDBACK AND EQUILIBRIUM

The concept of basal endpoint control was first developed by Carson and Kirkby (1972) as a means of understanding hillslope profiles. Thorne (1982) applied the idea to river banks, where it provides a useful means of understanding interactions between different bank erosion processes.

River banks are often subject to both mass failures and fluvial erosion. If a river bank fails, the failed material falls to the toe, or 'basal zone', of the bank. Its removal from this area is then dependent upon fluvial entrainment and transport, which is dependent upon flow conditions. Carson and Kirkby (1972) identified three possible states of basal endpoint control:

1. *Impeded removal:* if the near-bank river flow is insufficient to remove failed material at the rate at which it is supplied to the basal zone, then this material will accumulate at the bank toe. Such accumulation effectively buttresses the bank, decreasing the bank angle and increasing its stability. This diminishes the rate of sediment supply to the basal area, and the system tends towards the second state below.

2. *Unimpeded removal:* this represents an equilibrium condition, where the rate of sediment removal from the bank toe by fluvial forces matches the rate of sediment supply from above by bank failure. The river bank may continue to retreat, but the bank angle and overall form remain the same.

3. *Excess basal capacity:* if near-bank flow conditions remove sediment from the basal zone more rapidly than it is supplied from the bank above, basal scouring occurs. This effectively increases the bank height (as the base of the bank is lowered) and slope angle, making the river bank more unstable with respect to mass failures. The occurrence of such failures will then increase the rate of sediment supply to the basal zone, and the system tends towards the second state above.

The first and third states of basal endpoint control are examples of negative feedback, where the system functions in a manner that dampens the rate of change to the bank profile. The implication is that the overall rate of river bank retreat is determined by fluvial forces dictating the rate of sediment removal from the basal zone. Bank processes operate in equilibrium with fluvial erosion and transport processes. Nonlinearity and complexity challenge these kinds of equilibrium assumptions.

In some respects (Phillips, 2003) deterministic chaos aligned with ideas that were developing in physical geography around the same time. By the 1970s geomorphologists understood that some environments were characterised by positive feedback instead of negative feedback (King, 1970), exaggerating rather than minimising change. This may lead to **catastrophic** (large and sudden) events as internal system thresholds are crossed (Schumm, 1979). Evans and Clague's (1994) review of catastrophic events arising from climate-induced glacier ice loss provides multiple examples: glacier avalanches; landslides and debris flows; outbursts from moraine-dammed and glacier-dammed lakes (*jökulhlaups*). In the case of the latter, meltwater travelling through the glacier melts the ice around it by heat transfer, developing and enlarging a tunnel. As the tunnel grows, more meltwater can escape, increasing the heat transfer, melting more ice, and increasing the size of the tunnel further. The result is an exponential increase in discharge, producing a rapid flood that abates suddenly when the lake is drained.

Deterministic chaos, then, underlines the importance of nonlinear relations and feedback in natural systems. One of the significant implications is that the development of a complex system is unique. At each moment, the possible trajectories of change are determined by the present state of the system; and at each moment, the present state of the system is determined by its previous conditions. Development is said to be 'path dependent'. In other words, complex systems have a history, and history matters.

8.2.2 Path dependence

In the archives of the university where I work, there is a geography examination paper (for trainee teachers) dating from 1846. What particularly caught my eye about this paper is that it includes questions on regional geography, asking about the specificities of Great Britain and its colonial territories, and systematic geography, focusing on universally applicable relations between phenomena such as altitude and weather, or temperature and vegetation. There has long been some tension between these '**idiographic**' (identifying particularities) and '**nomothetic**' (seeking generalities) approaches to geography. This tension is easy to over-simplify as a 'humanities' versus 'science' approach; the **Quantitative Revolution** of the mid-twentieth century is often depicted as a shift from the former to the latter (Holt-Jensen, 2009). In practice, an understanding of both is needed to make sense of the world (Montello and Sutton, 2013), and that 1846 exam paper suggests that geographers have long been combining the two.

This combination of universal and particular is nowhere more evident than in river systems. A long history of hydrological, hydraulic and geomorphological research has yielded much in the way of universally applicable knowledge, such as the regular relations between downstream changes in discharge and channel cross-section (Leopold and Maddock, 1953), or between meander wavelength, radius of curvature and channel width (Leopold and Wolman, 1960). Yet few, if any, rivers conform exactly to the textbook examples. Local variations are always evident. As Lane and Richards (1997, p. 254) explained, 'The channel can ... be envisaged as being on a kind of trajectory, where what goes on in the future is critically dependent upon what happens in the present, what went on in the past, and what is taking place in reaches upstream and downstream of the reach in question.' In other words, the development of a river channel is path dependent; the place- and time-specific *story* of the river channel is important. Notions of **inheritance** and **contingency** in physical geography reflect path dependence, and sometimes the term 'state-dependence' is used (Woodroffe, 2007). Brierley et al. (2013) draw out the implications for applied work, advocating a 'place-based' approach to river management that explicitly aims to combine relevant generalised knowledge with an understanding of locally contingent dynamics.

If path dependence is important in natural systems, it is also relevant to social systems – indeed, the term 'path dependence' seems to be more commonly used by human geographers than physical geographers. In health geographies, Curtis and Riva (2010a, b) identify a variety of examples in contexts ranging from individuals to communities to global health initiatives. Among individuals, health in old age shows persistent associations with the socio-economic conditions of a person's place of childhood, such that individual life paths are important (Curtis et al., 2004). Curtis and Riva (2010b) highlight the implications for public health and policy initiatives, which often target populations in their current place of residence and therefore overlook such migration effects.

Notions of path dependency have perhaps been most popular in economic geography, with Brian Arthur and Paul David (both economists) identified as particular advocates. They use path dependency to account for the development of regional clustering in industries. While the details of their models differ, some common features can be identified (Martin, 2010; Martin and Sunley, 2010). These include:

- An early phase in which a new technology, product, industry or institution is explored.

- Some event, commonly attributed to chance or 'historical accident', which then establishes a particular development opportunity as preferred. This sets in train the path of development for that industry.

- The achievement of critical mass (for example, of businesses) in a region, resulting in 'lock-in'; the path becomes self-reinforcing through positive feedback.

- Once locked in, the developmental path is only disrupted by an external 'shock' to the industry.

In essence, path dependency has represented a revived interest in history among economic geographers. However, some have pointed out that the standard model depicted above has paid too little attention to *place* dependency. Boschma (2007) illustrates this with the example of the British automobile industry, which developed to concentrate around Coventry and Birmingham. The region already had coach and cycle manufacturing industries, which provided 'generic resources' of expertise that could be adapted to the manufacturing of cars. Lock-in is not necessarily down to a chance accident. Path dependency is a matter of history and geography in combination.

Arguments have been made that economic geographers' use of the notion of path dependency has been largely uncritical (Martin, 2010; Martin and Sunley, 2010; Henning et al., 2013). However, the idea of 'lock-in' introduces our next aspect of complexity theory for discussion, as it implies a particular form of attractor.

8.2.3 Attractors

Some systems, whatever their initial conditions, will eventually tend towards particular states. We can visualise all possible states of a system as a metaphorical 'space' defined by the variables or components of a system. This is known as 'phase space'. An attractor is a region of phase space – that is, a particular combination of values for the system components – towards which the system will evolve, regardless of where it started from.

Inkpen (2007) suggests that there may be attractors in the erosion rates found on **shore platforms**. The rate of erosion of the rocky surface is determined by a complex combination of four variables: material; environment; process; and history. These variables define the phase space, and the interactions between them constrain the possible erosion rates at any point on the rock surface. Inkpen depicts the phase space for this system as a landscape (Figure 8.2), where the high points represent the most likely erosion rates – the attractors. A single peak in the phase space landscape occurs if a particular erosion rate is most likely (Figure 8.2a). If a range of values is equally possible, a plateau landscape would occur. For a shore platform

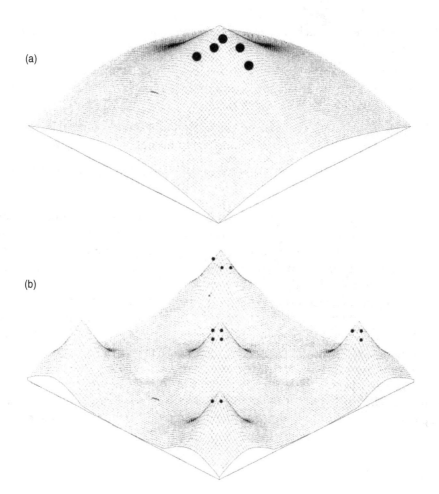

Figure 8.2 Representing constraints on movement of erosion rates about phase space. a) a single peak or 'typical' erosion value; b) multiple peaks representing a range of 'typical' erosion rates (Inkpen, 2007, p. 39).

with a number of different topographical units, the phase space landscape may well have multiple peaks, each representing the dominant erosion rate for a different topographical unit (Figure 8.2b).

In any system, an attractor represented by a point in phase space indicates a stable state. Economic geographers' discussions (and criticisms) of 'lock-in' seem to indicate a point attractor, where an industry is characterised by a particular, stable geographical configuration. But not all attractors are single points. Some form loops in the phase space, indicating a system that exhibits periodic behaviour (Baas, 2002). More intricate shapes, with multiple loops and bifurcations, are known as 'strange attractors', and these are indicators of chaotic behaviour.

A single system may have multiple attractors, and hence multiple possible states that it could tend towards. In **aeolian** environments, Nield and Baas's (2008) modelling work on the development of dune fields suggests that complex interactions between ecological and geomorphological components of the landscape are at work. Fast vegetation growth rates lead to the development of parabolic dunes. Medium growth rates result in transgressive transverse ridges, and slow growth rates yield highly sensitive, mixed dune-form systems. These dune form 'end states' represent different attractors. When a system reaches an attractor (a particular form of dune), it will be relatively stable in terms of remaining within the realms of that attractor. There will be some variation between sand dunes, and individual dunes will change and migrate over time, but the dominant overall dune form will remain the same. However, a disturbance such as vegetation removal due to drought, land clearance or fire can prompt the dune system to switch quite rapidly to another attractor, another dominant dune formation.

The stability of a system that has reached an attractor potentially presents a useful tool for environmental management. Thornes (2009) discusses the implications for river restoration. If the stable condition (attractor) associated with pool/riffle and meander wavelength can be identified, then the river can be engineered to this state and is likely to remain there, as a resilient, functioning system. He notes, however, that in any complex system there may be unknown and unexpected complications, and responses to extreme events can still be unpredictable.

8.2.4 Self-organisation and self-organised criticality

We began this chapter with the sand ripples at the mouth of the River Erme (Figure 8.1), noting that this patterned form is an emergent phenomenon. It would not be predictable from knowledge of the mechanisms by which individual sand grains are entrained, transported and deposited (the reductionist approach). The sand ripples are also an example of self-organisation, which can be defined as the emergence of order or structure from the interactions between components of a system (Baas, 2002; Green et al., 2008). In other words, it is the dynamics and feedback mechanisms *within* the system that produce order, rather than external influences on the system. Self-organisation is most obvious when it results in the production of visible spatial patterns, such as patterned ground (circles, polygons or stripes) in periglacial regions, or the periodic riffle/pool or step/pool sequences of river and stream channels (Clifford, 1993; Chin and Phillips, 2007). However, self-organisation has also been recognised in social systems such as local and global economies (Coe, 2011; Fløysand and Jakobsen, 2011).

Self-organisation highlights the cross-scale interdependence operating within a complex system, where feedback mechanisms (both positive and negative) are central. Small-scale processes such as the entrainment, transport and deposition of individual sand grains synthesise into larger-scale emergent phenomena such as sand ripples. The larger phenomena are dependent upon the smaller-scale processes.

Equally, those ripples then provide the environment for the individual sand grains, and so shape the smaller-scale processes. As Murray et al. (2008, p. 499) put it, 'causality extends in both directions through the scales', large scale affecting small scale and vice versa. Self-organisation may thus operate in tandem with chaos; a chaotic process at one scale (such as the movement of individual sand grains) can produce organised, structured patterns at a larger scale (such as sand ripples).

A well-known example of self-organisation in coastal geomorphology is that of **beach cusps** (Baas, 2002). Cusps occur as a series of regular concave embayments along the shoreline, separated by horns that extend seaward. Werner and Fink (1993) recognised these as self-organised features whose formation and continued existence is dependent upon feedback between beach morphology and the **swash flow** (Benavente et al., 2011). Incoming flow separates over the horns, depositing sediment there, and then converges in the embayments to erode sediment off the beach in the backwash (Figure 8.3). The divergence and convergence of flow thus results in sediment movement that ensures the continued existence of the cusps. The existence of cusps in turn causes the flow to diverge over the horns and converge in the embayments. Masselink and Pattiaratchi (1998) found this feedback mechanism to be dependent upon the relation between cusp spacing and swash circulation, in that it operates within a limited range: if the cusps are spaced too widely or are too subdued relative to the swash circulation, the embayments become infilled with sediment; if cusps are too narrow or too pronounced, the horns are eroded and the embayments infilled. Both circumstances eventually eliminate the cusp.

Beach cusps highlight an important feature of self-organisation. The beach is an **open system**, with a throughput of energy and matter, and this is generally thought to be essential to the development of self-organisation. Because of the constant supply of energy and matter, the system can be maintained in a far-from-equilibrium state.

Some self-organised systems persist in a critical state, where any small, localised event could have system-wide impacts. The idea of 'self-organised criticality' was first proposed by theoretical physicist Per Bak (1948–2002) and colleagues (Bak et al., 1987, 1988), and has since been applied to a variety of natural and social systems, from earthquakes (Scholz, 1991) and forest fires (Malamud et al., 1998; Song et al., 2001) to traffic jams (Nagel and Paczuski, 1995) and stock markets (Caldarelli et al., 1997).

The paradigmatic example of self-organised criticality is provided by a sand pile, described by Bak (1996). Imagine a flat table, onto which sand is dropped one particle (or clast) at a time. As more and more sand is added, it forms into a pile and the pile becomes bigger, with steeper and steeper sides. Small avalanches or 'sand slides' begin to occur. A single clast added to the pile might cause a local disturbance by triggering one of these slides, but it does not affect the whole pile. Eventually the sand pile grows to a size where the sides cannot get any steeper. In geomorphological terms, the sides of the sand pile have reached the **angle of repose** of the constituent sand material. With the continued addition of sand particles to the pile, each one may result in very little change, or it may trigger a small slide, or it may cause a huge avalanche across much of the sand pile. The overall result is that the amount of sand added to the pile is balanced by the

Figure 8.3 Beach morphology and swash flow interactions associated with beach cusps.
a) Incoming flow separates over the horns, ensuring continued deposition of sediment, and converges in the embayments, eroding sediment from the beach in the backwash.
b) Flow and sediment interactions at Seaton Beach, Cornwall. Although the cusps are not well developed here, the interaction between sediment and flow is apparent. The beach surface is higher where there are coarser sediments (the 'horns'), and the water fills the lower surface of the fine-grained embayments. (Photograph by Kevin Couper)

amount of sand leaving it, and this global (system-wide) effect, Bak argues, requires some kind of communication throughout the entire sand pile system. The sand pile has reached the self-organised critical state. It is critical because a single local event (a sand clast falling) can affect the entire system, and it is self-organised because there is no external force creating this pattern of behaviour (Frigg, 2003). The critical state is an attractor for the system (Bak and Creutz, 1994).

With a mixture of small and large events occurring, the relation between the magnitude of sand slides and their frequency is found to occupy a straight line when plotted on logarithmic axes. This is a power law relationship – more precisely, an inverse power law relationship: there is a high frequency of very small events, and a low frequency of very large events, so frequency decreases as magnitude increases. This inverse power law relationship was first noted in earthquakes, in which context it is known as the Gutenberg-Richter law. However, power laws of this type are characteristic of self-organised critical systems. Fonstad and Marcus (2003) identified inverse power law relations between the number and size of riverbank failures within drainage basins in the north-western Yellowstone area, and Van de Wiel and Coulthard (2010) found an inverse power law magnitude-frequency relation in river bedload. They note, though, that inverse power law relations should not be used as the *only* diagnostic of self-organised criticality, as this pattern can occur in other situations. Not all systems exhibiting power-law magnitude-frequency relations are self-organised critical systems.

Self-organised criticality is often related to the occurrence of fractal forms, to which we turn next.

8.2.5 Fractals

Figure 8.4 is, at first glance, an aerial view of a braided river system. Look closely at the centre of the image and you can see the multi-threaded channel, separated by ovate sediment deposits (braid bars), which themselves are crossed by traces of smaller channels. In the top-centre of the photograph is the rugged terrain of higher ground. The view is quite characteristic of rivers fed by glacial meltwater, such as the Waimakariri River in New Zealand or the Hulahula River in Alaska. The top left corner of the photograph, however, reveals that this is on a much smaller scale. Without the footprint it would be very difficult to tell how big this 'river system' really is. Braided rivers are self-similar across scales (a property known as scaling) and this self-similarity is a central characteristic of fractal phenomena.

In 1967, mathematician Benoît Mandelbrot (1924–2010) published a paper asking, 'How long is the coast of Britain?' This is a simple question, but it does not have a simple answer. Imagine measuring a length of coastline on a map. If we use a pair of dividers, set (for argument's sake) to measure 6cm intervals, then the overall length of our measured coastline will be n x 6cm, where n is the number of 'steps' of the dividers needed to get from one end of the line to the other. Now if we decrease the spacing of the dividers to 3cm and repeat the exercise, it would be reasonable to expect that with steps half as big we would need twice as many to get from one end of the line to the other. The overall measured length should therefore be $2n$ x 3cm. This expectation would hold true if we were measuring a straight line, but coastlines are not straight. Decreasing the divider steps allows us to account for more

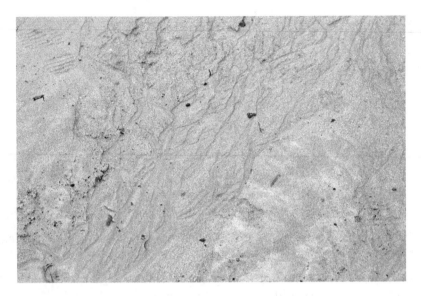

Figure 8.4 A braided 'river system' from above, but how big is it?
(Photograph by Kevin Couper)

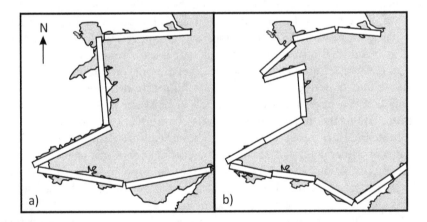

Figure 8.5 Measuring the coastline of mainland Wales. a) Using measurement lengths
of 100km, the distance from one end of the coast to the other is just five steps. b) Using
measurements lengths of 50km, covering the same stretch of coastline takes 11½ steps,
because we can follow the shape of the coastline more closely.

of the detail in the coastline, so we would actually end up with a longer measurement, taking more than twice as many steps (Figure 8.5). If we used smaller steps
still, we would 'see' even more of the detail and so get an even longer measurement.
All fractals exhibit this seeming anomaly, as more 'information' (in this case, detail
of the coastline) is available the closer in we focus.

EXERCISE 8.2

Measuring the coast

If you have access to a map of a coastal area, you could try measuring the coastline for yourself:

- Decide on a stretch of coast you want to measure.

- Choose your initial measuring length, bearing in mind that you will want a smaller measuring length later. You can use a ruler, but one of the simplest ways is to use a length of paper, which you can then tear into smaller pieces.

- Work your way along the coastline in 'steps' of your chosen length, counting how many steps it takes to get to the end, and make a note of the number.

- Repeat the exercise with a measuring length half the size, and compare the number of steps you need to measure the coastline.

The implication is that the length of a coastline is effectively undefinable, as it always depends on the length of the measuring unit used. The more irregular the line, the more it will increase in length as the measuring unit gets smaller. The amount of increase in detail as the measurement unit decreases is represented by the fractal dimension (D). We are used to the idea that lines are one-dimensional (D = 1), areas or planes are two-dimensional (D = 2), and volumes are three-dimensional (D = 3). Fractal phenomena have dimensions that fall in between these; they are fractional dimensions. The fractal dimension of the west coast of Britain was found to be 1.25 (Mandelbrot, 1967). In other words, the coastline is more than just a line (D = 1), and yet it is not an area (D = 2). Natural objects rarely conform to idealised 1D, 2D or 3D geometric shapes, and so fractal geometry attempts to 'summarize the messy complexity of shapes we see around us' (Halley et al., 2004, p. 254). The higher the fractal dimension (D), the more complex the object is.

Mandelbrot highlighted that the coastline is self-similar, in that each portion appears to be a reduced-scale image of the whole (just as the braided 'river' in Figure 8.2 appears to be a reduced-scale image of real braided river systems). However, there are two kinds of **self-similarity**. True self-similarity exists when each small portion is entirely geometrically identical to the whole, in all directions. Apart from snowflakes (Gao and Xia, 1996), few natural features are truly self-similar. Self-affinity is more common. This is where a portion of the feature looks like a scaled-down version of the whole, but the scaling is different in different directions (Mandelbrot, 1989). River systems exhibit this **anisotropic** scaling, the effect of gravity making the river scale differently in the downstream and cross-stream directions (Sapozhnikov and Foufoula-Georgiou, 1996).

In focusing on coastlines Mandelbrot's (1967) paper was clearly addressing a geographically oriented topic, but it was not until after the publication of his 1983 book, *The Fractal Geometry of Nature*, that the application of fractals really took off. This is an approach that has been widely used across the natural sciences to study phenomena from galactic structures to DNA sequences (Halley et al., 2004). Within geography, fractal characteristics have been identified in river systems, sediment deposits, soil hydrology, species distributions, plant community mosaics, deforestation patterns and Martian geomorphology, among others (Culver and Fong, 1994; Kent et al., 1997; Rodríguez-Iturbe and Rinaldo, 1997; Baas, 2002; Stepinski et al., 2004; Ni et al., 2011; Sun and Southworth, 2013). As with other aspects of complexity theory, fractal models have been used to understand the natural environment more than the social world, but they are not exclusively the preserve of physical geographers (as we shall see later in the chapter). The identification of fractal patterns, though, is essentially a descriptive step (Turcotte, 2007). In all cases it is important to follow that by considering the implications, and a key question lies in identifying the dynamics that drive the formation of self-similarity in the system being studied.

8.2.6 Implications of complexity

Chaos, path dependence, attractors, self-organization and fractals are, then, inter-related ideas that are all used to understand the dynamics of complex, nonlinear systems. These notions are interpreted and used in different ways by different people, though, both across geography and between disciplines. Harrison et al. (2006) distinguish between 'technical' and 'metaphorical' interpretations. Each of the ideas discussed here has been expressed mathematically, and some researchers work with these mathematical expressions to describe and interrogate the system dynamics that drive complexity. Others use the qualitative conceptual ideas, applying these as metaphors. There may be less distinction between the two than is apparent here (a point we will return to later), but the multitude of interpretations by different researchers raises the very real problem of miscommunication and misunderstanding. Equally, though, some commentators suggest that complexity has the potential to close the gap between human and physical geography, offering a means of understanding integrated natural–social systems in a holistic manner (Thornes, 2009; Grabbatin and Rossi, 2012).

The uptake of complexity theory has been widespread in physical geography and its related disciplines (such as geochemistry, geophysics and ecology) from the mid-1980s onwards. Indeed, a special issue of the journal *Geomorphology* focused on fractals as early as 1992. Complexity theory is inherently spatial (Thrift, 1999), and so perhaps this popularity should be no surprise. Phillips (2003) and Halley et al. (2004) suggest that the ideas introduced in this chapter are compatible with pre-existing ideas in geomorphology and ecology, such as notions of feedback, internal system thresholds and power laws. However, both also offer warnings against uncritical use of ideas such as self-organization and fractals, Phillips (2003) urging geomorphologists to remain focused on problems defined from a geomorphological perspective, rather than a nonlinear systems perspective. Geographical research should remain grounded in the geographies of the world.

Notwithstanding such cautions, complexity theory has had significant impact on the way we think about the natural world. The reductionism inherent in a positivist approach to science is of little use in explaining emergent phenomena, and complexity highlights that the drivers for change are not always external to the system under study. This presents particular problems for **palaeoenvironmental** research, where it has generally been assumed that large differences in sedimentary deposits were indicative of large changes in external factors such as climatic or tectonic conditions (Thornes, 2009; Van de Wiel and Coulthard, 2010). Coupled with the increasing availability of remote sensing technologies and large data sets, the impact of complexity on geomorphology has been particularly pronounced. Murray et al. (2008) described the discipline as having 'turned a corner' from a historic emphasis on qualitative, descriptive models, such that it 'is now accelerating along the leading edge of quantitative science' (p. 497). The extent of this change is also emphasised by Thornes (2009), who argues that complexity science begs an 'overall reconstruction' of both research and teaching in physical geography.

One of the significant challenges raised by complexity is the degree to which we can predict natural systems. Short-term forecasts are possible, but anticipating long-term consequences is much more difficult (Grabbatin and Rossi, 2012). The obvious everyday manifestation of this is weather forecasting, with the UK's Met Office providing detailed forecasts for no more than five days. Murray et al. (2008) identified four 'grand challenges' for Earth surface science, in which issues of prediction are central: they included both identifying the predictability of changes in the Earth surface system, and understanding how the Earth's surface will respond to climate change.

In human geography, Dittmer (2013) describes complexity theory as having been imported from the natural sciences in the 1990s. This depiction leaves geographers open to the charge of **naturalism**, the assumption that ideas from the natural sciences can be applied to social phenomena. However, Urry (2003) argues that this is not a naturalist move. Complexity theory is inherently applicable to all kinds of dynamic systems, regardless of the nature of the system. An emphasis on relationality and emergence is certainly seen as compatible with recent trends in human geography (Curtis and Riva, 2010a; Fløysand and Jakobsen, 2011; Dittmer, 2013), although Curtis and Riva (2010b) note that some ideas can equally be expressed through other theoretical frameworks.

8.3 Researching complexity

The focus of complexity research is on understanding the dynamics that arise within a system through the interactions of its component parts. Bak (1996) describes a three-step approach to such research: firstly, developing a mathematical model to describe a class of phenomenon (such as river networks or sand ripples); secondly, identifying the consequences of the model, either through analytical mathematics or numerical simulation (see Box 8.2); and thirdly, comparing the findings with empirical data from experiments and observations.

BOX 8.2   NUMERICAL AND ANALYTICAL MODELLING

Numerical modelling: In a numerical model, the status of the model is determined in incremental time-steps. The only way we can find out how the modelled system will develop is to run a simulation, re-calculating the state of the model for every time-step. If we want to vary the initial conditions of the model and find out what difference it makes, we have to start from the beginning again and run another simulation. A computer can be programmed to do this, making it much quicker. It is no coincidence that complexity science has developed in tandem with the development of computers.

Analytical modelling: In an analytical model it is possible to solve the equations that describe how the model functions. We can use mathematical techniques such as calculus and trigonometry to work out the solution, which saves having to re-calculate for every time-step. For many complex systems, analytical modelling is just not possible and so numerical modelling has to be used.

This description, though, seems to overlook an essentially preliminary step that can certainly be seen within geographical research – that of gathering empirical data to establish some sense of the phenomenon to be modelled and the kinds of complex dynamics that may be involved. There is little point in mathematical modelling unless we know what we are trying to model. This suggests that the first stage of complexity research should be defined more broadly as one of *describing the phenomenon of interest in terms of complexity*, culminating in the development of a mathematical model. This also better reflects Phillips' (2003) argument that research problems should be defined from the perspective of the discipline and current understanding of the system, rather than led by complexity theory alone. Box 8.3 thus presents an adapted version of Bak's three stages of complexity research.

It is probably unusual to see all three stages fully developed in a single journal article. However, the stages described in Box 8.3 providing a useful framing within which to consider individual studies, not least in terms of helping to consider where they might lead. The following sections provide examples of geographers' research within this framing.

**BOX 8.3   THREE STAGES OF
COMPLEXITY RESEARCH (ADAPTED
FROM BAK, 1996)**

1. Describing the phenomenon of interest in terms of complexity, ultimately through mathematical modelling.

2. Analysing the consequences of the model (through mathematical analysis or numerical simulation).

3. Comparing these consequences with empirical data.

8.3.1 Initial description or identification of complexity

The first question that arises in considering the application of complexity theory is one of defining the phenomena of interest and the model(s) of complexity most likely to be relevant. Research by Tschinkel (2013) on Namibian 'fairy circles' represents a very early stage of such work.

Fairy circles are near-circular barren patches of ground, ranging from 2 to 12 metres in diameter, within a sparse matrix of small grass species. Many of the individual circles have a surrounding 'halo' of taller grasses. Occurring in hundreds of thousands, fairy circles are found in regions of sandy soil with 50–100mm annual rainfall, between southern Angola and northern South Africa. The circles do appear on satellite images (Google Earth coordinates are provided on the companion website). They are not well understood.

Tschinkel (2013) explains that previous researchers have proposed a number of hypotheses for the cause of fairy circles. Some of these, such as soil nutrient or **microbiota** variations, radioactivity, or termite activity, are not supported by the empirical evidence. The most likely hypothesis is one of self-organization of vegetation growth, with positive and negative feedbacks between plants and physical processes operating at different scales. However, given that fairy circles are not well understood, Tschinkel (2013: 1) argues that 'it seems important to know exactly what needs to be explained'. His paper thus presents a descriptive account of fairy circles based on analysis of satellite and aerial photographs, historical records, and field observations and data. He identifies the range of variation in size, density and attributes of the circles, estimating rates of appearance and disappearance, and the lifespan and life stages of individual circles. While Tschinkel's paper does not present or test any specific hypothesis, his work has laid the foundations for that as a next step.

Zhang and Li (2012) provide an example of research that uses a model of complexity to describe a geographic phenomenon. More specifically, they examine the structure of road networks as a fractal structure. Rather than study the geometry (spatial form) of the roads, Zhang and Li are interested in the connectivity exhibited in road networks. They use the box-counting method to calculate the structural fractal dimension.

The box-counting method of obtaining the fractal dimension is simplest to understand in relation to geometric shapes. A grid of squares, each with sides of S length, is laid over the object of interest, and the number of boxes (n) that contain any part of the object is counted. Repeating this process with successively smaller boxes (reducing the value of S) provides a range of paired n and S values, which can be used for calculating the fractal dimension (D).

Zhang and Li (2012) explain how a network's *structure* can be represented diagrammatically, and the box-counting method then applied to establish the fractal dimension of the structure (as opposed to the geometry of the road network). They use this method to analyse the structural fractality of the road networks of the 50 most highly populated counties in the United States. The resulting structural fractal dimensions range from 2.94 to 4.90. (These are higher numbers than we would see if they were examining the geometry of the road network.) Zhang and Li conduct some more detailed analysis to examine particular properties of fractality, which will not be described here. Overall, though, they demonstrate that the irregularity and complexity of a city can be described by measuring the structural fractal dimension. They argue that this supports the idea of cities as complex adaptive and self-organizing systems, an idea which potentially has implications for understanding their development.

The first stage of complexity research, then, is essentially descriptive. Tschinkel (2013) was establishing a descriptive account of the phenomenon of interest (fairy circles) so that the relevance of complexity ideas, and specifically self-organization, can then be explored. Zhang and Li (2012) were applying a particular aspect of complexity theory (fractals) to find out whether it is of value in describing the structure of road networks.

8.3.2 Analysing the consequences of a model

Describing a phenomenon through a mathematical model then allows some assessment of the consequences of that model, which will potentially provide new insights into the phenomenon. Heffernan et al.'s (2013) work on the ridge-slough landscapes of the central Florida Everglades, USA, spans the first two stages of research defined in Box 8.3, developing a model and analysing it.

Ridges and sloughs are features of micro-topography that form a linear pattern in the landscape. The ridge-slough landscape is a **lotic** peatland area, but the ridges and sloughs organise vegetation into distinct assemblages. Elevated ridges and waterlogged slough depressions are described as being 50–150 metres in width, with sloughs being generally continuous and ridges varying in length (such that sloughs connect at either end of the ridges). The overall pattern is elongated in the direction of water flow. (Go to the companion website for Google Earth coordinates.)

Heffernan et al. begin by explaining that self-organised patterning of ecological systems results from the operation of spatially dependent feedbacks occurring over different distances. Patterned landscapes occur most commonly in wetlands and drylands. In such regions the presence or absence of water exerts strong control over vegetation, but vegetation also exerts strong control over water storage and movement, so there is feedback between the two. There is some suggestion that a combination of distal negative feedbacks and strong local positive feedbacks can lead to 'bi-stability', or the existence of two attractors for an ecosystem. This kind of patterned landscape and a homogeneous landscape could exist under the same conditions, each representing a different attractor.

Three hypotheses to account for the formation of ridge-slough patterns are outlined. The 'differential evapotranspiration' hypothesis suggests that different evapotranspiration rates between ridges and sloughs lead to differential phosphorous accumulations and hence to different level of productivity between the two 'patch' types. The 'differential sedimentation' hypothesis is relatively self-explanatory, in that higher rates of sediment deposition will produce ridges. Heffernan et al. point out limitations to both of these hypotheses. They then explain the 'discharge competence' hypothesis, which proposes that peat accretion and hydrology interact in such a manner that the landscape self-organises into a pattern that enables water to drain from the landscape most efficiently. For a finite amount of incoming water, an increased number of sloughs will reduce the water level, so that ridges expand. Ridge expansion, on the other hand, will increase water levels so that sloughs expand. Feedback is thus central to this hypothesis.

Heffernan et al. note that such complex patterned landscapes are often assessed using simulation modelling. This approach enables the spatial patterning to be simulated, but is limited in its capacity to provide insight into the specific feedback mechanisms at work. Mathematical analytical modelling, in contrast, is unable to reproduce the spatial patterns but can allow for more detailed assessment of feedback mechanisms. The researchers thus focus on the latter.

The development of their analytical model occurs in three stages. First they account for the reciprocal interactions between water depth and peat accumulation. They consider the implications of this model, and find that it would not explain the observed behaviours of the ridge-slough landscape. Secondly, the researchers extend their model to incorporate the interactions between microtopography and water flow, comparing two modelled patches of equal size and different soil elevation (a ridge and a slough). Their analysis reveals that the modelled system has two possible forms of equilibrium, indicating that the system has two attractors. Finally, analysing hydrological coupling between ridges and sloughs in a longitudinal direction allows them to assess the degree to which their modelled system is **anisotropic**, and so would produce linear features.

Heffernan et al. then identify that the consequences of their model align with empirical evidence from both ecological and palaeoenvironmental studies of the Everglades. They are quick to point out limitations and simplifications in their analytical model, though, and identify that alignment with empirical evidence does not necessarily allow them to rule out the differential evapotranspiration and differential sedimentation hypotheses. Indeed, it may be that a number of mechanisms are operating simultaneously to produce the patterned landscape. Ultimately, though, their study has established that the hypothesised discharge competence mechanism of self-organization would be capable of generating direction-dependent feedbacks to produce anisotropic patterning.

Modelling brings us back to Harrison et al.'s (2006) suggestion that there is less distinction between 'technical' and 'metaphorical' interpretations of complexity than might at first be obvious. Any model is necessarily a simplification of the system or object of interest. No matter how technical a model seems to be, a researcher constructing a model is really saying, 'I think it works like this.' A researcher using ideas such as chaos or path dependence (for example) metaphorically is also saying, 'I think it works like this.' The difference lies in the level of detail and precision being given, and so is more a difference of degree than of kind. The key test for any model, though, is comparison with empirical evidence.

8.3.3 Testing models against empirical data

On the morning of 22 August 2008, a plume of smoke could be seen rising from the Agios Isidoris area of central Rhodes, Greece (Figure 8.6a). Local residents initially tried to put out the fire, which had been started by accident, themselves, in an attempt to avoid a villager being arrested. By the time it had been extinguished five days later, an area of 13,240 hectares had been burnt (Figure 8.6b). The loss included 1,200 hectares of agricultural land, along with animals, machinery, storage buildings and a house. Suppression of the fire had taken a huge effort, involving 2,430 firefighters, military personnel and volunteers, using 121 vehicles, ten aeroplanes and nine helicopters. The total firefighting cost was in the region of €16 million. Restoration of the forest is expected to take 30–40 years (Theodoridis, 2010).

Research on wildfires (also known as forest fires or bush fires) has revealed that areas prone to fire disturbance experience a large number of low-intensity events, and very few catastrophic events like that described above. The size–frequency distribution generally conforms to a power law, which can be – although is not always – an indicator of self-organised criticality (D'Andrea et al., 2010). The boundaries of wildfires have also been found to be fractal (Adou et al., 2010). A number of wildfire researchers thus use complexity theory in their research, with cellular automata (CA) models quite popular.

CA models are used to simulate the spatial and temporal dynamics of complex, self-organizing systems. The space of interest is divided into a grid of cells (often square or rectangular, but not necessarily so). Each cell is assigned an initial status

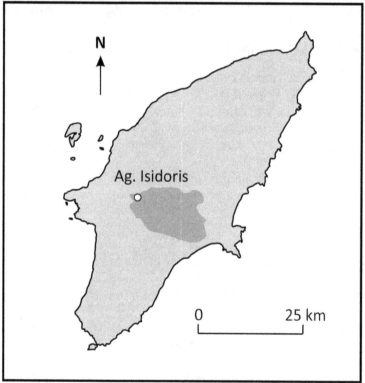

Figure 8.6 The Rhodes wildfire of 2008. a) Signs of a localised fire, shortly after it started (photograph by Kevin Couper). b) Location of its origin at Agios Isidoris, with shaded area indicating the approximate area affected by the fire.

reflecting the variables of interest; for forest fires, this is likely to describe vegetation in some way, indicating the presence or absence of fuel for the fire. Sets of rules and relations between neighbouring cells are then used to redefine the status of every cell in successive time steps. With each time step, the status of a single cell may stay the same or may change, depending on the status of its neighbours (and as determined by the rules and relations between cells). The result is a model that simulates the spatial behaviour of a system over time.

Favis-Mortlock (2004) explains that the relations between cells represent positive and negative feedbacks. Each cell is effectively an 'automaton' whose behaviour is determined by these feedbacks. Interactions are usually defined between adjacent cells, although in some cases the relations may extend to cells beyond those immediately adjacent. The key, though, is that the interactions are all 'local' (among neighbouring cells), yet system-wide responses may result.

Russo et al. (2013) describe the development and testing of a relatively simple CA model designed to simulate the spread of a wildfire. They use a grid of square cells. At any time, each cell will occupy one of four possible states:

1. No forest fuel (for cells containing un-vegetated land and/or sea)

2. Forest fuel that has not ignited

3. Forest fuel that is burning

4. Burnt

Four rules then determine the changes in cell status with each time step. Firstly, a cell with no forest fuel cannot catch fire, so must remain in the same state. Secondly, a cell that was burnt (state 4) in the previous time step remains burnt, as it cannot reignite. Thirdly, a burning cell (state 3) becomes burnt (state 4) in the next step. Fourthly, if a cell is burning, the probability that its neighbouring cells will catch fire (move to state 3) is determined by their vegetation type and density, along with the wind velocity and direction (with wind effects influenced by the ground slope).

Russo et al. (2013) use the Rhodes 2008 wildfire to confront their model. They define the initial conditions of each cell in terms of altitude and vegetation (type and density) using digital geospatial data of Rhodes. The fire is started in the cell representing the location that the actual fire began, and the simulation proceeded from there. The resulting shape and area of burned land at the end of the simulation is then compared with a satellite image of the actual burned area that resulted from the fire. This is a simple, qualitative comparison of the model with empirical data, but Russo et al. conclude that the CA model offers a satisfactory means of predicting wildfire spread. (Note that much more sophisticated, non-CA, models for simulating wildfire spread have been developed by others. Coen and Schroder (2013) provide one such example).

Russo et al. (2013) focused on simulating an individual wildfire, whereas D'Andrea et al. (2010) used another cellular automata model to examine wildfire regime, or the overall timing, frequency and magnitude of wildfire events in a region. They began with a long-established CA model for wildfire, but calibrated it for actual landscapes. This involved populating the CA model cells with observed vegetation types, and calculating probability values for the likelihood of fire spread and vegetation recovery for those specific vegetation types. The probability values were then used in the rules and relations determining cell status. The model simulated the occurrence of wildfires over a period of time, enabling the researchers to calculate the power law (magnitude–frequency) distribution as an indicator of wildfire regime.

D'Andrea et al. (2010) tested their calibrated model using empirical data from two regions. For the Mediterranean ecosystem of Liguria, Italy, the researchers used data for a 20-year period, constituting around 8,000 fires. For the subtropical environment of Alachua County, Florida, US, a period of 25 years gave them a record of around 1,400 fires. The power law distribution for a region was calculated from a random selection of 500 fires from the data set. D'Andrea et al. repeated that process 1,000 times for each region, giving them a range of power law distributions (and thus some indication of reliability).

The CA model was then used to run 1,000 simulations for each region, each simulation corresponding to the length of time for which data were available for that region. The researchers thus calculated 1,000 simulation power-law distributions for each region, enabling them to compare the resulting range with those from the empirical data. The outcome is a close correspondence between the two. D'Andrea et al. (2010) thus conclude that their CA model holds promise for simulating the effects of land use change (and hence land use policy) on wildfire regime for a region.

Through the framing of these three stages of work, then, we can see the procedures of research using complexity theory (at least in its 'technical' manifestation), and consider where such research might lead. Work through exercise 8.3 to have a go at this for yourself.

Philosophically, such research is **realist** in that it rests on the assumption that a real world exists, independently of us and our knowing of it (see Chapter 1 for further explanation). Epistemologically, the assumption that we can know the world through our senses (and with scientific instruments extending our senses) remains intact. On these points, then, complexity bears similarity with **positivism** (Chapter 2) and **critical rationalism** (Chapter 3). The significant difference from positivism is that complexity theory is anti-reductionist.

We have seen that the key test of models of complexity lies in comparison with empirical evidence. Sometimes this is more overtly presented as the development and testing of hypotheses. Indeed, Phillips (1999, 2003) and Kovalenko et al. (2012) consider this to be an essential component of complexity research in geomorphology and habitat research. This kind of technical complexity research is thus aligned with a critical rationalist philosophy of science (see Chapter 3).

EXERCISE 8.3

Characterising the rate of deforestation

Sun and Southworth (2013) present a fractal analysis of deforestation in the Amazon. Read their paper and try to answer the questions below. (The paper is freely accessible online, and there is a link to it on the companion website.)

NOTE: As with many journal articles, this one includes some quite technical details that can make for difficult reading. The questions below focus on the broad approach taken to the research, so try to get the gist of what was done even if you cannot follow all the details.

i) The research focuses on the 'MAP region'. What is this?

ii) What data were used as the basis of the research?

iii) Focusing on the calculation of fractal dimension:

  a. Which method did the authors use to determine the fractal dimension?

  b. What was the object for which they were calculating the fractal dimension?

iv) Their analysis did not cover the whole of the MAP area. How did they sample from within this? (Noting that the authors do not directly refer to sampling.)

v) According to the results of their analysis, how does the fractal dimension of non-forested land change as development increases?

vi) The main analysis focused on Areas Of Interest (AOIs), but the authors also undertook an analysis within a single AOI, dividing it into quarters. What was this for, and what did it reveal?

vii) Box 8.3 in this chapter identified three stages of complexity research. Which stage(s) is Sun and Southworth's research characteristic of? Try to explain your answer.

A link to Sun and Southworth's paper is on the companion website, along with answers to the questions. The full reference for the paper is:

Sun, J. and Southworth, J. (2013) 'Remote sensing-based fractal analysis and scale dependence associated with forest fragmentation in an Amazon tri-national frontier', *Remote Sensing* 5: 454–72. doi: 10.3390/rs5020454.

8.4 Complexity at the beach

The beginning of this chapter identified emergence and interdependence as two central features of self-organised systems. One starting point for research at the beach, then, might be to identify emergent forms and patterns, and/or the kinds of interconnections (relations) that give rise to interdependence. Such forms would clearly include sand ripples, dunes and beach cusps (all of which have featured earlier in the chapter), with interactions between their morphology and wave energy via sediment movement. Beach habitats may also provide a focus for study; Katrak et al. (2008) studied the fractal characteristics of crab burrows, for example. Looking beyond the immediate confines of the beach to consider the broader coastal environment, shore platforms and the fractal properties of the coastline itself have also made appearances in this chapter.

Our attention need not be restricted to physical geography either. Lazarus et al. (2011) provide an example of complexity research focusing on a 'coupled human-landscape system' (p. 990) in their work on **beach nourishment**. Local beach nourishment can be economically beneficial, both in affording protection to sea-front properties and as a tourist attraction generating income, but it is a direct intervention in the beach sediment system. Economic processes of coastal development and physical processes of shoreline change are thus inter-related.

In all of the examples described, the focus is on empirically observable phenomena. Once such a focus for research has been defined, it would be a matter of deciding which stage of research (as defined in Box 8.3) is most appropriate. Empirical data collection and modelling to describe the complex nature of the phenomenon of interest would be relevant if few prior studies have been undertaken. For features such as beach cusps, earlier research by others may generate hypotheses for testing. Finally, of course, all of this would require a clear notion of the complex dynamics at work; in other words, whether the focus is on chaotic behaviour, path dependence, identifying system attractors, self-organization or self-organised criticality, or fractal characteristics.

8.5 Complexity theory in summary

Complexity theory offers an approach to research that focuses on 'whole-system' dynamics, examing the ways in which the component parts of a system interact to generate collective behaviours. Developed from the 1960s onwards, 'complexity science' has rapidly grown into a multi-disciplinary field of research spanning the natural and social sciences, from physics to organisational management. Some of this research uses technical understandings of complexity, involving the use of mathematical models and quantitative data, while some uses the ideas of complexity as metaphors, in more loosely defined qualitative terms.

Within geography, complexity theory has had significant impact on physical geography, with some (such as Thornes, 2009) suggesting that an entire reorientation of teaching and research is necessary. Others are more cautious, pointing out that the ideas of complexity theory are often not so different from pre-existing concepts within the discipline, or can be expressed equally well through other theories. Within human geography, complexity theory has been directly used in economic geography and studies of urban development, in particular. Again, though, the general insights are considered to share some commonalities with **poststructuralist** and post-**phenomenological** relational geographies.

A number of basic ideas that fall under the umbrella of complexity have been introduced, including chaos, self-organization and fractals. The value of these, defined in strict terms, has been questioned. Frigg (2003) argues that self-organised criticality is not really a theory at all, as it is not 'about' anything in particular. Instead it offers a set of models. The same could be argued about all aspects of complexity theory. In similar vein, Halley et al. (2004) suggest that no natural phenomena conform to the ideal fractal, yet fractal analysis offers a useful tool for developing new insights. Complexity theory, then, could perhaps be seen as a group of tools that enable us to interrogate the nonlinear dynamics of a multitude of complex systems.

In focusing on whole-system dynamics, complexity research directly contrasts with the reductionist approach characteristic of positivism (Chapter 2). Adapting Bak's (1996) suggestion, complexity research can be characterised in three stages, involving: i) description of the phenomenon of interest in terms of complexity; ii) interrogating the implications of this; iii) testing these ideas against empirical evidence. This means that, in more formal terms, hypothesis-testing is a central facet of such research, although not all individual studies may reach that stage. In terms of philosophy, then, complexity research (using the 'technical' interpretations of complexity) aligns predominantly with the critical rationalist philosophy of science.

FURTHER READING

For further explanations

Bar-Yam, Y. (2011) *About Complex Systems*. Cambridge, MA: New England Complex Systems Institute. Online at http://www.necsi.edu/guide/.

Coco, G. and Murray, A.B. (2007) 'Patterns in the sand: from forcing templates to self-organization', *Geomorphology* 91 (3–4): 271–90.

Coulthard, T.J., Hicks, D.M. and Van de Wiel, M.J. (2007) 'Cellular modelling of river catchments and reaches: advantages, limitations and prospects', *Geomorphology* 90: 192–207.

Favis-Mortlock, D. and de Boer, D. (2003) 'Simple at heart? Landscape as a self-organizing complex system', in S. Trudgill and A. Roy (eds), *Contemporary Meanings in Physical Geography: From What to Why?* London: Arnold. pp. 127–72.

Grabbatin, B. and Rossi, J. (2012) 'Political ecology: nonequilibrium science and nature-society research', *Geography Compass* 6 (5): 275–89.

Halley, J.M., Hartley, S., Kallimanis, A.S., Kunin, W.E., Lennon, J.J. and Sgardelis, S.P. (2004) 'Uses and abuses of fractal methodology in ecology', *Ecology Letters* 7: 254–71.

Kovalenko, K.E., Sidinei, M.T. and Warfe, D.M. (2012) 'Habitat complexity: approaches and future directions', *Hydrobiologia* 685: 1–17.

Millington, J.D.A., Perry, G.L.W. and Malamud, B.D. (2006) 'Models, data and mechanisms: quantifying wildfire regimes', in C. Cello and B.D. Malamud (eds), *Fractal Analysis for Natural Hazards*. London: Geological Society Special Publications 261: 155–67.

Murray, A.B., Lazarus, E., Ashton, A., Baas, A., Coco, G., Coulthard, T., Fonstad, M., Haff, P., McNamara, D., Paola, C., Pelletier, J. and Reinhardt, L. (2009) 'Geomorphology, complexity, and the emerging science of the Earth's surface', *Geomorphology* 103: 496–505.

Phillips, J.D. (2011) 'Emergence and pseudo-equilibrium in geomorphology', *Geomorphology* 132: 319–26.

Stewart, I. (2010) 'The nature of fractal geometry', in N. Lesmoir-Gordon (ed.), *The Colours of Infinity: the Beauty and Power of Fractals*. London: Springer-Verlag. pp. 2–23.

Thornes, J.B. (2009) 'Time: change and stability in environmental systems', in N. Clifford, S. Holloway, S.P. Rice and G. Valentine (eds), *Key Concepts in Geography*. 2nd edition. London: Sage. pp. 119–39.

Turcotte, D.L. (1997) *Fractals in Geology and Geophysics*. 2nd edition. Cambridge: Cambridge University Press.

Wainwright, J. and Mulligan, M. (eds) (2013) *Environmental Modelling: Finding Simplicity in Complexity*. 2nd edition. Chichester: Wiley.

Progress in Human Geography and *Progress in Physical Geography* resources (available on the companion website)

Bekker, M.F. (2008) 'Linear forest patterns in subalpine environments', *Progress in Physical Geography* 32 (6): 635–53. doi: 10.1177/0309133308101384.

Curtis, S. and Riva, M. (2010a) 'Health geographies I: complexity theory and human health', *Progress in Human Geography* 34 (2): 215–23. doi: 10.1177/0309132509336026.

Curtis, S. and Riva, M. (2010b) 'Health geographies II: complexity and health care systems and policy', *Progress in Human Geography* 34 (4): 513–20. doi: 10.1177/0309132509336029.

Dittmer, J. (2013) 'Geopolitical assemblages and complexity', *Progress in Human Geography* doi: 10.1177/0309132513501405.

Gao, J. and Xia, Z.-G. (1996) 'Fractals in physical geography', *Progress in Physical Geography* 20 (2): 178–91.

Lau, S.S.S. and Lane, S.N. (2001) 'Continuity and change in environmental systems: the case of shallow lake ecosystems', *Progress in Physical Geography* 25 (2): 178–202. doi: 10.1177/030913330102500202.

Phillips, J.D. (1995) 'Self-organization and landscape evolution', *Progress in Physical Geography* 19 (3): 309–21. doi: 10.1177/030913339501900301.

Phillips, J.D. (2003) 'Sources of nonlinearity and complexity in geomorphic systems', *Progress in Physical Geography* 27 (1): 1–23. doi: 10.1191/0309133303pp340ra.

Phillips, J.D. (2009) 'Changes, perturbations, and responses in geomorphic systems', *Progress in Physical Geography* 33 (1): 17–30. doi: 10.1177/0309133309103889.

Examples

Heffernan, J.B., Watts, D.L. and Cohen, M.J. (2013) 'Discharge competence and pattern formation in peatlands: a meta-ecosystem model of the Everglades ridge-slough landscape', *PLoS ONE* 8 (5): e64174. doi: 10.1371/journal.pone.0064174.

Laub, B.G., Baker, D.W., Bledsow, B.P. and Palmer, M.A. (2012) 'Range of variability of channel complexity in urban, restored and forested reference streams', *Freshwater Biology* 57: 1076–95.

Murray, A.B., Coco, G. and Goldstein, E.B. (2014) 'Cause and effect in geomorphic systems: complex systems perspectives', *Geomorphology* doi: 10.1016/j.geomorph.2014.03.001.

Ni, H., Zheng, W., Liu, X. and Gao, Y. (2011) 'Fractal-statistical analysis of grain-size distributions of debris-flow deposits and its geological implications', *Landslides* 8: 253–9.

Nygaard, C. and Meen, G. (2013) 'The distribution of London residential property prices and the role of spatial lock-in', *Urban Studies* 50 (12): 2535–52.

Schwimmer, R.A. (2008) 'A temporal geometric analysis of eroding marsh shorelines: can fractal dimensions be related to process?', *Journal of Coastal Research* 24 (1): 152–8.

Verleysdonk, S., Krautblatter, M. and Dikau, R. (2011) 'Sensitivity and path dependence of mountain permafrost systems', *Geografiska Annaler: Series A, Physical Geography* 93 (2): 113–35.

9

Moral Philosophy and Ethics: Right and Wrong in Geography

9.1 Introduction: Understanding ethics

Picture yourself in the following scenario. It is your friend's birthday (girlfriend, boy-friend, housemate – whoever you like). Neither of you can afford to go out, but you would like to mark the occasion in some way. On your way home you call into a shop to buy a bottle of wine and some Pringles, your friend's favourite. It comes to £6.80. You hand over a £10 note, but you are given change for £20. Do you say anything, or do you keep the money? What *should* you do? The question is one of ethics. While this scenario is a simple one, an important point to take from it is that we all make ethical decisions every day, in all of our encounters with each other. We decide how to act with each other, guided by a sense of what is right and wrong, good and bad.

It is worth pausing here to note some terminology. In this chapter you will find reference to both 'ethics' and 'morals'. The two words have different roots: 'ethics' originates in the Greek *ethikos*, which is variously translated as ethos or character, or sometimes custom or usage (as in the customary way to behave in society). 'Morals' comes from the latin *moralis*, concerned with which actions are right or wrong. In practice the two are often used interchangeably (Vardy and Grosch, 1999). Within the context of geographical research, you are likely to come across reference to 'moral geographies' and 'research ethics'. I use that terminology here, but underlying both are questions of what is right and wrong, and how we should behave.

This chapter addresses two broad arenas of debate relating to geography and ethics (or morals): morality and the substantive content of geography – i.e. the things geographers focus on in their research; and ethics and the practices of geographical research. This should not be taken to imply that the two do not overlap. They do, in many different and complex ways, but it is convenient to draw boundaries (however fuzzy) somewhere. Before going any further, though, it is useful to understand something more of ethics.

So did you keep the money? Assuming you did, was that a good act or a bad act? Philosophers have established different approaches to deciding what is right or wrong. We shall consider four here, beginning with the three major **secular** ethical theories, and adding a feminist ethics of care.

9.1.1 Aristotle's virtue ethics

The Greek philosopher Aristotle (384–322 BCE) was born over 2,000 years ago, and remains one of the intellectual giants of philosophy. Aristotle's writings on ethics focused on human flourishing, on what constitutes the 'good' life, and on how to achieve such a life. Central to his ideas are the virtues: qualities of character (such as patience, courage and friendliness) and faculties of mind (such as knowledge, judgement and deliberation) that we all have potential to develop. Such virtues are understood to be intermediate positions between two extremes, one an excess and one a deficiency. Virtues thus lie at the mid-point between vices. An example would be the virtue of courage: a lack of courage is cowardice (vice), which renders people incapable of acting or making a decision, while too much courage can result in recklessness (vice), and taking unnecessary risks. Between those two extremes is the courageous person, who experiences fear proportional to the circumstances and is able to judge which dangers are worth facing and which are not, and act accordingly.

A virtuous person is one who has developed such virtues, along with the 'practical wisdom' that enables them to judge any situation and do the right thing. Such a person lives the good life. To judge whether an act is right or wrong, then, a virtue ethics approach would ask: what would a virtuous person do? The emphasis of virtue ethics is on the kind of person we ought to (strive to) be.

EXERCISE 9.1a

What would a virtuous person do?

Referring back to the scenario outlined at the start of the chapter, in which you were given extra change in the shop, try to decide what a virtuous person would do in such circumstances. What is the most relevant virtue here?
Look at the companion website for a response to this.

9.1.2 Kant's deontological ethics

Immanuel Kant (1724–1804) is generally considered to be the central figure of modern philosophy (that is, philosophy since the seventeenth century). His writings on morality represent only one strand of his work. In essence, Kant's view was that the social world is governed by moral laws in the same way that the natural world is governed by natural laws. He sought to identify these moral laws, the fundamental principles which form the basis for our moral choices. 'Deontological' stems from the Greek words *deon*, meaning duty, and *logos*, meaning science or 'study of'. Deontological ethics takes the position that we have a duty to behave according to moral laws or fundamental principles.

Vardy and Grosch (1999) explain that Kant distinguished between two kinds of imperative for action. 'Hypothetical imperatives' are those that lead us to act in a particular way to achieve a desired outcome. In simple terms, they are 'based on an "if"' (Vardy and Grosch, 1999, p. 56). If you want to increase your fitness, exercise more. If you want to achieve good grades, study hard. We can reject the imperative if we are prepared to reject the 'if', or the ends that the actions will lead us to. 'Categorical imperatives', in contrast, are ends in themselves. They would be followed by any rational person, because we have a duty to follow them. If you were to ask, 'Why should I do my duty?', the only possible response is 'Because it is your duty'. There is no other answer. Moral laws are categorical because they should be followed out of duty, and not as a means to particular ends.

Kant's deontological ethics thus emphasises the categorical imperative, for which he provided a number of formulations. We can summarise it in simple terms as:

- Always act in the way that you would want others to act in the same situation. In other words, act in such a way that the general principle guiding your action could be a law that held for everyone.

- Never use other people as a means to your own ends; all human beings should be respected 'as ends in themselves'.

If everyone acts in this way, the principles by which everyone acts will coincide, with any disagreements resolvable by rational arguments.

Deontological ethics, then, emphasises the reasons (motivations) for acting in a particular way. A good act is one undertaken because it is rationally judged to be the right way to act, based on a sense of duty. The outcomes of the act are irrelevant here, not least because there may be many external, unforeseen influences that impact on the outcome. Significantly, a deontological approach considers all (human) individuals to be worthy of equal moral consideration.

EXERCISE 9.1b

What are the motivations?

Return to the scenario at the start of the chapter, where you were given too much change in the shop. How should you act, according to deontological ethics? What are the right motivations here?

 Look at the companion website for a response.

9.1.3 Bentham's utilitarian ethics

Utilitarian ethics is primarily associated with Jeremy Bentham (1748–1832) and John Stuart Mill (1806–1873). Bentham was particularly interested in politics and the improvement of social conditions, and this influence can be seen in his utilitarian ethics. In Bentham's view, all humans are governed by two impulses: the maximisation of pleasure, and the minimisation of pain. A good act is therefore one which results in the greatest pleasure for the greatest number of people, and the least pain for the least number. This leads a utilitarian approach to focus on consequences. In effect this is a cost/benefit analysis, where both costs and benefits could take a variety of forms (such as physical, emotional, psychological or economic). It is worth noting that the emphasis on the greatest good for the greatest number means that minority interests are over-ruled by the interests of the majority.

EXERCISE 9.1c

What are the consequences?

Return again to the scenario at the beginning of the chapter, in which you were given extra change in the shop. According to utilitarian ethics, would keeping the money be judged as a good or bad act?

 Look at the companion website for a response, and a bit more on utilitarian ethics.

9.1.4 Feminist ethics of care

Feminist thinkers have criticised traditional approaches to ethics for (among other things) being highly gendered. The moral theories described above tend to prioritise traits that are culturally associated with masculinity: traits like rationality, objectivity, reason and intellect. Traits commonly associated with femininity, such as inter-dependence, community, sharing, trust and emotion are neglected. Similarly, these theories favour rules, impartiality and universality over relationships, partiality and particularity (Tong and Williams, 2011). In contrast, care ethics considers human relationships of care to be fundamental to moral considerations. Indeed, caring is part of what it is to be human. Care ethics is therefore universal (applying to every-one), but also particular, in that it foregrounds the specific circumstances in which care is needed and given. Good caring involves (Campbell, 2010):

1.   Attentiveness, recognising a need for care;

2.   Responsibility, taking responsibility to meet that need;

3.   Competence, in giving care, and;

4.   Responsiveness, in responding to care received from others.

Care ethics places emphasis on action or practice, rather than rules or principles. Such actions or practices are always context-specific. Some authors consider care ethics to be a particular form of virtue ethics, with care as the central virtue (Sander-Staudt, 2011). Campbell (2010) notes that the emphasis on practice, and associated lack of guiding principles, has led to some ambiguity over what care ethics really means.

EXERCISE 9.1d

What would a caring person do?

For the final time, think again about the scenario at the beginning of the chapter, in which you were given too much change in the shop. Try to work out what response a care ethics approach would lead you to make.
    Look at the notes on the companion website for a response.

The four approaches to ethics described here are all **normative** ethical theories. They set out to define how people should act – to establish norms for action. The scenario we have used to think through what each of these might mean in practice is relatively simple, directly involving only two people (you and the shop worker). Ethical consid-erations can be much more complex when the focus is on society more broadly.
    To take an example, in October 2013 the Policy Exchange, a right-wing think tank that seeks to promote new policy ideas in the UK, released a report examining pay conditions in the private and public sectors (Oakley, 2013). This report provides evidence that, in the less affluent areas of South West and North East England, people working in the public sector (such as in health or education) are paid more than those working in the private sector. In contrast, in London and the South East,

public sector workers are paid less than people in the private sector. The paper argues that this is because salaries in the public sector are established nationally, so do not reflect local labour markets, and that such national pay deals should be abolished. If we accept the evidence presented regarding pay differentials as reliable, what is a good act (or policy) in this situation?

On the one hand, national pay deals ensure that doctors, nurses and teachers are paid the same for the job they do, wherever in the country they do it. It could be argued that if this were not the case, no (or very few) qualified doctors, nurses or teachers would want to take jobs in the least affluent areas where they would receive the lowest salary. This could result in regional disparities in access to high-quality healthcare and education. Is that ethically good? On the other hand, it might be argued that the taxes paid by people working in the more affluent areas are subsidising education and healthcare provision in the less affluent regions. Is that ethically good? Working out what is morally right in such complex situations is much more difficult, and it is these kinds of situations that are often of interest to geographers.

9.2 Ethics and geography

Most of this book deals with **epistemology**, or theories of knowledge. Epistemology is concerned with describing how the world is. This chapter is concerned with ethics, or theories of morality. Ethics is concerned with establishing how people ought to act. The relation between the two is an issue of longstanding debate in philosophy, known as the 'is/ought' controversy (Vardy and Grosch, 1999).

Some philosophers argue that there is no logical step from 'is' to 'ought'. To adapt an example from Vardy and Grosch (1999):

- *'Is' statement*: 60 per cent of UK wildlife species (for which data are available) have declined in population during the last fifty years (State of Nature, 2013).
- *'Ought' statement*: that being the case, we ought to address the problem and prevent further decline.

There is a leap between these two statements. Knowledge that many of our wildlife species are in decline does not, in itself, tell us whether we should do anything about it. That is not to deny that it may be preferable, or even sensible, to increase our conservation efforts, but the second statement is not a logical consequence of the first statement. There is a clear division between 'is' (description) and 'ought' (prescription).

Other philosophers contend that a logical move from 'is' to 'ought' is possible in some circumstances, and that epistemology and ethics are connected. For example:

- *'Is' statement*: she is a conservationist.
- *'Ought' statement*: then she ought to do what conservationists do.

This is/ought controversy may seem like a rather abstract problem, but the two different responses to it are indicative of rather different geographies.

At various times in the discipline's history, geography's practitioners have styled geography as 'science'. This has often been for political reasons; seeking to secure a place in universities in the mid- to late-nineteenth century (Livingstone, 1992), to retain such a place in the mid-twentieth century (Holdt-Jensen, 2009), or more recently in efforts to secure greater funding (Royal Geographical Society, 2010). The 'scientific' forms of geography such as those that rose to prominence from the 1950s (underpinned by **positivist**, **critical rationalist** or, later, **critical realist** epistemologies) focus on describing the way the world is.

This emphasis on description was challenged in the 1970s with the emergence of radical geography, often associated with the use of Marxist theory (see Chapter 4). Harvey (1973) specifically argued that the fact/value (is/ought) distinction was problematic. Radical social geographers sought to both describe *and* challenge the inequalities of the world, addressing issues of social justice, political and economic domination, social deprivation, and various forms of discrimination (Smith, 2000). Geography became an explicitly political and ethical project.

David Smith (2000) explains that this concern with values continued through the development of **humanistic geography** in the 1970s and 1980s, with Yi-Fu Tuan (1986, 1989, 1993) particularly paying attention to moral issues. The early 1990s brought the advent of the 'cultural turn' and the influence of **postmodern, poststructuralist** and **feminist** thought (see Chapters 6 and 7), and human geographers were increasingly engaging with issues of morality. Geographers developed interest in issues of identity, representation and power, social justice, environmental justice and environmental ethics. David Smith particularly advocated a more concerted engagement with moral philosophy (Smith 1997, 1999, 2000, 2001, 2007). Creswell (1996) demonstrated that 'place' itself has normative dimensions. Our understandings of places involve normative conceptions of acceptable or deviant behaviour, and the inclusion or exclusion of social groups, in those places. In the twenty-first century, then, much human geography is directly concerned with social and cultural issues of moral significance.

In the case of participatory and activist geographies, this is accompanied by an explicit intention to make a difference, as the title of Castree et al.'s (2010) edited collection emphasises: *The Point is to Change It: Geographies of Hope and Survival in an Age of Crisis*. However, a number of commentators (Blomley, 2007; Olson and Sayer, 2009) suggest that, in the main, human geographers have focused too much on criticising the status quo without adequately developing a normative conception of human flourishing or 'good' to work towards. This may reflect the influence of poststructuralist theories in human geography (Popke, 2003). Poststructuralism is anti-foundationalist and anti-universalist, arguing that meaning is determined by language, convention and positionality, rather than having 'solid' foundations. This leads to an emphasis on difference and cultural relativity, challenging the possibility of establishing universal grounds for ethics.

So far we have considered only human geography, but it would be erroneous to think that ethical concerns did not also extend to physical geography. The science of physical geography places emphasis on understanding what 'is', but physical geographers have long been involved in applied work. Managing our interactions with the environment necessitates a move from 'is' to 'ought'. From conservation (Spellerberg and Sawyer, 1999; Ladle and Whittaker, 2011) to river management (Thorne et al., 1997; Maddock et al., 2013), landslide hazard management (Glade et al., 2006) or the mitigation of desertification (Imeson, 2011), for example, physical geography knowledge is used to shape decisions about our interaction with the environment. Regardless of whether such decisions are made from a conscious ethical position or not, they reflect values and (normative) ideas about how we ought to act. It is probably fair to say that few geographers working in these areas have directly engaged with moral philosophy, although there are some notable exceptions. Martin Haigh (2002), recounting some of his work in land reclamation, argued that geographers have a duty to 'be useful' and engage constructively with the world. Keith Richards (2003) explored the possibility of asserting ethical grounds for integrating human and physical geography. Both these authors drew on environmental ethics, which seeks to extend our moral concern to non-humans.

Geographers, then, have increasingly engaged with moral theory since the 1970s. The discussion above hints at two key issues among these deliberations. The first is a tension between universality and particularity, and how to reconcile the normative urge of moral theories with a concern for difference. The second, which is not unrelated to the first, is a question of how far (spatially and conceptually) our moral concerns should extend: in other words, which 'others' are we to be morally concerned with? These will be considered in turn.

9.2.1 Universality versus particularity: Normativity versus difference

Spatial difference is central to geography. Universal phenomena (such as the drainage basin hydrological cycle, or the production of food) appear different in different places and at different times. The scientific impulse, though, is to seek generalisable (universal) knowledge. A tension between universality and particularity has therefore long been of concern to geographers of all kinds. Ethical theories such as those described in the first part of this chapter are normative and universal, prescribing how all humans, everywhere, ought to behave. As Smith (2000) explains, the tension between universality and particularity leaves us with a problem of relativism. He identifies three types of relativism that are of concern:

- Relativism revealed in descriptive ethics. Descriptive ethics simply describes how people behave with regard to moral issues, and the values inherent in such behaviour. Relativism here tells us that beliefs about what is wrong or right, bad or good, differ between individuals, societies and cultures.

- Relativism in normative ethics. Normative ethics forms the focus of this chapter, prescribing what is good/bad, right/wrong. Relativism in normative ethics thus argues that what is actually right or wrong differs between individuals, societies and cultures. In other words, what people believe to be right or wrong *is* right or wrong, in their context.

- Relativism in meta-ethics. Meta-ethics refers to the forms of argument that people use to determine what is good or bad. Relativism here argues that there is no universal means of distinguishing right from wrong.

Geographers and anthropologists have provided plenty of empirical evidence that what people believe to be right or wrong differs. Indeed, we see this in the media frequently enough: recent examples in the UK have included debates around the Islamic practices of veil-wearing, arranged marriages and sharia law, or arguments for and against the legalisation of euthanasia for those who are terminally ill (a practice that is already legal in some countries). Relativism in normative ethics is rather more contentious. As Smith points out, to argue that all moral codes are worthy of equal respect, we would need to include those that legitimise torture and human sacrifice. Arguing that such moral codes are wrong, though, raises a meta-ethical question: on what basis, what (or whose) authority, do we judge some moral codes as inferior to others? Whose moral philosophy should be imposed on whom? The postmodern and poststructuralist resistance to 'grand narratives' conflicts with any attempt to impose a (single) normative theory of how society should function. On the other hand, geographers would be unable to argue for justice, or against oppression, if we take the view that what is 'good' is entirely culturally defined (Blomley, 2007).

Popke (2003) sees potential for a way out of this conundrum. Since the Enlightenment, most ethical thinking has been focused on 'the Cartesian subject'; humans as independent, autonomous individuals. Within this conception, our identity is dependent on our distinction from 'others', a distinction that involves drawing social and spatial boundaries. Poststructuralism acts to decentre this subject, emphasising the relational nature of identity; our identity is shaped in relation to those around us, and this holds potential for a more relational ethics. Popke makes reference to Doel's (1999) poststructuralist understanding of place as process, always in-the-making, rather than fixed and static. The implication is that this offers scope for attention to practical reason.

Following this through, a number of geographers have begun to emphasise a situational ethics of care or feminist ethics of care (Blomley, 2003; Smith, 2009; Lawson, 2009; Carmalt, 2011). Similarly, from the perspective of **non-representational theory** (Chapter 5) Nigel Thrift (2008) calls for an ethic that is open to the potential of every situation, oriented towards hope for the future. In effect, such ideas are offering a 'minimal' universalism, specifying only care for others as a universal norm. This is an ethics based more on an orientation towards particular ways of being, rather than prescribed rules for action. The implementation of such an ethics, its implications for practice, will always be dependent upon context. As we noted earlier in the chapter, there is some alignment with virtue ethics here (Barnett, 2010).

9.2.2 How far should our moral concerns extend?

If modern conceptions of identity have been based on distinguishing ourselves from others, effectively drawing boundaries, Popke (2003) highlights that much modern ethical thought has centred around a concern for the 'distant others' located beyond the boundaries. Geographers have particularly questioned our tendency to privilege local over distant strangers. It is not difficult to find public examples of this tendency. In the UK news media, reports of accidents or natural hazard events overseas usually highlight any Britons affected, as though they are somehow more important than non-British people. Smith (2000) provides a very readable discussion of the question of distant others. The account here draws heavily on his work, although necessarily without the nuances of his more extended consideration.

Smith notes a general degree of regret at the apparent loss of communities, and loss of the concern for those in proximity to us that is conventionally associated with communities. He points out that urbanisation has been accompanied by a diminution of place-based communities, as adults develop communities of choice based on similar interests or activities, rather than communities based on residence. The key question is how we might extend the care for those in our own communities to others.

Whilst geographers are increasingly seeing potential in an ethics of care, there is a danger that such an approach could become exclusionary. It could offer a defence for prioritising caring for our immediate others (friends, family, social group, nation). After all, those in close proximity to us – our family and friends – are those most affected by (or vulnerable to) what we do. Geographers are well attuned to the changing spatial organisation of human activities associated with globalisation; extended economic and political networks that mean we increasingly impact on distant others. This potentially affords grounds for extending the realm of our care to these others, although an obvious problem is that, when we buy our chocolate bars or cheap clothes, the distant others affected are often unknown or invisible to us (see Box 9.1). Traditional approaches to ethics appear to avoid this problem, emphasising sameness through the principle of universalisability. Deontological ethics, for example, accords the same moral worth to all humans, and this universalisability means that we should not discriminate against someone just because they are far away. The influence of postmodernism has been to diminish universal arguments, emphasising difference and particularity. It seems, then, that some middle ground is needed, some combination of the ethics of care with notions of universal justice. One option is to consider the ethics of care as a 'first-order' ethics associated with everyday life, and an ethics based on justice as a 'second-order' ethics operating at the level of society (Barry, 1995).

BOX 9.1   FOLLOW THE THINGS

'**Socks** *(made in Bulgaria, worn in the UK):* student David Roberts has never taken time to think about what his socks did for him, and what others had to do to get them onto his feet. What he finds is that he's treading in political economic geographies that he's been reading about in class and following in the news. He is not walking alone.' (www.followthething.com).

Having found out more about where his socks came from David (Roberts, 2006) wrote: 'Putting my foot into the oh-so-fluffy, comforting sock, it seems I'm helping to perpetuate the Arab–Israeli conflict, to disrupt the lives of hundreds of fellow Brits, and to contribute to the lives of thousands in Bulgaria. Who lives, dies, profits or suffers, depends, in a small part, on me. My socks have spoken, and what they have said matters. Oppression doesn't sit well with me. And what I do with my money. I can change what socks I buy. I must change. Sacrificing quality for ethics is a small price to pay. I may be just one person, but what I do makes a difference. To a lot of people. In a lot of different places.'

Ian Cook et al.'s 'follow the things' geographies are a means of uncovering the complex material relations between peoples, markets and things that are usually hidden in our everyday consumer lives. Taking a single commodity, multi-site ethnographic and/or online research provides insight into the multitude of people and relations that bring that commodity to our shopping bags. The Follow the Things website (www.followthethings.com) offers insights into a range of con-sumer products, from socks and t-shirts to foods, medicines and even money, that have been followed by students, journalists and filmmakers. References to some examples of Ian's work can be found in Further Reading at the end of the chapter.

Roberts, D. (2006) Socks. followthethings.com (www.followthethings.com/socks.shtml [accessed 28/10/13]).

If sameness and difference is an issue in determining how people (ought to) treat each other, it becomes more so when we turn our attention to the environment. The field of environmental ethics developed as a sub-discipline of philosophy from the 1970s, emerging more or less simultaneously in Australia, Norway and the United States. Its focal concern is to establish how we ought to behave in relation to the non-human world.

The issue at stake in the discussion above is the equivalence of moral worth among humans. Universal ethical theories assume that all individual humans have independent moral status – that is, they are deserving of our moral concern in themselves. We do not extend such moral concern to everything (see Box 9.2). A key concern in environmental ethics, then, is to determine *what*, rather than *who*, should be considered to have independent moral status.

BOX 9.2   INDEPENDENT MORAL STATUS

Your housemate has a library book that is due back today, but has fallen ill and so is unable to return it. You promise to return the book for them, as you need to go to the library anyway. Having made such a promise, you have a moral obligation to return the book. This obligation is to your friend, it is not an obligation to the book. The moral obligation that is associated with the book is entirely dependent upon its (and your) relation to your friend. The book has no independent moral status, whereas your friend does.

Vardy and Grosch (1999) identify three means of extending moral significance to non-human entities. These are:

- The libertarian extension. This posits that the libertarian emphasis on individuals should be extended to animals, or to individual living organisms (Cochrane, 2007), granting each the right to uninterrupted freedom of existence. One of the problems with this approach is deciding how far to go with it. Extending moral independence to all living organisms may seem intuitive when we think about monkeys, dogs or cats, but it also takes us into the realm of grasses, yeasts and bacteria. There is room for debate regarding what interests such non-sentient beings may have.

- Conservation ethics. This approach values the conservation and preservation of non-human nature specifically out of human interest. Ecosystems are not considered to have any intrinsic value, but only extrinsic value – a value entirely based on their utility to humans. Much of the **discourse** around climate change mitigation is based on this anthropocentric (human-centred) perspective, emphasising the impacts that changes in climate will have on human life.

- The ecological extension. This places value on the interconnectedness of the planet's geophysical and biophysical systems, and the diversity within this. The ecosystem is assumed to have intrinsic value in itself. As Aldo Leopold (1949, p. 240) put it, 'A thing is right when it tends to preserve the integrity, stability and beauty of the biotic community. It is wrong when it tends otherwise.'

Within the UK, as elsewhere, approaches to environmental management changed through the second half of the twentieth century from an emphasis on 'controlling' nature to an approach of 'working with' nature. This can be seen in changing approaches to river management (Downs and Gregory, 2004). In the 1970s rivers were controlled through the use of hard engineering structures such as concrete banks. By the start of the twenty-first century, river management and restoration emphasised the continuing operation of fluvial processes and habitats, with integrated river basin management, rather than just 'river management', becoming the preferred aim. Fryirs and Brierly (2009) highlight that individual river restoration schemes also reflect place-specific socio-economic, cultural and biophysical values (and, indeed, argue that this should be so). These different practices reflect not only differences in understanding of the river environment, but also different values, or ideas about how we ought to behave in relation to the environment.

Arguably, developed societies have not yet gone far enough. Radical ecologists (including ecofeminists) point out that the whole debate about moral extension fails to challenge the Western privileging of humans which has led to such serious environmental degradation in the first place. It uses humans as the paradigmatic example of morality, from which morality is extended outwards. Instead, our whole conception of humans and our place in the world needs re-thinking (Cochrane, 2007). One example of such re-thinking is provided by Bawaka Country et al. (2013). This paper takes up the Australian Yolŋu people's understanding of 'humans as one small part of a broader cosmos populated by diverse beings and diverse ways of being'. The emphasis is on everything and everyone entangled together in mutual interdependence, an 'ontology of co-becoming' (pp. 186–7). This is reflected in the authorship of the paper, in which the country itself is recognised as taking a role in shaping the content of the research.

From these two issues, of universality versus particularity, and of how far our moral concern should extend, we can see that geographers' engagements with moral philosophy appear to be increasingly turning towards relational understandings, advocating a feminist or situational ethics of care. This can be followed through to a relational concern for a more-than-human world.

9.3 Ethics and geographical research

9.3.1 Research integrity and research ethics

There is a notion that 'science' is an objective endeavour, its results independent of the individual carrying out the research. Even if we accept that objective knowledge is possible (for example, where theories have been tested by multiple people in multiple circumstances), it is easy to see that the content of knowledge is dependent upon the character of the researchers producing knowledge. The quality of society's knowledge depends on honesty: the honesty of researchers not to invent data (fabrication) and not to leave out data that might inconveniently falsify their hypothesis, for example. Researchers rely on each other to be honest about whose ideas, whose publications, have influenced any piece of work and give credit where it is due. In a review of referencing practices within physical geography, Haussman et al. (2013) argue that this kind of honesty is both ethically and scientifically important. These kinds of considerations, dependent upon a researcher's character, fall under the broad heading of 'research integrity'.

The term 'research ethics', in contrast, has come to be associated specifically with how we treat human participants in research. This is a rather more heavily policed, and hotly debated, aspect of research. To understand how it has arisen we need to turn briefly to medicine.

After the Second World War, the German town of Nuremberg became the venue for a series of thirteen war crimes trials, which extended from 1945 to 1949. Mostly those on trial were military, political and industrial leaders of Nazi Germany, but the Doctors' Trial (1946–7) saw 23 medical doctors charged with war crimes. They were accused of participating in the Nazi programme to euthanise prisoners of war, and of conducting medical experiments on prisoners. This included testing out poisons, and inflicting battlefield wounds on individuals in order to practise reconstructive surgery. One line of their defence was a (consequentialist) claim that the prisoners had been condemned to death anyway, so the experiments made no material difference to their fate. Sixteen of the doctors were found guilty of war crimes. The result of such practices coming to light was the establishment of the 'Nuremberg Code' for medical research, which was followed by the World Medical Association's (1964) 'Helsinki Declaration'. These documents set out ethical principles for medical research.

In 1972, news broke in the United States of the 'Tuskegee Study of Untreated Syphilis in the Negro Male'. This was a study that had begun forty years earlier, when around 400 poor and uneducated African American males were invited for free health checks. They were diagnosed with latent Syphilis (carrying the disease but showing no symptoms), told simply that they had 'bad blood', and asked to return regularly for further checks. They received hot meals and medicine for minor ailments during such checks, which would have provided significant incentive to return. The men were never actually treated for Syphilis though, as the doctors wanted to find out how the disease progressed. By the late 1940s it was known that Syphilis could be treated with Penicillin, but the men were never given any. By the time of the media outcry, over 70 of them had died of the disease, many had passed it to their wives, and several had children born with congenital Syphilis. The US Government subsequently established a National Commission to draw up ethical principles for the conduct of biomedical and behavioural research. The Commission's report (known as the Belmont Report, 1979), established three basic principles, with two of its authors extending this to four in a separate publication (Beauchamp and Childress, 1979). The four principles are:

- Respect: respecting the right of all individuals to autonomous self-determination, in other words, freedom to choose what happens to them, on an informed basis;

- Beneficence: endeavouring to do good;

- Non-maleficence: doing no harm;

- Justice: essentially, fairness in distribution of the costs and benefits of research.

While these notorious cases may seem somewhat remote from geography, they triggered a concern for human participants in research that now impacts on all subjects. In the decades since Beauchamp and Childress' publication, a veritable 'industry' of research ethics regulation and governance has developed, with guidelines produced by international, national and subject-based organisations (see the companion website for links to a variety). A concern for human participants in research thus stems from the biomedical sciences, but has spread to encompass any research involving people. This concern has been reactive, evolving as a series of responses to particularly significant cases of misconduct.

The four principles above are manifestations of deontological and utilitarian ethics. 'Respect' reflects Kant's categorical imperative, which requires people to act only as they would wish everyone else to act, and accords independent moral status to all individuals. Beneficence and non-maleficence are basically utilitarian – as, perhaps, is justice, although Mcfarlane (2009) suggests this is more aligned with John Rawls' conception of justice than with Bentham's utilitarianism. Overall, a 'traditional' conception of ethics, establishing principles or rules which everyone is obliged to follow, has rapidly become embedded in the way research is governed. In the UK and elsewhere this means that staff and students wishing to undertake research involving human participants must first have their research project approved by the university.

A number of critiques have been directed at this, by geographers and non-geographers alike. Probably one of the earliest concerns expressed by social scientists (and certainly the most widespread) is that the principles established for biomedical research are inappropriate for the social sciences. Dyer and Demeritt (2008) articulate this critique within geography, arguing that the doctor/patient relationship is more complex than that between social researcher and research participant. The doctor has other responsibilities and obligations towards the patient, outside of the research, and this is rarely the case in social research. The principle of avoidance of harm, combined with the deontological concern for all individuals, may also be at odds with human geographers' concerns to expose injustices in society.

A second criticism argues that *a priori* principles are inadequate for the messy and unpredictable practices of research. Horton (2008) and Morrow (2008) provide some detailed accounts of the ethically difficult, unanticipated situations they found themselves in when conducting research with children. This connects with a third criticism that the requirement for 'ethical approval' prior to conducting research necessarily front-loads 'ethics' at the start of the research process, when ethical practice requires continuous attention throughout (Macfarlane, 2009). The risk is that institutionalised ethics procedures engender a 'tick-box' approach to ethics, rather than encouraging on-going consideration of ethics-in-practice. Just as the moral turn in geography has led to arguments for 'practical reason' and an ethics of care, ethical conduct in undertaking research needs the same on-going, situation-specific attention.

Perhaps one of the most significant criticisms of research ethics regulation is that it is imposed on researchers in a potentially restrictive manner. Dyer and Demeritt (2008) assert that 'ethics creep' from biomedical sciences to social sciences (and beyond) has generated a regulatory regime of censorship, determining what research can or cannot be done. Another, particularly geographical, dimension of this imposition has been articulated by non-geographers. In an increasingly globalised research community, researchers working in non-Western cultures such as Japan are now being required to meet these Western research ethics expectations (Macfarlane and Saitoh, 2008). It is worth noting here that Trudeau (2012) provides some counter to Dyer and Demeritt's (2008) concerns. He points out that institutions have some flexibility in how they implement external research ethics requirements, and can do so in a constructive, supportive manner. Research ethics requirements *can* be used as an aid to ethical reflection.

9.3.2 Research and society

The term 'research ethics' has become synonymous with concern about the treatment of human participants in research, manifest in institutionalised procedures for vetting individual projects. This regulatory regime has developed to prevent particular kinds of (abusive) research being conducted. The broader issue here is the ethical question of what kinds of research society should, or should not, allow. This seems to be rarely discussed directly – although it is perhaps the direction in which Dyer and Demeritt (2002) were thinking when they raised concerns about research ethics regulation as a form of censorship. Two cases of disrupted research projects, both from 2008, are illustrative. The two projects were not by geographers, but both relate to issues of geographical interest: the first, inter-cultural relations and counter-terrorism; and the second, food production and environmental concerns.

In May 2008 Rizwaan Sabir, a Masters' degree student at the University of Nottingham, was arrested for downloading a training manual produced by the militant Islamic group Al-Qaeda. The university informed police that the materials had been downloaded. Sabir had emailed the training manual to a member of staff to print, and both men were arrested. The student was held in a police cell under the Terrorism Act for nearly a week, despite his supervisors insisting that the materials were directly relevant to his research on counter-terrorism. He was eventually released without charge (Curtis and Hodgson, 2008).

The following month, researchers in the Leeds University plant sciences laboratory led by Professor Howard Atkinson arrived at work to find an entire field trial of genetically modified potatoes destroyed (Atkinson, 2008). Around 400 plants had been pulled up overnight, thought to be the action of anti-GM protestors. Any such field trials require a licence, which involves scrutiny of the proposed work by the UK Advisory Committee on Releases to the Environment (ACRE). In this case ACRE considered the trial to be too small to pose any risk to the environment, and granted the licence. The field trial was the last stage in a three-year research project. As a result of the sabotage it had to be abandoned.

In both of these cases the disruption was a reaction against the researchers' actions. In the first, the University itself was the disruptive body (for which it attracted much criticism). In the second, it was an anonymous sector of 'the public'. The questions that arise, then, are whether or not it is wrong to conduct research on particular topics, who should decide, and how.

Both of the cases above prompted responses that made reference to the notion of 'academic freedom'. Broadly speaking, this posits that academic staff and students in universities should have the freedom to pursue knowledge in whatever fields they deem to be worthwhile, and to challenge received wisdom on the basis of such knowledge. The argument can be powerful: by understanding terrorism we will be better able to respond to terrorism; by interrogating arguments we are better able to identify, dismantle and challenge poor arguments. Underlying this is a normative assumption that knowledge is good.

A challenge to this assumption can be found in philosopher Clive Hamilton's (2013) discussion of 'geoengineering'. He defines geoengineering as 'deliberate, large-scale intervention in the climate system designed to counter global warming or offset some of its effects' (p. 1). Proposed geoengineering schemes are many and various, but Hamilton groups them into two broad classes: those designed to remove carbon dioxide from the atmosphere; and those designed to manage the solar radiation reaching the Earth's surface. These are technological solutions to climate change, including ideas such as changing the chemical composition of oceans, modifying cloud cover, or adding sulphate particles to the upper atmosphere to block sunlight. Is research into such technologies a good thing? Hamilton points out that geoengineering research is associated with a 'moral hazard'. There is every likelihood that such research would diminish incentive to reduce our carbon dioxide emissions, and it is highly questionable that such a result would be 'good'. Geoengineering also raises questions about global power. To implement such technologies would be to impose Western scientific solutions, founded on Western **anthropocentric** values and the domination of humans over nature, in ways that impact other cultures. Such questions are inherently geographical and moral.

These examples, then, highlight that the very act of undertaking research is a moral act, a manifestation of society's values.

9.4 Moral philosophy and ethics in summary

Ethics and moral philosophy address questions about how we ought to act. Such questions can be approached in different ways. Kant's deontological ethics and Bentham's utilitarian ethics begin with foundational principles, thought to be universally applicable. The former focuses on the reasons for an action (motivations), and the latter on the outcomes (consequences). In contrast, Aristotle's virtue ethics and theories of care ethics emphasise a particular way of being that we should strive to achieve. We may each have different preferences, finding ourselves more convinced by one approach or the other, but a basic awareness of these different approaches enables us to look at a situation in different ways, and perhaps see different possibilities.

Geography's quantitative revolution of the mid-twentieth century emphasised the discipline as a descriptive science, seeking to reveal how the world is. From the 1970s this emphasis on 'is' was contested, radical geographers explicitly setting out to expose, challenge and counter inequalities and injustices in society. We should not assume, though, that questions of ethics are not also relevant to physical geography. Any intervention in the natural environment is also normative, based on – or establishing through practice – assumptions about how we ought to act.

The very pursuit of knowledge is, then, a normative act; a performance of values either conscious or unconscious. Institutionalised regulatory regimes tend to place emphasis on particular aspects of how we conduct research, but geographers' ethical awareness and intention has long gone beyond such regimes. There is always room for improvement, of course. The lack of attention to geographies in languages other than English (or, alternatively, the imposition of English as an international *lingua franca* for research) is a normative move, and one that I am guilty of reinforcing through this book. Alongside this has been a deficit in attention to others' geographies, other peoples' ways of knowing the world. Undoubtedly there are moves to address this issue, through participatory modes of research in both social and environmental dimensions of the discipline. In a complex world, it seems, there is endless scope for moral debate.

FURTHER READING

For further explanations

Caitlin, C., Sultana, F. and Pain, R. (eds) (2007) 'Special Thematic Issue: Participatory Ethics', *ACME: An International E-Journal for Critical Geographies* 6 (3). http://www.acme-journal.org/volume6-3.html.

Carmalt, J.C. (2011) 'Human rights, care ethics and situated universal norms', *Antipode* 43 (2): 296–325.

Horton, J. (2008) 'A "sense of failure"? Everydayness and research ethics', *Children's Geographies* 6 (4): 363–83.

Lawson, V. (2009) 'Instead of radical geography, how about caring geography?' *Antipode* 41 (1): 210–13.

Morrow, V. (2008) 'Ethical dilemmas in research with children and young people about their social environments', *Children's Geographies* 6 (1): 49–61.

Simandan, D. (2011) 'The wise stance in human geography', *Transactions of the Institute of British Geographers* NS 36: 188–92.

Smith, D.M. (2000) *Moral Geographies: Ethics in a World of Difference*. Edinburgh: Edinburgh University Press.

Smith, S. (2009) 'Everyday morality: where radical geography meets normative theory', *Antipode* 41 (1): 206–9.

Progress in Human Geography and *Progress in Physical Geography* resources

Barnett, C. (2010) 'Geography and ethics: justice unbound', *Progress in Human Geography* 35 (2): 246–55. doi: 10.1177/0309132510370672.

Barnett, C. (2011) 'Geography and ethics: placing life in the space of reasons', *Progress in Human Geography* 36 (3): 379–88. doi: 10.1177/0309132510397463.

Blomley, C. (2007) 'Critical geography: anger and hope', *Progress in Human Geography* 31 (1): 53–65. doi: 10.1177/0309132507073535.

Cook, I. (2006) 'Geographies of food: following', *Progress in Human Geography* 30 (5): 655–66. doi: 10.1177/0309132506070183.

Dyer, D. and Demeritt, D. (2008) 'Un-ethical review? Why it is wrong to apply the medical model of research governance to human geography', *Progress in Human Geography* 33 (1): 46–64. doi: 10.1177/0309132508090475.

Hulme, M. (2012) 'Climate change: climate engineering through stratospheric aerosol injection', *Progress in Physical Geography* 36 (5): 694–705. doi: 10.1177/0309133312456414.

Popke, J. (2003) 'Poststructuralist ethics: subjectivity, responsibility and the space of community', *Progress in Human Geography* 27 (3): 298–316. doi: 10.1191/0309132503ph429oa.

Popke, J. (2009) 'Geography and ethics: non-representational encounters, collective responsibility and economic difference', *Progress in Human Geography* 33 (1): 81–90. doi: 10.1177/0309132508090441.

Smith, D.M. (1997) 'Geography and ethics: a moral turn?' *Progress in Human Geography* 21 (4): 583–90. doi: 10.1191/030913297673492951.

Smith, D.M. (1998) 'How far should we care? On the spatial scope of beneficence', *Progress in Human Geography* 22 (1): 15–38. doi: 10.1191/030913298670636601.

Smith, D.M. (1999) 'Geography and ethics: how far should we go?' *Progress in Human Geography* 23 (1): 119–25. doi: 10.1191/030913299674152414.

Smith, D.M. (2000) 'Moral progress in human geography: transcending the place of good fortune', *Progress in Human Geography* 24 (1): 1–18. doi: 10.1191/030913200671792325.

Smith, D.M. (2001) 'Geography and ethics: progress, or more of the same?', *Progress in Human Geography* 25 (2): 261–8. doi: 10.1191/030913200678580511.

Wilcock, D., Brierley, G. and Howitt, R. (2013) 'Ethnogeomorphology', *Progress in Physical Geography* 37 (5): 573–600. doi: 10.1177/0309133313483164.

Examples

Charlesworth, A. (2004) 'A corner of a foreign field that is forever Spielberg's: understanding the moral landscapes of the site of the former KL Płaszow, Kraków, Poland', *Cultural Geographies* 11: 291–312.

Cook, I. (2004) 'Follow the thing: papaya', *Antipode* 36 (4): 642–64.

Cook, I. and Harrison, M. (2007) 'Follow the thing: "West Indian Hot Pepper Sauce"', *Space and Culture* 10 (1): 40–63.

Haigh, M.J. (2002) 'Land reclamation and deep ecology: in search of a more meaningful physical geography', *Area* 34 (3): 242–52.

Jansson, A. (2013) 'The hegemony of the urban/rural divide: cultural transformations and mediatized moral geographies in Sweden', *Space and Culture* 16 (1): 88–103.

Richardson-Ngwenya, P. and Richardson, B. (2013) 'Documentary film and ethical food-scapes: three takes on Caribbean sugar', *Cultural Geographies* 20 (3): 339–56.

Wohling, M. (2009) 'The problem of scale in indigenous knowledge: a perspective from northern Australia', *Ecology and Society* 14 (1): 1; [online] url: http://www.ecologyandso ciety.org/vol14/iss1/art1/ [accessed 29/10/13].

Thinking, Doing, Constructing Geography

The aim of this book was to provide introduction to some key philosophical and theoretical positions that have been influential in shaping geographic thought since the mid-twentieth century, considering the implications of each for the methodological practices of research. Both human geography and physical geography have been addressed, and the book is intentionally *not* separated into 'human geography' and 'physical geography' sections. This chapter provides a reminder of the philosophies and theories, before considering the debates around geography's two halves.

10.1 Back to the beach! A summary of philosophies and theories in methodological terms

Philosophies and theories are by their very nature rather abstract, and it can often be difficult to see how they connect to 'doing' geography. For this reason, Chapters 2 to 8 have examined some examples of research and then considered how we might approach research at the beach. The point was to provide a means of connecting the abstract ideas of **philosophy** and **theory** with the methodological issues of defining and organising a research project. Considering all of those 'beach' research ideas together thus enables some kind of comparison.

The emphasis of **positivist** research (Chapter 2) is establishing the truth of synthetic statements, the kind of statements that make claims about the way the world is (as opposed to analytical statements, which are logically true by virtue of their meaning alone). This leads to a focus on **empirical** (observable) evidence. Positivist research usually involves the collection of large, quantitative data sets, aiming to reveal universally applicable patterns or relations and thereby establish 'laws'. Positivism is inherently **reductionist**, seeking to explain phenomena through reference to simpler components. Ultimately, mathematics and physics (the simplest and most generally applicable) provide the foundation for knowledge.

In practical terms this means that positivist research at the beach would focus on empirical, material phenomena. These could include the morphology and sediments of the beach itself, and their interactions with waves and tide. Beach inhabitants, both human and non-human, are also observable phenomena in terms of their presence, absence and spatio-temporal distribution. Quantitative methods of surveying and measuring, including through the use of questionnaire surveys for social research, would be on the agenda.

Critical rationalism (Chapter 3) shares with positivism an emphasis on empirical evidence, but actively seeks to falsify theories. To philosopher of science Karl Popper, the distinction between science and non-science is that scientific theories involve a risk of being wrong. A strictly critical rationalist research **methodology** begins with a theory, develops risky predictions from that theory, and then tests those predictions against empirical evidence.

The first step in undertaking a critical rationalist study on the beach is to identify (select or develop) a theory relevant to the focus of interest. The example considered in Chapter 3 came from previous research, in Ariza and Leatherman's (2012) suggestion that imposing a smoking ban on beaches is good for tourism, as it reduces litter and increases visitor numbers. This general theory would allow us to develop hypotheses – that is, specific predictions of what we would expect to see on particular beaches if the theory is true. (This is a **deductive** move, going from general to particular.) Once we have the hypotheses, we can establish what data collection methods we would need to test these hypotheses.

The same methodological sequence is also commonly used in the application of **complexity theory** (Chapter 8), revealed in the three-stage approach to research recommended by complexity theorist Per Bak (1996). Adapting his proposal to more accurately reflect the practices of geographers gave us the three steps of: describing and modelling the phenomenon of interest in terms of complexity; analysing the model to identify the implications, which provides us with the hypotheses for testing; and assessing the hypotheses against empirical evidence. Quite often 'complexity' research addresses only one or two of those three stages. Such research at the beach might involve using cellular automata to model the **self-organization** of sand ripples or beach cusps, for example. Equally, the ideas of complexity can be used in a metaphorical way, such as in examining **path dependence** in a local economy.

Marxist and **critical realist** research were treated together in Chapter 4. Both are **structuralist**, in that they seek to identify the structures underlying events in the world. Bhaskar's critical realism was influenced by Marx, and it is not unusual for geographers to identify their work as both Marxist and critical realist. In such research, a process of **abstraction** is used, carefully thinking through a particular aspect of the world in depth to identify the processes and relations at work. Intensive, case study research can then be used to refine those abstractions. Extensive research can either inform the development of the abstractions or further test them, providing empirical evidence of regularities. Research can thus oscillate between intensive and extensive modes.

This approach was illustrated through a consideration of the environmental pressures associated with beach tourism on the Mediterranean island of Mallorca. Using prior research by Garcia and Servera (2003), it may be possible to abstract (conceptualise) the ecological relations and social relations associated with tourism. These are likely to range from the place images used by package holiday companies to promote their services to potential customers, to local decision-makers' access to knowledge of beach ecosystems, to the ecological relations of sea-grass communities and beach sediments. Intensive case study research in specific locations would then enable us to distinguish between the necessary and contingent relations that give rise to particular outcomes in beach management. Such research might involve interviews and documentary analysis, but could also involve physical geography research on the beach itself.

Moving to **phenomenology** and post-phenomenological ideas (Chapter 5) brings a shift in emphasis, from the 'objective', 'external' world to the subjective world of interpretation and meaning. While the development of **humanistic geography** in the 1970s was distinctly phenomenological, more recent (post-humanist) developments prioritising **materialism**, embodiment, **non-representational** and relational geographies extend into the post-, or certainly more-than-, phenomenological. Through such perspectives the multi-sensory ways in which we experience places become paramount. A beach must surely offer rich potential for such research; from sunbathing to sand-castle-making to surfing, embodied experience seems central to the (Western) popular understanding of beaches. Qualitative ethnographic and auto-ethnographic methods are likely to take centre stage.

Finally, this brings us to a loose grouping of ideas that can be understood as **social constructionist**, or at least developed out of social constructionist orientations. **Feminist** research might specifically focus on gender roles and relations, in the lives of lifeguards and their interactions with the beach-going public, or in family groups. Taking a feminist standpoint, the focus would specifically be on the lived experiences of the females – or of other marginalised groups – on and around beaches.

The ways in which beach norms are constructed and perpetuated through cultural representations of beaches, such as in film or fiction, take us into the realm of **poststructuralism** (including poststructuralist feminism). Social categories of gender, age, ethnicity, (dis)ability, religion and class operate to include or exclude particular people from particular places, and so the beach space becomes intertwined with issues of identity and power. This is perhaps particularly so if we keep in mind international beach tourism. The very notion of beach as 'escape' (and we could substitute that with other words, such as fun, freedom, play, holiday) is worthy of interrogation. The postmodern themes of **hyperreality** and simulation might be relevant here; images selling us the perfect beach, the perfect beachgoer. Researching these kinds of themes might involve ethnographic methods of observation, participant observation, interviewing and diaries. Equally, analysis of cultural representations in film, TV, holiday brochures, news media, fiction or video games would be relevant.

We have, then, a range of philosophical and theoretical perspectives that can lend themselves to some quite different research projects. There are two points to be made here. Firstly, the summary of these different perspectives above runs the risk of giving the impression that philosophy and theory come first, prior to methodology. Research does not necessarily – perhaps not even often – work in that order. Many researchers will begin with an interest in a particular object, experience, event, problem or idea. That starting point may itself prescribe or proscribe particular kinds of data, particular kinds of methods. If you really want to understand *why* some people are afraid to swim in the sea, then an intensive, qualitative study using methods that enable expression of those fears is likely to give you greater insight than a large-scale questionnaire survey or – worse still – observation of lots of beachgoers. Appropriate philosophical and theoretical framings follow from there. This should not be seen as an excuse for trying to avoid philosophy and theory! The very act of identifying a research focus itself involves assumptions about what exists and how we know things, so philosophy and theory are no less important. It is simply that they are not necessarily the starting point in defining a research project.

Secondly, in the summary provided above, physical geography features in the earlier approaches to research (positivism, critical rationalism and complexity theory, critical realism). Human geography runs throughout, but the later approaches seem to be solely the preserve of human geographers. This raises the contentious issue of the relation between the two, and it is to this that we turn next.

10.2 Some thoughts on human geography and physical geography

Histories of geography tell us that, in its entry into universities, geography was particularly promoted as an integrative subject, encompassing nature and culture together (Unwin, 1992; Herbert and Matthews, 2004; Johnston, 2005). One of the key concepts enabling this synthesis was the region, with many academic geographers prior to the 1950s specialising in the comprehensive study of a selected region. From the 1950s onwards, systematic geography took primacy over regional syntheses, such that the latter half of the twentieth century was characterised by divergence rather than cohesion. Urban and Rhoads (2003) described the idea of geography as an integrated discipline as nothing more than an 'idealised notion'. Human geographers and physical geographers have different focal interests, draw on different bodies of theory, use different methods, and target different communities in their publication practices (Johnston, 2005). Are they really separate disciplines?

The end of the twentieth century was marked by debate about the 'divide' and how to cross it (Massey, 1999, 2001; Lane, 2001; Raper and Livingstone, 2001), and such efforts at dialogue have been continuing in both Anglophone and German geography (Egner and von Elverfeldt, 2009). Matthews and Herbert's (2004) edited text, *Unifying Geography: Common Heritage, Shared Future,* directly set out to promote aspects of the discipline that offer potential for generating unity, identifying space, place, environment and maps as points of commonality. Rather than reiterate their approach here, I instead want to interrogate some points of difference.

10.2.1 Ontological and epistemological differences

The immediately obvious difference between human geography and physical geography is that of subject matter. Human geographers study the world of human society and culture, and physical geographers study the world of non-human entities. Embedded in this is a notion that humans are somehow different from non-human beings, with culture (and hence humans) irreducible to nature. This nature/culture divide has a long history in Western thought, traceable at least to the sixth or seventh centuries BC (Urban and Rhoads, 2003). It is embedded in Christian understandings of nature, and was continued through the dualist philosophy of Descartes (emphasising mind/body distinction) to become embedded in Western science. Anderson (2014) traces how the nineteenth-century science of comparative anatomy further perpetuated the human/non-human dualism.

A problem arises in that such rigid distinction between humans and non-humans has been dismantled by research in the natural sciences. Ecology and biology provide increasing evidence of culture among some non-human animals, particularly great apes and cetaceans. Each dolphin has a 'signature whistle', a sound unique to the individual making it, and such whistles appear to be used in both identifying each other and maintaining group cohesion (Kershenbaum et al., 2013). Bottlenose dolphins have long social memories, remembering other individual dolphins for 25 years or more (Bruck, 2013). Orcas display population-specific feeding behaviours, different groups catching different prey, using different hunting methods, and making different sets of vocal sounds while doing so (Deecke et al., 2011). Among such animal species more generally, Whitehead et al. (2004) identify that culture can be transmitted 'horizontally' within generations, individuals learning from their peers, or 'vertically' between generations. If culture exists in non-human animals, then culture does not offer a clear **ontological** distinction between humans and non-humans.

Philosopher Ian Hacking (1999), in his analysis of social constructionism, distinguished between 'interactive' and 'indifferent' kinds of research subjects. Humans are interactive, in that people respond to, perhaps accept or reject, the classifications assigned to them. As Hacking explains, 'It can really matter to someone to be classified as a woman refugee; if she is not thus classified, she may be deported or go into hiding, or marry to gain citizenship' (p. 11). In contrast, non-human objects are indifferent to the ways we think about or describe them. Whether we describe Ben Nevis as a mountain or a hill makes no difference to the peak itself. Hacking suggests that, at some level, this difference between interactive and indifferent kinds reflects a fundamental distinction between the natural and social sciences (and so, by implication, between physical geography and human geography).

This distinction appears to work well enough, until we begin to consider the applications of research. The way we conceptualise or classify non-living entities shapes our actions in relations to those entities (Tadaki et al., 2012), and even non-living entities can respond to actions. A river or hillslope will respond to our management interventions – that it is the whole point of such interventions – and so is responding, albeit indirectly, to our classification of it. The idea of interactive and indifferent kinds still does not provide a clear ontological distinction between humans and non-humans.

The fact remains, though, that some human geographers draw on a group of philosophical and theoretical positions that is not open to physical geographers studying non-human and non-living entities. Perhaps the most convincing explanation for this difference is epistemological rather than ontological. Our capacity for communication and empathy within-species far outweighs our capacity for communicating with, and understanding, other species. As Buller (2014, p. 315) puts it (hinting at Wittgenstein's later philosophy), 'we can never know what it is like to be a bat and can only imagine what a lion would say'. Even conducting positivist research using quantitative data about individuals we have never met, we know what it is to be human 'from the inside', in a way that we can never know what it is to be anything else. (This is essentially a phenomenological argument.) We have the option of taking up a different epistemology when studying humans than when studying anything non-human.

Having recognised this distinction, it is notable that at least since the mid-1990s human geographers have not confined themselves to the study of humans. People share spaces and places with non-human animals, from dogs and cats to cows to wolves or kangaroos. The development of poststructuralist, materialist, non-representational (or more-than-representational) and relational geographies has lent itself to an extension of human geographers' concerns to our non-human cohabitants, to the extent that Buller (2013) notes some hesitancy around the label 'human' geography.

Particularly significant to the discussion here is recognition of the occurrence – even necessity – of trans-species communication. The animals we live with or encounter are not passive receptacles, but themselves have agency; they respond to us and we respond to them, in multiple ways (Haraway, 2008; Brown and Dilley, 2012). In a particularly powerful account of intra-species bonds, philosopher Mark Rowlands' (2008) book *The Philosopher and the Wolf* reveals the ways that sharing our living spaces with non-human others can impact on our understanding of ourselves and the world. We may never know what it is to be a dog or cat, but even episte-mologically the distinction between human and non-human is not as clear-cut as it might at first seem.

In sum, it seems difficult to maintain any argument for a clear-cut binary division between human geography and physical geography on the basis of subject content, assuming a culture/nature, human/non-human distinction. Ontologically the case seems weak. Epistemologically the difference is a little clearer, but some fuzziness, some 'ifs' and 'buts', remain even here. On this basis, then, it should not surprise us that the 'divide' between physical geography and human geography is not clear-cut either (Matthews and Herbert, 2004; Viles, 2005; Couper, 2007).

10.2.2 A socially constructed 'divide'

Recognising the point above is not to argue that there is no division within geog-raphy. Massey (1999, 2001), Lane (2001), Matthews and Herbert (2004) and others have clearly been debating something! If we accept that there is a 'divide' of some sort, then we can identify it as socially constructed (whatever 'it' is).

Referring back to Berger and Luckmann's (1966) explanation of the processes by which social construction occurs (Chapter 6), it is possible to identify at least three of them at work here. Geography students are surrounded by books on human geography and on physical geography, and journals such as *Progress in Human Geography* and *Progress in Physical Geography*, or *Geografiska Annaler Series A: Physical Geography* and *Geografiska Annaler Series B: Human Geography*. Degree courses usually include separate human geography and physical geography compo-nents (although there may be elements of convergence as well). Academic job advertisements usually specify whether a human geographer or physical geogra-pher is required. *Institutionalisation* is at work here: all of these objects and practices institutionalise the divide between physical geography and human geography. In being institutionalised, it then forms part of the objective, external reality encoun-tered by individuals; it is *objectivated*. Education is a formal means of *socialisation*, and so the divide is perpetuated, students being socialised into seeing themselves as (predominantly) human geographers or physical geographers. When we refer to ourselves as a 'physical geographer' or 'human geographer', we reinforce the divide. Donovan et al. (2011) provide interesting accounts of the difficulties that may be encountered when setting out to resist such boundaries.

The broader social contexts within which academics work undoubtedly serve to reinforce this division. Specialisation is rewarded. With an ever-increasing number of articles being published in ever-increasing numbers of journals worldwide, keep-ing up with a specialist interest can be difficult enough. Encompassing the breadth of the discipline to any depth becomes impossible. Specialised, technical language can further limit communication to a small community (Demeritt, 1996). Johnston (2003) identified that physical geographers and human geographers are largely tar-geting different audiences in their publication practices, the former focusing their efforts on journals shared with other earth/environmental science communities, and the latter tending to publish in geography journals.

The binary divide between human geography and physical geography is, then, a social construction. It is an artefact of our concepts, language and practices. There are both differences and similarities between geographers of all kinds, in terms of what they study and how they study it. With culture existing among non-human animals, and cultural geographers' studies encompassing animals, differences in subject focus are not necessarily clear-cut. Some human geographers and some physical geographers use complexity theory (Chapter 8), and the work of some human geographers and some physical geographers can be characterised by a critical rationalist (Chapter 3) or critical realist (Chapter 4) philosophy. Physical geography and human geography are both social practices that can be understood using the social theories introduced in Chapters 5–7. It is not that there are no differences; rather, there are multiple modes of difference and similarity, such that reference to *the* divide is over-simplistic. If we follow Hacking's (1999) description of social constructionist arguments, the implication is that whatever is socially constructed does not have to be as it is. Things could be different.

10.2.3 Is this the geography we need?

Some geographers argue for reunification of the discipline, a return to a vision of geography as a single, coherent discipline. Reviewing these arguments, Viles (2005) identifies three types:

1. The heritage argument, that geography has always been united and so should stay that way;

2. The holistic argument, that 'geography simply *is* the study of human-environment relations' (p. 32) and so the component parts cannot be separated;

3. The pragmatic argument, that human geography and physical geography would be too weak as individual disciplines to survive in an academic climate of underfunding. Disciplinary identity and politics come to the fore.

Each kind of argument may have some merit, each may persuade some individuals, and each could also be opposed quite reasonably. Arguments for a reunification, though, presuppose division. If geography were not 'divided', there would be no need to argue for reunification. If we accept that geography is divided, then the only available argument against that situation appears to be one of unification. The key question is whether this binary is a useful way of understanding and representing the discipline.

Alongside my PhD studies I also worked for a geoconservation (or 'earth heritage' conservation) group. Some of the group's work focused on documenting and recording what was where, designating sites as regionally important and worthy of some protection. Some of our work focused on public engagement, organising events or creating posters and displays to promote understanding and appreciation of the physical landscape. A constant stream of funding applications and tenders for contracts was produced in the background, without which the group would not exist. It was a good place to work; a happy bunch of geomorphologists and geologists. Gradually, though, I realised that the work was raising questions for me that were not primarily geomorphological or geological. They were questions about how 'ordinary people' (not geologists or geomorphologists) relate to landscape and place. Conservation is a social and political act. Education – including informal, public education – is a social and political act. To influence people it helps to understand people. Having studied geography at university I at least had some awareness that there were different dimensions to what we were trying to do, even though I had not studied cultural geographies of landscape directly myself.

It has become evident that a scientific (biophysical) understanding of nature is insufficient to address the big issues faced by society globally; issues of food production, access to fresh water, and climate change, for example. Society, culture, economics and politics are all important. Equally, a scientific understanding of environmental systems is essential, as a social science approach alone is also insufficient to understand and tackle such issues. We need the two in combination (Unwin and Rose, 2004; Egner and Elverfeldt, 2009). There is also an increasing sense that global capitalist society needs a different (that is, ontologically different) understanding of the planet and our place within it, a different way of relating to nature and valuing nature. This is certainly being recognised and addressed in other disciplines, including philosophy (Toadvine, 2009; Clingerman et al., 2014), sociology (Newton, 2007), education (Bonnet, 2009) and fictional writing such as Hayden Gabriel's (2004) *A Wonderful Use for Fire* or Barbara Kingsolver's (2013) *Flight Behaviour.*

Geographers *are* addressing such issues, working collaboratively on flood risk, river and land management (McEwen and Jones, 2012; Bracken and Oughton, 2013; Emery et al., 2013), for example. Geographers are certainly attempting to rethink the human/non-human binary (Urban and Rhoads, 2003; Jöns, 2006; Panelli, 2010; Rautio, 2013), and making efforts to work with alternative (indigenous) world-views (Bawaka Country, 2013; Blaser, 2014). In some cases, individuals have worked at the intersection of the two 'sides' (Evans and Randalls, 2008; Donovan et al., 2011).

We have seen that ontologically and epistemologically a dualistic understanding of geography seems over-simplistic. We can now add that practically, in terms of what geographers actually do, it is also problematic. There are two (and probably more) issues arising from this. The first is another pragmatic and political argument. Thinking about geography in terms of a human/physical binary has potential to leave a gap at the intersection, exactly where some of the big challenges for society lay. Alongside the urge to put geographical knowledge to good use and make a difference, there is also a concern that other disciplines are addressing that gap and so geographers should be (seen to be) too. Such arguments are perhaps strongest when we consider that geographers working in universities are the minority, far outweighed by geography graduates who go on to work in all sorts of fields, tackling all sorts of problems. As Castree (2012) points out, too much of the 'divide' debate focuses solely on research. An appreciation of the different dimensions of geography, and of science, social science and humanities perspectives, can be a valuable thing.

The second consideration is ethical. Individuals who work at the intersection of human geography and physical geography, developing their expertise in that domain, risk exclusion from either of the dominant social categories by which geographers define themselves. They may be neither and both 'physical geographer' and 'human geographer'. This raises issues of identity, as well as more pragmatic matters such as which journals to target for publication and which conferences to attend (for researchers), or even which jobs to apply for.

This could be misinterpreted as an argument for unity – and, in particular, what Castree (2012) refers to as 'muscular unity', imposed on everyone. Similarly, it could be misinterpreted as an argument for geographers to become 'integration generalists' (Urban and Rhoads, 2003). It is neither. Rather, it is a suggestion that perhaps the time has come for greater acknowledgement of plurality. We need to recognise that the binary separation of human and physical has become 'real' through our social practices, yet the actual work of geographers – the focal concerns, the philosophies, theories and methodologies that shape their work – does not divide so neatly. The obvious metaphor is that geographers are not black or white, but black, white and all shades of grey in between. Some geographers may prefer to work with a focus solely on social inequalities, urban public spaces or local economies. Others may prefer to focus entirely on sand dune dynamics, species migration or glacier hydrology. Still more may find themselves somewhere in between, and all deserve acknowledgement. Is it time to dismantle the divide, and to call ourselves 'geographers'?

FURTHER READING

For further explanations

Castree, N., Rogers, A. and Sherman, D. (2005) *Questioning Geography*. Oxford: Blackwell.

Dixon, D., Hawkins, H. and Straughan, E. (2012) 'Of human birds and living rocks: remaking aesthetics for post-human worlds', *Dialogues in Human Geography* 2 (3): 249–70.

Donovan, K., Sidaway, J.D. and Stewart, I. (2011) 'Bridging the geo-divide: reflections on an interdisciplinary (ESRC/NERC) studentship', *Transactions of the Institute of British Geographers* NS 36: 9–14.

Lane, S.N. (2001) 'Constructive comments on D. Massey's "Space-time, 'science' and the relationship between physical geography and human geography"', *Transactions of the Institute of British Geographers* 26 (2): 243–56.

Massey, D. (1999) 'Space-time, "science" and the relationship between physical geography and human geography', *Transactions of the Institute of British Geographers* 24: 261–76.

Matthews, J.A. and Herbert, D.T. (eds) (2004) *Unifying Geography: Common Heritage, Shared Future*. Abingdon: Routledge.

Trudgill, S. and Roy, A. (2003) *Contemporary Meanings in Physical Geography: From What to Why?* London: Arnold. [See particularly the chapters by Thornes and McGregor, Urban and Rhoads, and Richards.]

Progress in Human/Physical Geography resources

Buller, H. (2014) 'Animal geographies I', *Progress in Human Geography* 38 (2): 308–18. doi: 10.1177/0309132513479295.

Douglas, I. (1987) 'The influence of human geography on physical geography', *Progress in Human Geography* 11: 517–40. doi: 10.1111/j.0020-2754.1999.00261.x.

Gerber, J. (1997) 'Beyond dualism – the social construction of nature and the natural and social construction of human beings', *Progress in Human Geography* 21 (1): 1–17. doi: 10.1191/030913297671906269.

Johnston, C. (2008) 'Beyond the clearing: towards a dwelt animal geography', *Progress in Human Geography* 32 (5): 633–49. doi: 10.1177/0309132508089825.

Panelli, R. (2010) 'More-than-human social geographies: posthuman and other possibilities', *Progress in Human Geography* 34 (1): 79–87. doi: 10.1177/0309132509105007.

Wainwright, S.P. (2012) 'Science studies in physical geography: an idea whose time has come?' *Progress in Physical Geography* 36 (6): 768–812. doi: 10.1177/0309133312450997.

Wilcock, D., Brierley, G. and Howitt, R. (2013) 'Ethnogeomorphology', *Progress in Physical Geography* 37 (5): 573–600. doi: 10.1177/0309133313483164.

Glossary

abduction A form of reasoning or inference, often referred to (in philosophy of science) as 'inference to the best explanation'. To borrow an example from Douven (2011), walking along the beach, you see what looks like a picture of Winston Churchill in the sand. It might be that what you are looking at is actually the trace of an ant crawling on the beach. 'The much simpler, and therefore (you think) much better, explanation is that someone intentionally drew a picture of Churchill in the sand. That, in any case, is what you come away believing.' Like **induction**, abduction draws conclusions that go beyond the information that we start with (for example, from observations). The difference is that abduction makes an appeal to *explanation* to provide grounds for the conclusion.

abstraction In Marxist and critical realist research, isolating a phenomenon of interest in thought to analyse it in depth. The aim is often to identify the processes and relations at work, or the necessary (essential) and contingent (incidental) characteristics of the phenomenon of interest.

actant In Bruno Latour's Actor Network Theory, 'actants' are anything in a given situation that modifies other actors in that situation. In other words actants are 'acting agents', or 'interveners', people or things that make a difference to (have a part in shaping) the situation. Actants can be human and non-human (and hybrid). Latour used the word instead of 'actors' to emphasise the inclusion of non-human entities; to 'rid the word of any trace of anthropomorphism' (2005, p. 75). The term 'actant' thus emphasises the relations between human and non-human (and hybrid) entities.

aeolian Wind-blown, as in aeolian processes and aeolian landforms.

affective Associated with (but not quite the same as) feelings, emotions, attitudes, moods. Affect is relational, a pre-cognitive sensation arising from our interactions with people, things and places.

angle of repose The steepest angle of slope (measured in degrees from horizontal) at which a granular material (such as sand or gravel), piled up, will come to rest.

anisotropic Having properties that vary with direction (are directionally dependent).

anthropocentric Human-centred. In environmental ethics, anthropocentric world views prioritise human interests above all else, valuing the environment only in terms of its utility to humans.

a priori A Latin term used in philosophy to denote knowledge that is independent of ('comes before' or is 'prior to') experience. This refers to statements that are logically true without reference to the state of things in the world. For example, 'a bachelor is an unmarried man' is true, regardless of whether any specific men are married or unmarried. This contrasts with *a posteriori* statements, whose truth is dependent upon the state of things in the world (and hence knowledge that is dependent on observation or experience).

assemblage Particularly associated with the ideas of philosopher Gilles Deleuze (1925–1995), for example in Deleuze and Guattari (1987). Deleuze described the social world as conststing of assemblages, or combinations of things in relations with each other. 'Things', in this case, can be material objects and people, but they can also be non-material, such as events, utterings, ideas or signs. Smith and Protevi (2013) describe an assemblage as 'an emergent unity joining together heterogeneous bodies in a 'consistency".

attractor A set of states or properties towards which a dynamic system will evolve, regardless of its starting conditions. Some systems have multiple attractors, and so multiple possible sets of conditions that the system could tend towards.

beach cusps In geomorphology, beach cusps form as a series of concave embayments separated by 'horns' of coarser material pointing seawards. An example of self-organization, where small-scale process dynamics combine to create larger-scale patterns.

beach nourishment A form of beach management that involves importing sediment (sand or gravel) to replenish an eroding beach.

berm In coastal geomorphology, the flat upper surface of a ridge or terrace formed on the landward part of the beach.

Cartesian Relating to the works of French mathematician and philosopher René Descartes (1596–1690). His philosophical works provided the modern version of the mind–body problem, a dualist distinction between mental and material phenomena. In mathematics, Descartes developed a coordinate system by which a point on a plane can be described by two coordinates, indicating the distance of the point from two fixed lines which are perpendicular to each other (axes). This Cartesian coordinate system provides a link between Euclidean geometry and algebra.

catastrophic events (e.g. in geomorphology) Large and sudden events, usually rare in human timescales.

chaos In science, the notion of chaos describes a deterministic system (one whose state at any one time determines its future states) that is difficult to predict. We often think that deterministic systems should be easily predictable, but in a chaotic system, what happens in the future is highly sensitive to the current state of the system. Minor differences can give rise to very different outcomes.

closed system In physical sciences, a system (consisting of inputs, throughputs and outputs) which has inputs and outputs of energy but not matter.

complexity theory A collection of ideas that provide an approach to science which focuses on the relationships between parts of a system, the collective behaviours generated by these relationships, and how the system interacts with its environment.

contingent Circumstances or events that are dependent upon particular conditions. Contrasts with those circumstances that are *necessary* for something to happen.

critical rationalism A philosophy of science developed by Karl Popper. Critical rationalism emphasises deductive arguments and the falsification (as opposed to verification) of hypotheses and theories.

critical realism A philosophy of science originating with Roy Bhaskar, and promoted within the social sciences through the work of Andrew Sayer, in particular. Bhaskar developed 'transcendental realism' as a philosophy of science, and 'critical naturalism' for social science. Others used the term 'critical realism' to refer to these in combination. Critical realism distinguishes between the empirical (our observations of events), the actual (events as they occur), and the real (mechanisms or structures that cause events). Critical realist geography thus seeks to uncover underlying, unobservable structures or mechanisms.

cultural turn A movement within human geography and the social sciences more broadly to emphasise the role of culture in social life, drawing attention to practices of meaning-making and signification. Influenced by poststructuralist and postcolonial ideas, the cultural turn has been particularly strong in British cultural geography, developing from the late 1980s and through the 1990s. Valentine (2001) provides a useful review of the cultural turn and its influence on social geography.

cycle of erosion The model of large-scale, long-term landscape development developed by William Morris Davis in the late nineteenth century (Davis, 1899 and subsequent works). Originally intended as a generally applicable model, it was developed on the basis of experience in humid temperate environments. As Davis encountered other environments (such as arid regions or glacial regions) he tried to produce modified versions to encompass these. The Cycle of Erosion is perhaps best known for the characterisation of landscapes (and rivers) as 'young', 'mature' or 'old-age'. Davis' work had a profound impact on geomorphology in the early twentieth century, but his Cycle of Erosion was heavily criticised. It fell out of favour by the mid-twentieth century as emphasis shifted to focus on the physical, chemical and biological bases for geomorphological processes.

deduction A form of argument that moves from generally applicable theories to specific cases. This form of argument was promoted by Karl Popper in his critical rationalist philosophy of science. Beginning with a generally applicable theory, we can apply it to a specific case to develop 'risky predictions' (hypotheses), and then use empirical evidence to test whether or not the theory is true.

dialectical In Marxist theory, a method of examining things from opposite perspectives, for example considering identity and difference, or quality and quantity.

discourse In general use, discourse refers to spoken (conversational) and written language. Foucault demonstrated that language is inseparable from how we understand the world (our concepts and ideas), and so inseparable from what we do in the world. Discourse thus extends beyond purely language to encompass our actions and practices.

drainage basin An area of land that drains into a single river system. Sometimes referred to as the 'watershed' (often in North American literature), although this term can also be used to denote the boundary between drainage basins.

drumlin A landform consisting of glacial debris, sometimes with a bedrock core, in the shape of an elongated or streamlined hillock. The long axis of the drumlin lies parallel to the flow direction of the glacier under which it formed. Drumlins occurring together can create what is sometimes termed a 'basket of eggs' topography.

emergence In complexity theory, complex systems or patterns arise from – emerge from – the multiple interactions of smaller-scale phenomena. Emergence thus refers to collective behaviour or, as Bar-Yam (2011) puts it, 'what parts of a system do together that they would not do alone'.

empirical (Knowledge) based on observable evidence or experience, rather than on logical reasoning or theory.

empiricism In philosophy, the doctrine that all knowledge is gained from sense experience.

epistemology The branch of philosophy concerned with the nature and scope of knowledge. Issues of what constitutes knowledge, and of how we can know something, are central to epistemology.

Euclidean geometry A mathematical conception of space thought to have been developed by Greek mathematician Euclid, and the only known form of geometry for 2,000 years. Euclidean geometry describes objects in space in terms of points, lines, areas and volumes, using the dimensions of length, height and width. In simple terms, this is space as an 'empty container' in which objects exist and events happen.

feminism A collection of philosophical and theoretical ideas centred on the role of gender in shaping social life, but extending to encompass other social categorisations. In particular, feminist thought challenges hierarchical inequalities and the use of binary classifications.

fractals Infinitely complex patterns in which every part has the same statistical properties as the whole (self-similarity across scales). Fractals occupy fractional dimensions, between 1D and 2D (lines and planes), or between 2D and 3D (planes and objects).

grey literature Written material that is not available through commercial publishing outlets. This includes a range of materials from a variety of sources, such as reports, technical specifications and standards, theses, policy documents, fact sheets, working papers and other 'official documents' that are not published commercially (such as reports by governments or non-governmental organisations). Some consider 'grey literature' to encompass anything other than books and journal articles.

grounded theory A social research methodology that aims to develop theory from data (rather than applying pre-existing theory), through progressively identifying categories of meaning emerging from the data. The origins of this approach lay in the work of Glaser and Strauss (1967), but grounded theory has since been utilised across many different disciplinary fields.

haptic Relating to the sense of touch. Haptic geographies thus emphasise bodily sensations.

humanistic geography A form of geography that developed in the 1970s, and that placed humans – in terms of their experiences, perceptions, actions and agency – at the centre of geography. Humanistic geography's focus is on people's behaviour and relations with the world around them; the meanings, ideas and emotions through which such relations are manifest; and the creative capacity of human thoughts and actions.

hyperreality A simulation that is exaggerated in comparison to reality, better than the 'real thing'. Associated with the (poststructuralist) theories of Jean Beaudrillard.

idealism There are various forms of idealism. In its strictest sense, idealism is the doctrine (associated with Bishop Berkeley) that nothing exists outside of human minds; all is mental or spiritual in nature. Social scientists tend to use a broader conception of idealism, associated with the German idealist philosophers of the late eighteenth and early nineteenth centuries. The focus here is on things as they appear to us, without necessarily making assumptions as to whether things exist in themselves (outside of our conception of them).

idiographic Relating to particularities, rather than general laws or principles. Regional geography is an example of idiographic geography, seeking to understand the particular characteristics of individual regions. Contrasts with **nomothetic** (or systematic) geography.

imperialism Policy and associated practices that seek to extend the power or influence of one state over others. Often associated with colonisation and empire (the source of the term), imperialism takes many forms (cultural, social, economic).

induction A form of argument that moves from observation of specific cases to generally applicable theories. The problem with induction is that we cannot be sure the theories derived in this way are 'true'; there is no logical basis for assuming that future observations and experiences will always conform to past observations and experiences.

inheritance (in physical geography) Inherited landscapes and landforms are those which formed under different environmental (e.g. climatic or tectonic) conditions than the present. In the UK, processes in the Late Glacial period formed much of the physical landscape that we now see. Inherited features thus include misfit valleys, much larger than the streams that now occupy them, and the U-shaped valleys characteristic of glacial landscapes (with some particularly good examples in Scotland and the Lake District).

instrumentalism A mode of thought that values an activity (such as research, or education) only for the purposes it serves or outcomes it yields, and not for its own sake.

liminal Relating to a transition, threshold or boundary, neither one thing nor another. A liminal place is a place where normal rules do not apply, perhaps because such places are hard to reach, or they have become places associated with unlawful activities, or they are marginal in some way.

lotic An environment characterised by moving freshwater.

materialism In philosophy, the metaphysical thesis that everything that exists is matter, or stems from matter. (This is often considered to be synonymous with 'physicalist', although the two have not always been seen as the same thing.) In geography, materialism denotes a focus on physical, material objects. In Marxist geographies this takes the form of emphasising the role of material productive technologies and capacities in shaping society (historical materialism). Cultural geography's recent (re)turn to materialism takes a relational focus, emphasising the agency of the material world in the social world and vice versa.

metaphysics The branch of philosophy that deals the ultimate nature of reality; the first principles of abstract concepts such as being, time, space and identity. Ontology is a major branch of metaphysics.

methodology The overall system of methods used to conduct research.

microbiota The micro-organisms of a habitat or site.

morphodynamic An approach to understanding the physical landscape that focuses on the interactions between (or mutual adjustments of) form and process. The morphodynamic approach to coasts thus considers coastal geomorphology, the fluid dynamics of moving water, the processes of sediment transport that result from their interaction, and the resulting feedbacks between them.

naturalism The idea that the social world can be studied by the same methods as the natural world.

nomothetic Law-like. Nomothetic, or systematic, geography seeks to understand particular types of phenomena and produce generally applicable (law-like) statements about them. Contrasts with **idiographic** geography.

nonlinear In science (including physical geography), a linear relation is where two quantities are proportional to each other. Doubling one has the effect of doubling the other. A nonlinear relation is any relation that is not linear. A nonlinear system is thus one in which the outputs are not proportional to the inputs.

non-representational theory A theory or group of theories that emphasise *experience*, in that the world is experienced before it is represented. The practices of everyday life, our being-in-the-world and the ways in which space, places and beings are always-becoming (and hence always have potential) are emphasised. (See Chapter 5 for more.)

normative Establishing a standard or norm (e.g. of behaviour), i.e. that applies or should apply to everyone, or to which everyone is supposed to conform.

ontology The major branch of **metaphysics**, that deals with questions of existence and what exists.

open system In the natural sciences, an open system is a system (consisting of inputs, throughputs and outputs) that has inputs and outputs of both energy and matter. This is in contrast to closed systems (which have inputs/outputs of energy but not matter) and isolated systems (with no inputs or outputs). In the social sciences, an open system describes a situation in which there are non-deterministic relationships between entities, those entities being both material and non-material (such as ideas), human and non-human.

palaeoenvironmental Relating to past environments or environmental conditions.

paradigm Commonly taken to mean the frame of reference within which an academic discipline operates, and which legitimates the kinds of questions asked and the kinds of methodological approaches adopted. The term also refers to a typical example of something (the 'paradigmatic' example). 'Paradigm' is typically associated with Thomas Kuhn's conception of the progress of science (see Chapter 6, for more on the use of the term).

path dependence When current circumstances are shaped by the past trajectory of events or decisions made. Future possibilities are thus dependent on (or constrained by) the history of the system or situation of interest. The term 'path dependence' seems more common in human geography than physical geography. A similar notion of 'contingency' is found in geomorphology, where the future possibilities for landscape change are dependent (contingent) upon the current circumstances, which are in turn shaped by the historical trajectory of change.

phenomenology A philosophical movement that sought to understand things as they appear to us, or as we experience them. Associated with Husserl, Heidegger, Sartre (existential phenomenology) and Merleau-Ponty in particular. See Chapter 5.

philosophy The academic discipline concerned to understand the fundamental nature of reality, existence and knowledge.

political ecology Broadly, the study of environmental issues in the context of political, economic and social relations. However, there is no clear consensus on a definition.

political economy The production, distribution and consumption of resources understood as constituted in and by social relations (and particularly power relations).

positivism A philosophy of science developed by French philosopher Auguste Comte in the nineteenth century, and then taken further by the logical positivists of the Vienna Circle in the early twentieth century. Positivism emphasises: empirical evidence as the basis of knowledge; mathematical analysis of data (mathematics being the simplest and most generally applicable 'science'); identification of patterns to infer causal relations; promotion of the unity of the sciences (through method or language). (See Chapter 2.)

postmodernism Refers to a style, era and theory (or mode of thought) considered to have developed after, and in reaction to, modernism. Postmodernism is characterised by an eclecticism, consciously (and self-consciously) drawing on and amalgamating a range of influences, and a distrust of 'meta-theory' (overarching theory that provides explanation of, or justification for, everything). Associated with Baudrillard and Lyotard (although only the latter described his own work as postmodernist). (See Chapter 7.)

poststructuralism Closely associated with postmodernism, in that the boundaries between the two are not distinct. Poststructuralism rejects structuralist explanations of society, understanding meaning as relational. This often leads poststructuralists to challenge binary categorisations, focusing on the ways that meanings and identities are produced and resisted. Associated with Derrida and Foucault (and others). (See Chapter 7.)

pragmatism A philosophical movement in which the meaning of an idea or proposition is considered to lie in its practical consequences. If the practical implications of two ideas are the same, then there is nothing to judge between those ideas.

Quantitative Revolution The transition from qualitative, descriptive regional studies to quantitative, systematic studies that occurred in Anglo-American geography around the middle of the twentieth century.

realism The assumption or belief that objects are real, existing independently of our minds. *Scientific realism* adds to this the assumptions that our scientific theories are true (the semantic commitment), and that it is possible for us to know the truth about real observable and unobservable objects (the epistemological commitment).

reductionism A means of analysing and describing a complex or complicated phenomenon in terms of its simpler component parts. In physical geography this often implies using the basic principles of chemistry and physics, a move that is consistent with a **positivist** philosophy of science.

reflexivity In research, a process by which the researcher continually reflects on themselves as researcher, and their relations with research participants. In particular, such reflection attends to the researcher's social situation (particularly in relation to research participants), knowledge, experiences and values, and how these may be influencing the knowledge produced through the research.

relativism An understanding of truth, knowledge and morality as existing in relation to social, cultural or historical context. Relativism thus contends that there is no absolute right or wrong, no absolute truth or falsity, and no certainty in knowledge.

secular Not associated with spiritual or religious matters. Secular ethics thus addresses issues of what is right and wrong without reference to religion.

self-organization A type of emergent behaviour found in complex systems, whereby the dynamics and feedbacks operating *within* a system (rather than imposed from outside the system) lead to the development of a pattern of behaviour or form. Examples discussed in Chapter 8 include sand ripples, patterned ground and beach cusps.

self-similarity A mathematical term to describe something that is an approximate copy of itself at different scales.

semantic Relating to meaning.

shore platform A horizontal or gently sloping rocky platform occurring at the base of sea cliffs. Shore platforms can occur at high tide level, or can be inter-tidal (between high and low tide levels) or sub-tidal (only exposed by the very lowest tides).

social constructionism A mode of thought that considers our knowledge and concepts to be products of our social lives and practices (weak social constructionism). Strong social constructionists would argue that the entities we perceive are socially produced. (See Chapter 6.)

structuralism A perspective that seeks to explain events and processes through reference to underlying structures or causal mechanisms.

swash flow The circulation of water in the nearshore shallow part of the beach, the zone of wave breaking and uprush.

transcendental In philosophy, transcendental arguments are those that identify conditions that are necessary, in order for us to have coherent experiences or knowledge. Such arguments therefore 'go beyond' (transcend) our experience or knowledge.

theory A supposition or set of ideas providing explanation for something. A generalised, abstract set of ideas about how phenomena are related.

References

Ackerman, E.A. (1945) 'Geographic training, wartime research, and immediate professional objectives', *Annals of the Association of American Geographers* 35 (4): 121–43.

Adamson, G. and Pavitt, J. (2011) 'Postmodernism: style and subversion', in G. Adamson and J. Pavitt (eds) *Postmodernism: Style and Subversion, 1970–1990.* London: V&A Publishing. pp. 12–97. http://researchonline.rca.ac.uk/630/1/Postmodernism2011.xyz.pdf [accessed 19/07/13].

Adou, J.K., Billaud, Y., Brou, D.A., Clerc, J.-P., Consalvi, J.-L., Fuentes, A., Kaiss, A., Nmira, F., Porterie, B., Zekri, L. and Zekri, N. (2010) 'Simulating wildfire patterns using a small-world network model', *Ecological Modelling* 221: 1463–71.

Agger, B. (1991) 'Critical theory, poststructuralism, postmodernism: their sociological relevance', *Annual Review of Sociology* 17: 105–31.

Aitchison, C.C. (2005) 'Feminist and gender perspectives in tourism studies', *Tourist Studies* 5 (3): 207–24.

All Night Long (1983) Lionel Ritchie. Can't Slow Down. ZK72020. Detroit, MI: Motown.

Allen-Collinson, J. (2011) 'Feminist phenomenology and the woman in the running body', *Sport, Ethics and Philosophy* 5 (3): 297–313.

Anderson, B. and Harrison, P. (eds) (2010) *Taking Place: Non-Representational Theories and Geography.* Farnham: Ashgate.

Anderson, J. (2012) 'Relational places: the surfed wave as assemblage and convergence', *Environment and Planning D: Society and Space* 30 (4): 570–87.

Anderson, K. (2014) 'Mind over matter? On decentring the human in Human Geography', *Cultural Geographies* 21 (1): 3–18.

Andreski, S. (ed.) (1974) *The Essential Comte.* London: Croom Helm.

Ariza, E. and Leatherman, S.P. (2012) 'No-smoking policies and their outcomes on US beaches', *Journal of Coastal Research* 28 (1A): 143–7.

Atkinson, H. (2008) 'Vandalism of GM crop puts British academic freedom under threat', *Times Higher Education* 04/09/08. http://www.timeshighereducation.co.uk/403403.article [accessed 27/10/13].

Avatar (2009) Cameron, J. California: Twentieth Century Fox Film Corporation. [Film].

Baas, A.C.W. (2002) 'Chaos, fractals and self-organization in coastal geomorphology: simulating dune landscapes in vegetated environments', *Geomorphology* 48: 309–28.

Bak, P. (1996) *How Nature Works: the Science of Self-Organized Criticality.* New York: Springer-Verlag.

Bak, P. and Creutz, M. (1994) 'Fractals and self-organized criticality', in A. Bunde and S. Havlin (eds) *Fractals in Science.* Amsterdam: Springer-Verlag. pp. 26–47.

Bak, P., Tang, C. and Wiesenfeld, K. (1987) 'Self-organised criticality: an explanation of $1/f$ noise', *Physical Review Letters* 59: 381–4.

Bak, P., Tang, C. and Wiesenfeld, K. (1988) 'Self-organised criticality', *Physical Review* 38 (A): 364–74.

Baker, A. (2007) 'Occam's razor in science: a case study from biogeography', *Biology and Philosophy* 22: 193–215.

Bakewell, O. (2010) 'Some reflections on structure and agency in migration theory', *Journal of Ethnic and Migration Studies* 36 (10): 1689–1708.

Barnes, T. (2009) 'Placing ideas: genius loci, heterotopia and geography's quantitative revolution', *Progress in Human Geography* 28 (5): 565–95.

Barnett, C. (2010) 'Geography and ethics: justice unbound', *Progress in Human Geography* 35 (2): 246–55.

Barratt, P. (2012) '"My magic cam": a more-than-representational account of the climbing assemblage', *Area* 44 (1): 46–53.

Barry, B. (1995) *Justice as Impartiality: A Treatise on Social Justice, Vol. 2*. Oxford: Clarendon Press.

Bar-Yam, Y. (2004) *Making Things Work: Solving Complex Problems in a Complex World*. Cambridge, MA: New England Complex Systems Institute/Knowledge Press.

Bar-Yam, Y. (2011) *About Complex Systems*. Cambridge, MA: New England Complex Systems Institute. http://www.necsi.edu/guide/study.html [accessed 19/03/04].

Baschlind, E. (2002) Being Feminist in Geography - Feminist Geography in the German-Speaking Academy: History of a Movement', in P. Moss (ed.) *Feminist Geography in Practice: Research and Methods*. Oxford: Blackwell. pp. 25–30.

Baudrillard, J. (1981) *Simulacra and Simulation* (trans. S.F. Glaser, 1994). Michigan: University of Michigan Press.

Bavendamm, G., Hagemann, K. and James, L. (2004) 'The Revolutionary and Napoleonic Wars: New approaches and future questions of research. Report on the workshop of the international research project, working group and network on "NATIONS, BORDERS, IDENTITIES: The Revolutionary and Napoleonic Wars in European Experiences and Memories." (1st Nov, 2004, Military History Research Institute)'. http://www.unc.edu/nbi/texte/W1-report.pdf [accessed 26/01/14].

Bawaka Country including Suchet-Pearson, S., Wright, S., Lloyd, K. and Burarrwanga, L. (2013) 'Caring *as* country: towards an ontology of co-becoming in natural resource management', *Asia Pacific Viewpoint* 52 (2): 185–97.

Beauchamp, T.L. and Childress, J.F. (1979) *Principles of Biomedical Ethics*. New York: Oxford University Press.

de Beauvoir, S. (1949/2010) *The Second Sex*. Trans. C. Borde and S. Malovany-Chevalier London: Vintage/Random House.

Bee, B. (2011) 'Women weathering the climate: gendered knowledge and adaptive capacities in Central Mexico'. PhD thesis, Pennsylvania State University. https://etda.libraries.psu.edu/paper/12428/7746 [accessed 05/10/13].

Bee, B. (2013) 'Who reaps what is sown? A feminist inquiry into climate change adaptation in two Mexican *ejidos*', *ACME: An International E-Journal for Critical Geographies* 12 (1): 131–54.

Benavente, J., Harris, D.L., Austin, T.P. and Vila-Concejo, A. (2011) 'Medium term behaviour and evolution of a beach cusps systems in a low energy beach, Port Stephens, NSW, Australia', *Journal of Coastal Research* SI 64: 170–4.

Berg, L.D. (1993) 'Between modernism and postmodernism', *Progress in Human Geography* 17 (4): 490–507.

Berger, P.L. and Luckmann, T. (1966) *The Social Construction of Reality: Everything That Passes for Knowledge in Society*. London: Penguin.

Bergoffen, D. (2010) 'Simone de Beauvoir' in E.N. Zalta (ed.) *The Stanford Encyclopedia of Philosophy* (Fall 2010 edition). http://plato.stanford.edu/archives/fall2010/entries/beauvoir/ [accessed 25/08/13].

Berry, B. and Garrison, W.L. (1958) 'The functional bases of the central place hierarchy', *Economic Geography* 34: 145–54.

Berthling, I. (2011) 'Beyond confusion: rock glaciers as cryo-conditioned landforms', *Geomorphology* 131: 98–106. http://www.uio.no/studier/emner/matnat/geofag/GEG2130/h12/berthling-rock-glacier-confusion-2012.pdf.

Bhaskar, R. (1975) *A Realist Theory of Science*. Hassocks: Harvester Press.

Bhaskar, R. (1979/2005) *The Possibility of Naturalism: A Philosophical Critique of the Contemporary Human Sciences* (3rd edition). London: Routledge (Taylor & Francis e-Library).

Bhaskar, R. (1989) 'Societies.' Chapter 2 of *The Possibility of Naturalism*, Hemel Hempstead: Harvester Wheatsheaf, reproduced in M. Archer, R. Bhaskar, A. Collier, T. Lawson and A. Norrie (eds) *Critical Realism: Essential Readings*. Abingdon: Routledge. pp. 206–57.

Bhaskar, R. (1998)' General introduction', in M. Archer, R. Bhaskar, A. Collier, T. Lawson and A. Norrie (eds) *Critical Realism: Essential Readings*. Abingdon: Routledge. pp. ix–xxiv.

Bird, A. (2000) *Thomas Kuhn*. Chesham: Acumen Publishing Limited.

Bird, A. (2013) 'Thomas Kuhn', in E.N. Zalta (ed.) *The Stanford Encyclopedia of Philosophy* (Spring 2013 edition). http://plato.stanford.edu/archives/spr2013/entries/thomas-kuhn/ [accessed 19/03/13].

Bishop, M. and Shroder, J.F. (2004) *Geographic Information Science and Mountain Geomorphology*. Amsterdam: Springer.

Blaikie, P.M. (1985) *The Political Economy of Soil Erosion in Developing Countries*. London: Longman.

Blaikie, P.M. and Brookfield, H.C. (1987) *Land Degradation and Society*. London: Methuen.

Blaser, M. (2014) 'Ontology and indigeneity: on the political ontology of heterogeneous assemblages', *Cultural Geographies* 21 (1): 49–58.

Blomley, C. (2007) 'Critical geography: anger and hope', *Progress in Human Geography* 31 (1): 53–65.

Bluck, B.J. (2011) 'Structure of gravel beaches and their relationship to tidal range', *Sedimentology* 58: 994–1006.

Bonnet, M. (2009) 'Systemic wisdom, the "selving" of nature, and knowledge transformation: education for the "greater whole"', *Studies in Philosophy of Education* 28: 39–49.

Booker, K.M. (2007) *Postmodern Hollywood: What's New in Film and Why It Makes Us Feel So Strange*. Westport, CT: Praeger.

Bortolotti, L. (2008) *An Introduction to the Philosophy of Science*. Cambridge: Polity Press.

Boschma, R. (2007) 'Path creation, path dependence and regional development', in J. Simmie and J. Carpenter (eds) *Path Dependence and the Evolution of City Regional Economies*. Working Paper series no. 197. Oxford: Oxford Brookes University. pp. 40–55.

Boschma, R., Eriksson, R. and Lindgren, U. (2008) 'How does labour mobility affect the performance of plants? The importance of relatedness and geographical proximity', *Journal of Economic Geography* 9: 169–90.

Bouillon, H. (1998) 'Book review: Gunnar Andersson, Criticism and the History of Science. Kuhn's, Lakatos's and Feyerabend's Criticisms of Critical Rationalism (Philosophy of History and Culture, Vol. 13). Leiden, New York, Köln: Brill', *Journal for General Philosophy of Science* 29: 133–45.

Bowell, T. (2011) 'Feminist standpoint theory', in J. Fieser and B. Dowden (eds) *Internet Encyclopedia of Philosophy*. http://www.iep.utm.edu/fem-stan/ [accessed 23/08/13].

Bracken, L.J. and Oughten, E.A. (2013) 'Making sense of policy implementation: the construction and uses of expertise and evidence in managing freshwater environments', *Environmental Science & Policy* 30: 10–18.

Braun, B. and Wainwright, J. (2001) 'Nature, poststructuralism, and politics', in N. Castree and Braun, B. (eds) *Social Nature: Theory, Practice, and Politics*. Oxford: Blackwell. pp. 41–63.

Brierley, G., Fryirs, K., Callum, C., Tadaki, M., Huang, H.Q. and Blue, B. (2013) 'Reading the landscape: integrating the theory and practice of geomorphology to develop place-based understandings of river systems', *Progress in Physical Geography* 37 (5): 601–21.

Brown, A. Fleetwood, S. and Robert, J. (2001) 'The marriage of critical realism and Marxism: happy, unhappy or on the rocks?' in A. Brown, S. Fleetwood and J. Roberts (eds) *Critical Realism and Marxism*. Abingdon: Routledge. pp. 1–22.

Brown, H. (1999) 'The methodological roles of theory in science', in B. Rhoads and C. Thorn (eds.) *The Scientific Nature of Geomorphology*. Chicester: Wiley. 4–20.

Brown, K. and Dilley, R. (2012) 'Ways of knowing for "response-ability" in more-than-human encounters: the role of anticipatory knowledges in outdoor access with dogs', *Area* 44 (1): 37–45.

Browne, K., Norcup, J., Robson, E. and Sharp, J. (2013) 'What's in a name? Removing women from the Women and Geography Study Group', *Area* 45 (1): 7–8.

Bruck, J.N. (2013) 'Decades-long social memory in bottlenose dolphins', *Proceedings of the Royal Society B: Biological Sciences* 280 (1768): 20131726. doi: 10.1098/rspb.2013.1726.

Buller, H. (2014) 'Animal geographies I', *Progress in Human Geography* 38 (2): 308–18.

Butler, J. (2004) 'Jacques Derrida', in *London Review of Books* 26 (21): 32. http://www.lrb.co.uk/v26/n21/judith-butler/jacques-derrida [accessed 14/08/13].

Buttimer, A. (1974) *Values in Geography*. Commission on College Geography Resource Paper 24. Washington, DC: Association of American Geographers.

Cadman, L. (2009) 'Non-representational theory/Non-representational geographies', in R. Kitchin, and N. Thrift (eds) *International Encyclopaedia of Human Geography*. Amsterdam: Elsevier. pp. 456–63.

Calberac, Y. (2011) 'Why should geographers lost in the field read Roland Barthes?' *ACME* 20 (1): 21–41.

Caldarelli, G., Marsili, M. and Zhang, Y.-C. (1997) 'A prototype model of stock exchange', *Europhysics Letters* 40 (5): 479.

Campbell, T. (2010) 'Ethics of care', in R.H. Corrigan and M.E. Farrell (eds) *Ethics: A University Guide*. Gloucester: Progressive Frontiers Press. pp. 79–108.

Carmalt, J.C. (2011) 'Human rights, care ethics and situated universal norms', *Antipode* 43 (2): 296–325.

Carson, M.A. and Kirkby, M.J. (1972) *Hillslope Form and Process*. Cambridge: Cambridge University Press.

Castree, N. (1994) 'Teaching history, philosophy and theory: notes on representing Marxism and "Marxist geography"', *Journal of Geography in Higher Education* 18 (1): 33–42.

Castree, N. (2005) 'Is Geography a science?' In N. Castree, A. Rogers and D. Sherman (eds) *Questioning Geography*. Oxford: Blackwell. pp. 57–79.

Castree, N. (2008) 'The Limits to Capital (1982): David Harvey', in P. Hubbard, R. Kitchin, and G. Valentine (eds) *Key Texts in Human Geography*. London: Sage. pp. 61–70.

Castree, N. (2011) 'David Harvey', in P. Hubbard, and R. Kitchin (eds) *Key Thinkers on Space and Place*. London: Sage. pp. 234–41.

Castree, N. (2012) 'Progressing physical geography', *Progress in Physical Geography* 36 (3): 298–304.

Castree, N., Chatterton, P.A., Heynan, N., Larner, W. and Wright, M.W. (eds) (2010) *The Point Is to Change It: Geographies of Hope and Survival in an Age of Crisis*. London: Wiley-Blackwell.

Cavagna, A. and Giardina, I. (2008) 'The seventh starling', *Significance* 5 (2): 62–6.

Chamberlin, T.C. (1890) 'The method of multiple working hypotheses', *Science* (old series) 15: 92-6; reprinted 1965, 148: 754-9.

Chappell, J.E. Jr (1991) 'On realism, in geography and elsewhere', *The Professional Geographer* 43 (2): 228–31.

Chin, A. and Phillips, J.D. (2007) 'The self-organization of step-pools in mountain streams', *Geomorphology* 83: 346–58.

Church, M. (2010) 'The trajectory of geomorphology', *Progress in Physical Geography* 34 (3): 265–86. doi: 10.1177/0309133310363992.

Clarke, S. (1981) *The Foundations of Structuralism: A Critique of Lévi-Strauss and the Structuralist Movement*. Brighton: Harvester Press.

Clifford, N. (1993) 'Formation of riffle-pool sequences: field evidence for an autogenetic process', *Sedimentary Geology* 85 (1–4): 39–51.

Clingerman, F., Treanor, B., Drenthen, M. and Utsler, D. (2014) *Interpreting Nature: The Emerging Field of Environmental Hermeneutics*. New York: Fordham University Press.

Cloke, P., Philo, C. and Sadler, D. (1991) *Approaching Human Geography: An Introduction to Contemporary Theoretical Debates*. London: Paul Chapman Publishing.

Cochrane, A. (2007) 'Environmental ethics', in J. Fieser and B. Dowden (eds) *Internet Encyclopedia of Philosophy*. http://www.iep.utm.edu/envi-eth/ [accessed 25/10/13].

Coe, N.M. (2011) 'Geographies of production I: an evolutionary revolution?' *Progress in Human Geography* 35 (1): 81–91.

Coen, J.L. and Schroeder, W. (2013) 'Use of spatially refined satellite remote sensing fire detection data to initialize and evaluate coupled weather-wildfire growth model simulations', *Geophysical Research Letters* 40: 5536–41.

Colacino, C. and Grehan, J.R. (2003) 'Suppression at the frontiers of evolutionary biology: Léon Coizat's case'. English version of 'Ostracismo alle frontiere della biologia evoluzionistica: il caso Léon Croizat', in M. Capria (ed), *Scienza e Democrazia*. Napoli: Liguori Editore: pp. 195–220. Available online at http://www.academia.edu/2072287/LEON_CROIZATS_CASE [accessed 12/05/2014].

Collier, A. (1994) *Critical Realism: An Introduction to Roy Bhaskar's Philosophy*. London: Verso.

Colls, R. (2011) 'Feminism, bodily difference and non-representational geographies', *Transactions of the Institute of British Geographers* NS 37: 430–45.

Comte, A. (1830) *Course de Philosophie Positive*. Reproduced in S. Andreski (ed.) (1974) *The Essential Comte*. London: Croom Helm.

Cope, M. (2002) 'Feminist epistemology in Geography', in P. Moss (ed.) *Feminist Geography in Practice: Research and Methods*. Oxford: Blackwell. pp. 43–56

Corson, M.W. and Palka, E.J. (2004) 'Geotechnology, the US Military, and War', in S.D. Brunn, S.L. Cutter and J.W. Harrington, Jr (eds) *Geography and Technology*. Dordrecht: Kluwer Academic Publishers. pp. 401–30.

Cosgrove, D. and della Dora, V. (eds) (2008) *High Place: Cultural Geographies of Mountains, Ice and Science*. London: IB Tauris.

Couper, P.R. (2007) 'Fluvial geomorphology and semiotics: a Wittgensteinian perspective of the "divide" between human and physical geography'. *Transactions of the Institute of British Geographers* NS 32: 279–94.

Couper, P.R. and Ansell, L. (2012) 'Researching the outdoors: exploring the unsettled frontier between science and adventure', *Area* 44 (1): 14–21.

Couper, P. and Maddock, I. (2001) 'Subaerial river bank processes and interaction with other bank erosion mechanisms on the River Arrow, Warwickshire, UK', *Earth Surface Processes and Landforms* 26 (6): 631–46.

Crawford, C.S. (2004) 'Actor-Network Theory' in G. Ritzer (ed.) *Encyclopedia of Social Theory*. London: Sage. 1–4.

Creswell, T. (1996) *In Place/Out of Place: Geography, Ideology, and Transgression*. Minneapolis: University of Minnesota Press.

Creswell, T. (2013) *Geographic Thought: A Critical Introduction*. Chichester: Wiley-Blackwell.

Culver, D.C. and Fong, D.W. (1994) 'Small scale and large scale biogeography of subterranean crustacean faunas of the Virginias', *Hydrobiologia* 287: 3–9.

Curry, M.R. (1996) 'Commentary 1', in M.R. Curry, R. Lee and A. Buttimer (1996) 'Buttimer, A. 1974: Values in geography. Commission on College Geography Resource Paper 24. Washington DC. Association of American Geographers', *Progress in Human Geography* 20 (4): 513–19.

Curtis, P. and Hodgson, M. (2008) 'Student researching al-Qaida tactics held for six days', *Guardian* 24/05/08. http://www.theguardian.com/education/2008/may/24/highereducation.uk [accessed 27/05/13].

Curtis, S. and Riva, M. (2010a) 'Health geographies I: complexity theory and human health', *Progress in Human Geography* 34 (2): 215–23.

Curtis, S. and Riva, M. (2010b) 'Health geographies II: complexity and health care systems and policy', *Progress in Human Geography* 34 (4): 513–20.

Curtis, S., Southall, H., Congdon, P. and Dodgeon, N. (2004) 'Area effects on health variation over the life-course: analysis of the longitudinal study sample in England using new data on area of residence in childhood', *Social Science and Medicine* 58: 57–74.

Dancing on the Ceiling (1986) Lionel Ritchie. Dancing on the Ceiling. 6158ML. Detroit, MI: Motown.

D'Andrea, M., Fiorucci, P. and Holmes, T.P. (2010) 'A stochastic forest fire model for future land cover scenarios assessment', *Natural Hazards and Earth System Sciences* 10: 2161–7.

Datta, A. (2012) '"Where is the global city?" Visual narratives of London among east European migrants', *Urban Studies* 49 (8): 1725–40.

Davies, A. (2013) 'Identity and the assemblages of protest: the spatial politics of the Royal Indian Navy Mutiny, 1946', *Geoforum* 48: 24–32.

Davis, W.M. (1899) 'The geographical cycle', *The Geographical Journal* 14 (5): 481–504.

Davis, W.M. (1915) 'The principles of geographical description', *Annals of the Association of American Geographers* 5: 61–105.

Daya, S. (2011) 'Performing place, mobility and identity in South Africa', *Area* 43 (4): 488–94.

Dear, M.J. (1988) 'The postmodern challenge: reconstructing Human Geography', *Transactions of the Institute of British Geographers* NS 13: 262–74.

Dear, M.J. (2000) *The Postmodern Urban Condition*. Oxford: Blackwell.

Dear, M. and Wassmansdorf, G. (1993) 'Postmodern consequences', *Geographical Review* 83 (3): 321–6.

Deecke,V.B.,Nykänen, M., Foote,A.D. and Janik,V.M. (2011) 'Vocal behaviour and feeding ecology of killer whales Orcinas orca around Shetland, UK', *Aquatic Biology* 13: 79-88.

Deleuze, G. and Guattari, F. (1987) *A Thousand Plateaus* (trans. B. Massumi). Minneapolis: University of Minnesota Press.

Demeritt, D. (1996) 'Social theory and the reconstruction of science and geography', *Transactions of the Institute of British Geographers* 21: 484–503.

Derrida, J. (1976) *On Grammatology* (trans. G.C. Spivak). Baltimore: Johns Hopkins University Press.

Desbiens, C. (2010) 'Step lightly, then move forward: exploring feminist directions for northern research', *The Canadian Geographer* 54 (4): 410–16.

Dewsbury, J.D. and Naylor, S. (2002) 'Practising geographical knowledge: fields, bodies and dissemination', *Area* 34: 253-60.

Dittmer, J. (2006) 'Teaching the social construction of regions in regional geography courses: or, why do vampires come from Eastern Europe?' *Journal of Geography in Higher Education* 30 (1): 49–61.

Dittmer, J. (2013) 'Geopolitical assemblages and complexity', *Progress in Human Geography* doi: 10.1177/0309132513501405.

Dixon, D.P. and Jones, J.P. III (2006) 'Feminist geographies of difference, relation, and construction', in S. Aitken and G. Valentine (eds) *Approaches to Human Geography*. London: Sage. 42–56.

Doel, M.A. (1999) *Poststructuralist Geographies: The Diabolical Art of Spatial Science*. New York: Rowman & Littlefield.

Doel, M.A. (2007) 'Classics in human geography revisited: Dear, M. 1988: The postmodern challenge: reconstructing human geography. Transactions of the Institute of British Geographers NS 13, 262–74: Commentary 1', *Progress in Human Geography* 31 (5): 675–8.

Dolphin Tale (2011) Smith, C. M. California: Warner Bros. [Film].

Donovan, K., Sidaway, J.D. and Stewart, I. (2011) 'Bridging the geo-divide: reflections on an interdisciplinary (ESRC/NERC) studentship', *Transactions of the Institute of British Geographers* NS 36: 9–14.

Dorling, D. (2010) 'All connected? Geographies of race, death, wealth, votes and birth', *The Geographical Journal* 176 (3): 186–98.

Dorling, D. (2013) 'Fairness and the changing fortunes of people in Britain', *Journal of the Royal Statistical Society A* 176 (1): 97–128.

Douven, I. (2011) 'Abduction', in E. Zalta (ed) *The Stanford Encyclopedia of Philosophy* (Spring 2011 edition). http://plato.stanford.edu/archives/spr2011/entries/abduction/ [accessed 19/03/14].

Downs, P.W. and Gregory, K.J. (2004) *River Channel Management: Towards Sustainable Catchment Hydrosystems*. London: Arnold.

Durrheim, K. and Dixon, J. (2001) 'The role of place and metaphor in racial exclusion: South Africa's beaches as sites of shifting racialization', *Ethnic and Racial Studies* 24 (3): 433–50.

Dyer, D. and Demeritt, D. (2008) 'Un-ethical review? Why it is wrong to apply the medical model of research governance to human geography', *Progress in Human Geography* 33 (1): 46–64.

Egner, H. and von Elverfeldt, K. (2009) 'A bridge over troubled waters? Systems theory and dialogue in geography', *Area* 41 (3): 319–28.

Elavsky, M. (2009) 'United as ONE: Live 8 and the politics of the global music media spectacle', *Journal of Popular Music Studies* 21 (4): 384–410.

Elder-Vass, D. (2012) *The Reality of Social Construction.* Cambridge: Cambridge University Press.

Emery, S.B., Perks, M.T. and Bracken, L.J. (2013) 'Negotiating river restoration: the role of divergent framing in environmental decision-making', *Geoforum* 47: 167–77.

Entrikin, N. (1976) 'Contemporary humanism in Geography', *Annals of the Association of American Geographers* 66 (4): 615–32.

Evans, J. and Randalls, S. (2008) 'Geography and paratactical interdisciplinarity: views from the ESRC–NERC PhD studentship programme', *Geoforum* 39 (2): 581–92.

Evans, S. (2013) Gendered Frontiers: Reporting from the RGS Expeditions Archive. Royal Geographical Society (with Institute of British Geographers) Annual International Conference, London, August 2013.

Evans, S.G. and Clague, J.J. (1994) 'Recent climatic change and catastrophic geomorphic processes in mountain environments', *Geomorphology* 10: 107–28.

Evers, C. (2009) '"The Point": surfing, geography and a sensual life of men and masculinity on the Gold Coast, Australia', *Social and Cultural Geography* 10 (8): 893–908.

Farid, F. (2009) 'Terror at the beach: Arab bodies and the somatic violence of white cartographic anxiety in Australia and Palestine/Israel', *Social Semiotics* 19 (1): 59–78.

Favis-Mortlock, D. (2004) 'Self-organization and cellular automata models', in J. Wainright and M. Mulligan (eds) *Environmental Modelling: Finding Simplicity in Complexity.* Chichester: Wiley. pp. 349–70.

Favis-Mortlock, D. and de Boer, D. (2003) 'Simple at heart? Landscape as a self-organizing complex system', in S. Trudgill and A. Roy (eds) *Contemporary Meanings in Physical Geography: From What to Why?* London: Arnold. pp. 127–72.

Feminist Pedagogy Working Group (2002) 'Defining feminism?' in P. Moss (ed.) *Feminist Geography in Practice: Research and Methods.* Oxford: Blackwell. pp. 21–4.

Ferrarotti, F. (1999) 'The social character of science: the lessons of positivism', *International Journal of Politics, Culture, and Society* 12 (4): 535–53.

Feyerabend, P. (1975) *Against Method.* London: Humanities Press.

Flowerdew, R. (2011) 'Peter Haggett', in P. Hubbard and R. Kitchin (eds) *Key Thinkers on Space and Place* (2nd edition). London: Sage. pp. 205–10.

Fløysand, A. and Jakobsen, S.-E. (2011) 'The complexity of innovation: a relational turn', *Progress in Human Geography* 35 (3): 328–44.

Fonstad, M.A. and Marcus, W.A. (2003) 'Self-organized criticality in riverbank systems', *Annals of the Association of American Geographers* 93 (2): 281–96.

Ford, N. and Brown, D. (2006) *Surfing and Social Theory: Experience, Embodiment and Narrative of the Dream Glide.* Abingdon: Routledge.

Forsyth, T. (2008) 'Political ecology and the epistemology of social justice', *Geoforum* 39: 756–64.

Foucault, M. (1969) *Archaeology of Knowledge* (trans. A.M.S. Smith, 2002). London and New York: Routledge.

Foucault, M. (1975) *Discipline and Punish: The Birth of the Prison* (trans. A. Sheridan, 1977). New York: Vintage Books.

Frick, W.F., Hayes, J.P. and Heady, P.A. III (2008) 'Island biogeography of bats in Baja California, Mexico: Patterns of bat species richness in a near-shore archipelago', *Journal of Biogeography* 35: 353–64.

Frigg, R. (2003) 'Self-organized criticality – what it is and what it isn't', *Studies in History and Philosophy of Science* 34: 613–32.

Frost-Arnold, G. (2005) 'The large scale structure of logical empiricism: unity of science and the elimination of meta-physics', *Philosophy of Science* 72: 826–38.

Fryirs, K. and Brierly, G. (2009) 'Naturalness and place in river rehabilitation', *Ecology and Society* 14 (1): 20 [online]. URL: http://www.ecologyandsociety.org/vol14/iss1/art20/ [accessed 28/10/13].

Fuller, M.R. and Peckarsky, B.L. (2011) 'Does the morphology of beaver ponds alter downstream ecosystems?' *Hydrobiologia* 668: 35–48.

Gabriel, H. (2004) *A Wonderful Use for Fire*. London: Pan Books.

Gale, T. (2009) 'Urban beaches, virtual worlds and "the end of tourism"', *Mobilities* 4 (1): 119–38.

Gallagher, M. (2011) 'Sound, space and power in a primary school', *Social & Cultural Geography* 12 (1): 47–61.

Galt, R.E. (2010) 'Scaling up political ecology: the case of illegal pesticides on fresh vegetables imported into the United States, 1996-2006', *Annals of the Association of American Geographers* 100 (2): 327-55.

Gao, J. and Xia, Z.-G. (1996) 'Fractals in physical geography', *Progress in Physical Geography* 20 (2): 178–91.

Garcia, C. and Servera, J. (2003) 'Impacts of tourism development on water demand and beach degradation on the island of Mallorca (Spain)', *Geografiska Annaler: Series A, Physical Geography* 85 (3–4): 287–300.

Geldof, B. (1986) *Is That It?* London: Sidgwick & Jackson.

Giere, R.N. (1996) 'From Wissenschaftliche Philosophie to Philosophy of Science', in R.N. Giere and A.W. Richardson (eds) *Origins of Logical Empiricism*. Minneapolis: University of Minnesota Press. pp. 335–54.

Glade, T., Anderson, M.G. and Crozier, M.J. (eds) (2006) *Landslide Hazard and Risk*. Chichester: John Wiley & Sons.

Glaser, B.G. and Strauss, A.L. (1967) *Discovery of Grounded Theory: Strategies for Qualitative Research*. Chicago: Aldine.

Glassman, J. (2011) 'Critical geography III: critical development geography', *Progress in Human Geography* 35 (5): 705–11.

Gleick, J. (1988) *Chaos: The Amazing Science of the Unpredictable*. (reproduced 1997) London: Minerva.

Gökarıksel, B. (2012) 'The intimate politics of secularism and the headscarf: the mall, the neighbourhood, and the public square in Istanbul', *Gender, Place and Culture* 19 (1): 1–20.

Gower, B. (1997) *Scientific Method: Historical and Philosophical Introduction*. Abingdon: Routledge.

Grabbatin, B. and Rossi, J. (2012) 'Political ecology: nonequilibrium science and nature-society research', *Geography Compass* 6 (5): 275–89.

Green, D.G., Leishman, T.G. and Sadedin, S. (2008) 'Dual phase evolution – a mechanism for self-organization in complex systems', in A. Minai, D. Braha and Y. Bar-Yam (eds) *Unifying Themes in Complex Systems: Proceedings of the Sixth International Conference on Complex Systems*. Berlin: Springer. pp. 58–65.

Gregory, K.J. (2000) *The Changing Nature of Physical Geography*. London: Arnold.

Gregson, N., Kothari, U., Cream, J., Dwyer, C., Holloway, S., Maddrell, A. and Rose, G. (1993) 'Gender in feminist geography', in Women and Geography Study Group, *Feminist Geographies: Explorations in Diversity and Difference*. Harlow: Longman. pp. 49–85.

Hacking, I. (1999) *The Social Construction of What?* Cambridge, MA: Harvard University Press.

Haggett, P. (1961) 'Land use and sediment yield in an old plantation tract of the Serra do Mar, Brazil', *Geographical Journal* 127: 60–62.

Hague, S., Street, J. and Savigny, H. (2008) 'The voice of the people? Musicians as political actors', *Cultural Politics* 4 (1): 5–24.

Haigh, M.J. (2002) 'Land reclamation and deep ecology: in search of a more meaningful physical geography', *Area* 34 (3): 242–52.

Haines-Young, R.H. and Petch, J.R. (1980) 'The challenge of critical rationalism for methodology in physical geography', *Progress in Physical Geography* 4 (1): 63–77.

Haines-Young, R.H. and Petch, J.R. (1981) 'Causal and functional relationships in geomorphology: a reply', *Earth Surface Processes* 6: 207–9.

Haines-Young, R.H. and Petch, J.R. (1983) 'Multiple working hypotheses: equifinality and the study of landforms', *Transactions of the Institute of British Geographers* 8 (4): 458–66.

Haines-Young, R.H. and Petch, J. (1986) *Physical Geography: Its Nature and Methods.* London: Harper & Row Ltd.

Halley, J.M., Hartley, S., Kallimanis, A.S., Kunin, W.E., Lennon, J.J. and Sgardelis, S.P. (2004) 'Uses and abuses of fractal methodology in ecology', *Ecology Letters* 7: 254–71.

Hamilton, C. (2013) *Earthmasters: The Dawn of the Age of Climate Engineering.* London: Yale University Press.

Hammond, M., Howarth, J. and Keat, R. (1991) *Understanding Phenomenology.* Oxford: Blackwell.

Hanfling, O. (1981) 'Introduction', in O. Hanfling (ed.) *Essential Readings in Logical Positivism.* Oxford: Blackwell. pp. 1-25.

Haraway, D. (2008) *When Species Meet.* Minneapolis: University of Minnesota Press.

Harman, C. (2000) *How Marxism Works* (6th edition). London: Bookmarks Publications Ltd. http://users.comcen.com.au/~marcn/redflag/archive/harman/hmw/index.html [accessed 23/02/13].

Harman, E. (1983) 'Capitalism, patriarchy and the city', in C. Baldock and B. Cass (eds) *Women, Social Welfare and the State in Australia.* Sydney: Allen & Unwin. pp. 103–20.

Harrison, S. (2001) 'On reduction and emergence in geomorphology', *Transactions of the Institute of British Geographers* 26: 327–39.

Harrison, S., Massey, D. and Richards, K. (2006) 'Complexity and emergence (another conversation)', *Area* 38 (4): 465–71.

Harvey, D. (1969) *Explanation in Geography.* London: Edward Arnold.

Harvey, D. (1973) *Social Justice and the City.* London: Arnold.

Harvey, D. (1982) *The Limits to Capital.* Oxford: Blackwell.

Harvey, D. (2002) 'Agency and community: a critical realist paradigm', *Journal for the Theory of Social Behaviour* 32 (2): 163–94.

Hausman, R., Tyson, L. and Zahidi, S. (2012) *The Global Gender Gap Report.* Geneva: World Economic Forum. http://www3.weforum.org/docs/WEF_GenderGap_Report_2012.pdf [accessed 09/09/13].

Haussman, N.S., McIntyre, T., Bumby, A.J. and Loubser, M.J. (2013) 'Referencing practices in physical geography: how well do we cite what we write?' *Progress in Physical Geography* 37 (4): 543–9.

Heffernan, J.B., Watts, D.L. and Cohen, M.J. (2013) 'Discharge competence and pattern formation in peatlands: a meta-ecosystem model of the Everglades ridge-slough landscape', *PLoS ONE* 8 (5): e64174. doi: 10.1371/journal.pone.0064174.

Heidegger, M. (1953) *Being and Time: A Translation of Sein und Zeit* (trans. J. Stambaugh, 1996). New York: SUNY Press.

Heidegger, M. (1971) 'Building dwelling thinking', in *Poetry, Language, Thought* (trans. A. Hofstadter). New York: Harper Perennial. pp. 143–59.

Heidegger, P. and Jenssen, I. (2013) 'Press release – NGOs publish 2013 list of toxic ship dumpers: German and Greek shipping companies amongst the world's worst', *NGO Shipbreaking Platform*. http://www.shipbreakingplatform.org/press-release-ngos-publish-2013-list-of-toxic-ship-dumpers-german-and-greek-shipping-com panies-amongst-the-worlds-worst/ [accessed 02/03/14].

Henning, M., Stam, E. and Wenting, R. (2013) 'Path dependence research in regional economic development: cacophony or knowledge accumulation?', *Regional Studies* 47 (8): 1348–62.

Herbert, D.T. and Matthews, J.A. (2004) 'Geography: roots and continuities', in H.A. Matthews and D.T. Herbert (eds) *Unifying Geography: Common Heritage, Shared Future*. Abingdon: Routledge. pp. 3–18.

Hesse-Biber, S. and Leavy, P. (2006) *The Practice of Qualitative Research*. London: Sage.

Heyt, F. (1999) 'Popper's Vienna: a contribution of the history of the ideas of critical rationalism', *Innovation: the European Journal of Social Science Research* 12 (4): 525–41.

Higher Education Statistics Agency Ltd (2013) 'Table 1: All staff in UK HE institutions by activity, mode of employment and gender, 2011/13', Statistics: Staff Employed at UK HE Institutions. http://www.hesa.ac.uk/index.php?option=com_content&task =view&id=1898&Itemid=239 [accessed 08/09/13].

Holt-Jensen, A. (2009) *Geography: History and Concepts: A Student's Guide* (4th edition). London: Sage.

Horton, J. (2008) 'A "sense of failure"? Everydayness and research ethics', *Children's Geographies* 6 (4): 363–83.

Horton, R.E. (1945) 'Erosional development of streams and their drainage basins; hydro-physical approach to quantitative morphology', *Geological Society of America Bulletin* 56: 275–370.

Hubbard, P., Kitchin, R., Bartley, B. and Fuller, F. (2002) *Thinking Geographically: Space, Theory and Contemporary Human Geography*. London: Continuum.

Hudson, R. (2006) 'On what's Right and keeping Left: or why Geography still needs Marxian political economy', *Antipode* 38 (2): 374–95.

Huggel, C., Clague, J. and Korup, O. (2012) 'Is climate change responsible for changing landslide activity in high mountains?', *Earth Surface Processes and Landforms* 37 (1): 77–91.

Ihde, D. (2009) *Postphenomenology and Technoscience*. New York: SUNY Press.

Imeson, A. (2011) *Desertification, Land Degradation and Sustainability*. Chichester: John Wiley & Sons.

Inkpen, R. (2005) *Science, Philosophy and Physical Geography*. Abingdon: Routledge.

Inkpen, R. (2007) 'Interpretation of erosion rates on rock surfaces', *Area* 39 (1): 31–42.

Introna, L. (2011) 'Phenomenological approaches to ethics and information technology', in E.N. Zalta (ed.) *The Stanford Encyclopedia of Philosophy* (Summer 2011 edition). http://plato.stanford.edu/archives/sum2011/entries/ethics-it-phenomenology/ [accessed 21/09/13].

Jackson, P. (1989) *Maps of Meaning: An Introduction to Cultural Geography*. London: Unwin Hyman.

Jackson, P. and Smith, S. (1981) *Social Interaction and Ethnic Segregation*. London: Academic Press.

Jackson, P. and Taylor, J. (1996) 'Geography and the cultural politics of advertising', *Progress in Human Geography* 20 (3): 356–71.

Jacobs, H. (1861) *Incidents in the Life of a Slave Girl*. Boston: Published for the Author.

Jameson, F. (1988/1998) 'Postmodernism and the consumer society', in E.A. Kaplan, (ed.) *Postmodernism and its Discontents: Theories, Practices*. London: Verso. Reproduced in F. Jameson (1998) *The Cultural Turn: Selected Writings on the Postmodern, 1983–1998*. London: Verso. pp. 1-20

Jin, Jong-Heon (2008) 'Paektudaegan: science and colonialism, memory and mapping in Korean high places', in D. Cosgrove and V. della Dora (eds) *High Places: Cultural Geographies of Mountains, Ice and Science*. London: IB Tauris. pp. 196–215.

Johnston, R. (1986) *On Human Geography*. Oxford: Blackwell.

Johnston, R. (2003) 'Geography: a different sort of discipline?' *Transactions of the Institute of British Geographers* NS 28: 133–41.

Johnston, R. (2005) 'Geography – coming apart at the seams?' in N. Castree, A. Rogers and D. Sherman (eds) *Questioning Geography*. Oxford: Blackwell. pp. 9–25.

Johnston, R. (2009) 'Geography and the social sciences tradition', in N.J. Clifford, S.P. Holloway and G. Valentine (eds) *Key Concepts in Geography* (2nd edition). London: Sage. pp. 45–65.

Johnston, R. and Sidaway, J. (2004) *Geography and Geographers: Anglo-American Human Geography since 1945* (6th edition). Abingdon: Routledge.

Jones, A. and Murphy, J.T. (2010) 'Theorizing practice in economic geography: foundations, challenges and possibilities', *Progress in Human Geography* 35 (3): 366–92.

Jöns, H. (2006) 'Dynamic hybrids and the geographies of technoscience: discussing conceptual resources beyond the human/non-human binary', *Social and Cultural Geography* 7 (4): 559–80.

Katrak, D., Dittman, S. and Seuront, L. (2008) 'Spatial variation in burrow morphology of the mud shore crab *Helograpsus haswellianus* (Brachyura, Grapsidae) in South Australian saltmarshes', *Marine & Freshwater Research* 59 (10): 902–11.

Keller, E.F. (2009) 'Organisms, machines, and thunderstorms: a history of self-organization, part two. Complexity, emergence, and stable attractors', *Historical Studies in the Natural Sciences* 39 (1): 1–31.

Kellner, D. (2013) 'Jean Baudrillard', in E.N. Zalta (ed.) *The Stanford Encyclopedia of Philosophy* (Spring 2013 edition). http://plato.stanford.edu/archives/spr2013/entries/baudrillard/ [accessed 08/04/13].

Kent, M., Gill, W.J., Weaver, R.E. and Armitage, R.P. (1997) 'Landscape and plant community boundaries in biogeography', *Progress in Physical Geography* 21 (3): 315–53.

Kershenbaum, A., Sayigh, L.S. and Janik, V.M. (2013) 'The encoding of individual identity in dolphin signature whistles: how much information is needed?', PLoS ONE 8 (10): e77671. doi: 10.1371/journal.pone.0077671.

Khamis, S. (2010) 'Braving the Burqini™: re-branding the Australian beach', *Cultural Geographies* 17 (3): 379–90.

Kill Bill: Vol. 1 (2003) Q. Tarantino, Santa Monica, CA: Miramax. [Film].

King, C.A.M. (1970) 'Feedback relationships in geomorphology', *Geografiska Annaler Series A: Physical Geography*. 52 (3/4): 147–59.

Kingsolver, B. (2013) *Flight Behaviour*. London: Faber & Faber.

Kovalenko, K.E., Thomaz, S.M. and Warfe, D.M. (2012) 'Habitat complexity: approaches and future directions', *Hydrobiologia* 685: 1–17.

Kruse, R.J. III (2012) 'The making of the *Piano Bar*: landscape, art, and discourse in Biscayne Bay', *Southeastern Geographer* 52 (2): 131–45.

Kuhn, T. (1962/2012) *The Structure of Scientific Revolutions* (50th anniversary edition) (2012). Chicago: University of Chicago Press.

Kuhn, T. (1969) 'Postscript', in T. Kuhn (2012) *The Structure of Scientific Revolutions* (50th anniversary edition). Chicago: University of Chicago Press. pp.173–208.

Kuhn, T. (1974) 'Second thoughts on paradigms', in F. Suppe (ed.) *The Structure of Scientific Theories*. Urbana, IL: University of Illinois Press. pp. 459–82.

Kwan, M.-P. and Schwanen, T. (2009) 'Quantitative revolution 2: the critical (re)turn', *The Professional Geographer* 61 (3): 283–91.

Ladle, R.J. and Whittaker, R.J. (eds) (2011) *Conservation Biogeography*. Chichester: John Wiley & Sons.

Ladyman, J. (2002) *Understanding Philosophy of Science*. Abingdon: Routledge.

Lane, S.N. (2001) 'Constructive comments on D. Massey's "Space-time, 'science' and the relationship between physical geography and human geography"', *Transactions of the Institute of British Geographers* 26 (2): 243–56.

Lane, S.N. and Richards, K.S. (1997) 'Linking river channel form and process: time, space and causality revisited', *Earth Surface Processes and Landforms* 22: 249–60.

Langford, M. and Higgs, G. (2010) 'Accessibility and public service provision: evaluation of the impacts of the Post Office Network Change Programme in the UK', *Transactions of the Institute of British Geographers* NS 35: 585–601.

Latham, A. (2011) 'Edward W. Soja', in P. Hubbard and R. Kitchin (eds) *Key Thinkers on Space and Place* (2nd edition). London: Sage. pp. 380–6.

Latour, B. (1987) *Science in Action: How to Follow Scientists and Engineers Through Society*. Cambridge, MA: Harvard University Press.

Latour, B. (2004) *Politics of Nature: How to Bring the Sciences into Democracy*. Cambridge, MA: Harvard University Press.

Latour, B. and Woolgar, S. (1979) *Laboratory Life: The Construction of Scientific Facts*. London: Sage.

Lawson, V. (2009) 'Instead of radical geography, how about caring geography?' *Antipode* 41 (1): 210–13.

Lawson, V. and Staeheli, L. (1991) 'On critical realism, human geography, and arcane sects!' *The Professional Geographer* 43 (2): 231–3.

Lazarus, E.D., McNamara, D.E., Smith, M.D., Gopalakrishnan, S. and Murray, A.B. (2011) 'Emergent behaviour in a coupled economic and coastline model for beach nourishment', *Nonlinear Processes in Geophysics* 18: 989–99.

Leach, E. (1970) *Claude Lévi-Strauss*. Chicago: University of Chicago Press.

Lee, E. (2013) 'The energies of activism: rethinking agency in contemporary climate change activism', PhD Thesis, University of Durham. http://etheses.dur.ac.uk/6953/ [accessed 27/06/13].

Leopold, A. (1949) *A Sand County Almanac and Sketches Here and There*. Oxford: Oxford University Press. Reproduced in C. Meine (ed.) (2013) *Aldo Leopold: A Sand County Almanac & Other Writings on Ecology and Conservation*. New York: Literary Classics of the United States (Library of America).

Leopold, L.B. and Maddock, T. Jr (1953) *The Hydraulic Geometry of Stream Channels and Some Physiographic Implications.* US Geological Survey Professional Paper No. 252.

Leopold, L.B. and Wolman, L.G. (1960) 'River meanders', *Bulletin of the Geological Sciences of America* 71: 769–94.

Ley, D. (1981) 'Cultural/humanistic geography', *Progress in Human Geography* 5 (2): 249–57.

Life of Pi (2012) A. Lee, Los Angeles, CA: Fox 2000 [Film].

Livingstone, D.N. (1992) *The Geographical Tradition.* Oxford: Blackwell.

Lorimer, H. (2005) 'Classics in human geography revisited: Jackson, P. (1989) Maps of Meaning: an introduction to cultural geography. London: Unwin Hyman', *Progress in Human Geography* 29 (6): 741–3.

Lyotard, J.-F. (1984) *The Postmodern Condition: A Report on Knowledge* (trans. G. Bennington and B. Massumi) (1984). Manchester: Manchester University Press.

Macfarlane, B. (2009) *Researching with Integrity: The Ethics of Academic Research.* Abingdon: Routledge.

Macfarlane, B. and Saitoh, Y. (2008) 'Research ethics in Japanese higher education: faculty attitudes and cultural mediation', *Journal of Academic Ethics* 6 (3): 181–95.

Mackin, J.H. (1948) 'Concept of the graded river', *Bulletin of the Geological Society of America* 59: 463–512.

Maddock, I., Harby, A., Kemp, P. and Wood, P.J. (eds) (2013) *Ecohydraulics: An Integrated Approach.* Chichester: John Wiley & Sons.

Maddrell, A. (2009) *Complex Locations: Women's Geographical Work in the UK, 1850–1970.* London: Wiley-Blackwell.

Malamud, B.D., Morein, G. and Turcotte, D.L. (1998) 'Forest fires: an example of self-organized critical behavior', *Science* 281: 1840–2.

Mallon, R. (2013) 'Naturalistic approaches to social construction', in E.N. Zalta (ed.) *The Stanford Encyclopedia of Philosophy* (Fall 2013 edition) http://plato.stanford.edu/archives/fall2013/entries/social-construction-naturalistic/ [accessed 22/09/13].

Mandelbrot, B.B. (1967) 'How long is the coast of Britain? Statistical self-similarity and fractional dimension', *Science* NS 156: 636–8.

Mandelbrot, B.B. (1983) *The Fractal Geometry of Nature.* New York, NY: Henry Holt & Co.

Mandelbrot, B.B. (1989) 'Fractal geometry: what is it, and what does it do?' *Proceedings of the Royal Society of London A* 423: 3–16.

Martin, R. (2010) 'Roepke Lecture in Economic Geography – rethinking regional path dependence: beyond lock-in to evolution', *Economic Geography* 86 (1): 1–27.

Martin, R. and Sunley, P. (2010) 'The place of path dependence in an evolutionary perspective on the economic landscape', in R. Boschma and R. Martin (eds) *Handbook of Evolutionary Economic Geography.* Chichester: Edward Elgar. pp. 62–92.

Marx, W. and Bornmann, L. (2012) 'The emergence of plate tectonics and the Kuhnian model of paradigm shift: a bibliometric case study based on the Anna Karenina principle', *Scientometrics* 94: 595–614.

Masselink, G. and Pattiaratchi, C.B. (1998) 'Morphological evolution of beach cusps and associated swash circulation patterns', *Marine Geology* 146: 93–113.

Massey, D. (1999) 'Space-time, "science" and the relationship between physical geography and human geography', *Transactions of the Institute of British Geographers* 24: 261–76.

Matthews, J.A. and Herbert, D.T. (eds) (2004) *Unifying Geography: Common Heritage, Shared Future.* Abingdon: Routledge.

May, J. (2011) 'Zombie geographies and the undead city', *Social & Cultural Geography* 11 (3): 285–98.

Mayo, D.J. (2010) 'Toward progressive critical rationalism: exchanges with Alan Musgrave', in D.J Mayo and A. Spanos (eds) *Error and Inference: Recent Exchanges on Experimental Reasoning, Reliability, and the Objectivity and Rationality of Science.* Cambridge: Cambridge University Press. 113–24. http://www.phil.vt.edu/dmayo/personal_website/Ch%203%20Crit%20progressive%20rationalism%20Musgrave.pdf [03-01-131].

Mayo, D.J. (2013) 'Critical rationalism and its failure to withstand critical scrutiny', in C. Cheyne, and J. Worrall (eds) *Rationality and Reality.* Amsterdam: Springer. pp. 1–96.http://www.phil.vt.edu/dmayo/personal_website/XXXX%282006%29%20Critical%20Rationalism%20and%20Its%20Failure%20to%20Withstand%20Critical%20Scrutiny.pdf [accessed on 12/05/2014].

McAuliffe, C. (2012) 'Graffiti or street art? Negotiating the moral geographies of the creative city', *Journal of Urban Affairs* 34 (2): 189–206.

McCormack, D. (2012) 'Geography and abstraction: towards an affirmative critique', *Progress in Human Geography* 36 (6): 715–34.

McDowell, L. (1993a) 'Space, place and gender relations: Part I. Feminist empiricism and the geography of social relations', *Progress in Human Geography* 17 (2): 157–79.

McDowell, L. (1993b) 'Space, place and gender relations: Part II. Identity, difference, feminist geometries and geographies', *Progress in Human Geography* 17 (3): 305–18.

McEwen, L. and Jones, O. (2012) 'Building local/lay flood knowledges into community flood resilience planning after the July 2007 floods, Gloucestershire, UK', *Hydrology Research* 43 (5): 675–88.

McMahon, E. (2005) '*Puberty Blues* takes feminist generationalism to the beach', *Australian Feminist Studies* 20 (48): 281–9.

McQuillan, C. (2012) 'German Idealism', in J. Fieser and B. Dowden (eds) *Internet Encyclopedia of Philosophy.* http://www.iep.utm.edu/germidea/ [accessed 12/11/13].

Merleau-Ponty, M. (1945) *Phenomenology of Perception* (trans. C. Smith 1958), reprinted (2002). London: Routledge.

Miller, A.J. and Sassler, S. (2012) 'The construction of gender among working-class cohabiting couples', *Qualitative Sociology* 35 (4): 427–46.

Mitchell, D. (2011) 'Peter Jackson', in P. Hubbard, and R. Kitchin (eds) *Key Thinkers on Space and Place.* London: Sage. pp. 257–63.

Mitchelson, M.L., Alderman, D.H. and Popke, E.J. (2007) 'Branded: the economic geographies of streets named in honor of Reverend Dr. Martin Luther King Jr.', *Social Science Quarterly* 88 (1): 120–45.

Monk, J. and Hanson, S. (1982) 'On not excluding half of the human in human geography', *The Professional Geographer* 34: 11–23. Reproduced in T.S. Oakes and P.L. Price (eds) (2008) *The Cultural Geography Reader.* Abingdon: Routledge. pp. 365–72.

Montello, D.R. and Sutton, P.C. (2013) *An Introduction to Scientific Research Methods in Geography and Environmental Studies* (2nd edition). London: Sage.

Morrow, V. (2008) 'Ethical dilemmas in research with children and young people about their social environments', *Children's Geographies* 6 (1): 49–61.

Müller, M. (2006) 'Discourses of postmodern epistemology: radical impetus lost?' *Progress in Development Studies* 6 (1): 306–20.

Murdoch, J. (2005) *Post-structuralist Geography: A Guide to Relational Space.* London: Sage.

Murray, A.B., Lazarus, E., Ashton, A., Baas, A., Coco, G., Coulthard, T., Fonstad, M., Haff, P., McNamara, D., Paola, C., Pelletier, J. and Reinhardt, L. (2009) 'Geomorphology, complexity, and the emerging science of the Earth's surface', *Geomorphology* 103: 496–505.

Murzi, M. (2005) 'Jules Henri Poincaré', in J. Fieser and B. Dowden (eds) *Internet Encyclopedia of Philosophy*. http://www.iep.utm.edu/poincare/ [accessed 30/12/13].

Musgrave, A.E. (2010) 'Critical rationalism, explanation and severe tests', in D. G. Mayo and A. Spanos (eds) *Error and Inference: Recent Exchanges on Experimental Reasoning, Reliability, and the Objectivity and Rationality of Science*. Cambridge: Cambridge University Press. pp. 88–112.

Nagakawa, Y. and Payne, P.G. (2011) 'Experiencing beach in Australia: study abroad students' perspectives', *Australian Journal of Environmental Education* 27 (1): 94–108.

Nagel, K. and Paczuski, M. (1995) 'Emergent traffic jams', *Physical Review* E 51: 2909–18.

Nakhnikian, G. (1964) 'Introduction', in E. Husserl, trans. W.P. Alston and G. Nakhnikian 1964/1990, *The Idea of Phenomenology*. London: Kluwer Academic Press. pp. ix–xxii.

Newton, T. (2007) *Nature and Sociology*. Abingdon: Routledge.

Ni, H., Zheng, W., Liu, X. and Gao, Y. (2011) 'Fractal-statistical analysis of grain-size distributions of debris-flow deposits and its geological implications', *Landslides* 8: 253–9.

Nield, J.M. and Baas, A.C.W. (2008) 'The influence of different environmental and climatic conditions on vegetated aeolian dune landscape development and response', *Global and Planetary Change* 64: 76–92.

Nussbaum, M. (2011) 'Reinventing the civil religion: Comte, Mill, Tagore', *Victorian Studies* 54 (1): 7–34.

Oakley, M. (2013) *Public and Private Sector Pay: 2013 Update*. Policy Exchange [available online at http://www.policyexchange.org.uk/publications/category/item/public-and-private-sector-pay-2013-update], [accessed 23/10/13].

O'Hear, A. (1980) *Karl Popper*. London: Routledge & Kegan Paul.

Okruhlik, K. (2004) 'Logical empiricism, feminism and Neurath's auxiliary motive', *Hypatia* 19 (1): 48–72.

Ollman, B. (2003) *Dance of the Dialectic: Steps in Marx's Method*. Illinois: University of Illinois Press.

Olson, E. and Sayer, A. (2009) 'Radical geography and its critical standpoints: embracing the normative', *Antipode* 41 (1): 180–98.

O'Loughlin, J. and Witmer, F.D. (2011) 'The localized geographies of violence in the North Caucasus of Russia, 1999–2007', *Annals of the Association of American Geographers* 101 (1): 178–201.

O'Rourke, K.H. (2006) 'The worldwide economic impact of the French Revolutionary and Napoleonic Wars, 1798–1815', *Journal of Global History* 1: 123–49.

Overton, J., Murray, W.E. and Banks, G. (2012) 'The race to the bottom of the glass? Wine, geography, and globalization', *Globalizations* 9 (2): 273–87.

Pain, R. (1991) 'Space, sexual violence and social control: integrating geographical and feminist analyses of women's fear of crime', *Progress in Human Geography* 15 (4): 415–31.

Panelli, R. (2010) 'More-than-human social geographies: posthuman and other possibilities', *Progress in Human Geography* 34 (1): 79–87.

Papanicolaou, A.N., Dermisis, D.C. and Elhakeem, M. (2011) 'Investigating the role of clasts on the movement of sand in gravel bed rivers', *Journal of Hydraulic Engineering* 137 (9): 871–83.

Parker, B. (2011) 'Material matters: gender and the city', *Geography Compass* 5/6: 433–47.

Paul, T. (2011) 'Space, gender, and fear of crime: some explorations from Kolkata', *Gender, Technology and Development* 15 (3): 411–35.

Pearson, A. (2002) 'Allied military model making during World War II', *Cartography and Geographic Information Science* 29 (3): 227–41.

Pedynowski, D. (2003) 'Science(s) – which, when and whose? Probing the metanarrative of scientific knowledge in the social construction of nature', *Progress in Human Geography* 27 (6): 735–52.

Phillips, J.D. (1999) 'Divergence, convergence, and self-organization in landscapes', *Annals of the Association of American Geographers* 89 (3): 466-88.

Phillips, J.D. (2003) 'Sources of nonlinearity and complexity in geomorphic systems', *Progress in Physical Geography* 27 (1): 1–23.

Phillips, M. (2008) 'Uneven Development (1984): Neil Smith', in P. Hubbard, R. Kitchin and G. Valentine (eds) *Key Texts in Human Geography*. London: Sage. pp. 71–81.

Philo, C. (2011) 'Michel Foucault', in P. Hubbard, and R. Kitchin (eds) *Key Thinkers on Space and Place* (2nd edition). London: Sage. pp. 162–70.

Pons, O. (2007) 'A haptic geography of the beach: naked bodies, vision and touch', *Social & Cultural Geography* 8 (1): 123-41.

Pons, O. (2009) 'Building castles in the sand: repositioning touch on the beach', *Senses and Society* 4 (2): 195-210.

Poole, S.P. (1944) 'The training of military geographers', *Annals of the Association of American Geographers* 34 (4): 202–6.

Poon, J. (2003) 'Quantitative methods: producing quantitative methods narratives', *Progress in Human Geography* 27 (6): 753–62.

Poon, J. (2004) 'Quantitative methods: past and present', *Progress in Human Geography* 28 (6): 807–14.

Poon, J. (2005) 'Quantitative methods: not positively positivist', *Progress in Human Geography* 29 (6): 766–72.

Popke, J. (2003) 'Poststructuralist ethics: subjectivity, responsibility and the space of community', *Progress in Human Geography* 27 (3): 298–316.

Popper, K.R. (1972) *The Logic of Scientific Discovery* (3rd edition). London: Hutchinson.

Popper, K.R. (1974) *Conjectures and Refutations: The Growth of Scientific Knowledge* (5th edition). Abingdon: Routledge.

Porter, R. '(1993) 'Baudrillard: history, hysteria and consumption', in C. Rojek, and B.S. Turner (eds) *Forget Baudrillard?* Abingdon: Routledge. 1–21.

Powell, R. (2010) 'Spaces of informalisation: playscapes, power and the governance of behaviour', *Space and Polity* 14 (2): 189–206.

Pratt, A.C. (2011) 'Andrew Sayer', in P. Hubbard, and R. Kitchin (2011) *Key Thinkers on Space and Place* (2nd edition). London: Sage. pp. 352–8.

Pulp Fiction (1994) Q. Tarantino, Santa Monica, CA: Miramax. [Film].

Raper, J. and Livingstone, D. (2001) 'Let's get real: spatio-temporal identity and geographic entities', *Transactions of the Institute of British Geographers* NS 26: 237–42.

Rautio, P. (2013) 'Children who carry stones in their pockets: on autotelic material practices in everyday life', *Children's Geographies* 11 (4): 394–408.

Redding, P (2012) 'Georg Wilhelm Friedrich Hegel', in E. Zalta (ed.) *The Stanford Encyclopedia of Philosophy* (Summer 2012 edition). http://plato.stanford.edu/archives/sum2012/entries/hegel/ [accessed 12/11/13].

Relph, E.C. (1976) *Place and Placelessness*. London: Pion Limited.

Relph, E.C. (1981) 'Phenomenology', in M.E. Harvey and B.P. Holly (eds) *Themes in Geographic Thought*. London: Croom Helm. pp. 99–114.

Rennett, M. (2012) 'Quentin Tarantino and the director as DJ', *Journal of Popular Culture* 45 (2): 391–409.

Reservoir Dogs (1992) Q. Tarantino, Santa Monica, CA: Miramax. [Film].

Reuter, D. (2013) 'Press release – shipping industry's beach dumping of toxic ships revealed in new online database', *NGO Shipbreaking Platform*. http://www.shipbreakingplatform.org/press-release-shipping-industrys-beach-dumping-of-toxic-ships-revealed-in-new-online-database/ [accessed 02/03/14].

Reynolds, J. (2005) 'Maurice Merleau-Ponty (1908-1961)', in J. Fieser and B. Dowden (eds) *Internet Encyclopedia of Philosophy*. http://www.iep.utm.edu/merleau/ [accessed 19/11/13].

Rhoads, B.L. and Thorn, C.E. (1994) 'Contemporary philosophical perspectives on physical geography with emphasis on geomorphology', *Geographical Review* 84 (1): 90–102.

Rhoads, B.L. and Thorn, C.E. (1999) 'Towards a philosophy of geomorphology', in B.L. Rhoads and C.E. Thorn (eds) *The Scientific Nature of Geomorphology*. Chichester: Wiley. pp. 115–43.

Richards, K. (1999) 'Samples and cases: generalisation and explanation in geomorphology', in B.L. Rhoads and C.E. Thorn (eds) *The Scientific Nature of Geomorphology*. Chichester: Wiley. pp. 172–90.

Richards, K. (2003) 'Ethical grounds for an integrated geography', in S. Trudgill and A. Roy (eds) *Contemporary Meanings in Physical Geography: From What to Why?* London: Arnold. pp. 233–58.

Richards, K., Watson, E., Bulkeley, H. and Powell, R. (2002) 'Some ideas and reflections on teaching "ideas" in geography', *Journal of Geography in Higher Education* 26 (1): 33–47.

Richards, K.S. (1990) 'Editorial: "Real" geomorphology', *Earth Surface Processes and Landforms* 15: 195–7.

Riley, M. (2009) '"The next link in the chain": children, agri-cultural practices and the family farm', *Children's Geographies* 7 (3): 245–60.

Ritzer, G. (1997) *Postmodern Social Theory*. London: McGraw-Hill.

Roberts, J.M. (2001) 'Realist spatial abstraction? Marxist observations of a claim within critical realist geography', *Progress in Human Geography* 25 (4): 545–67.

Rodaway, P. (2011) 'Yi-Fu Tuan', in P. Hubbard and R. Kitchin (eds) *Key Thinkers on Space and Place*. London: Sage. pp. 426–31.

Rodríguez-Iturbe, I. and Rinaldo, A. (1997) *Fractal River Basins: Chance and Self-Organization*. Cambridge: Cambridge University Press.

Roig, F.X., Rodríguez-Perea, A., Martín-Prieto, J.A., and Pons, G.X. (2009) 'Soft management of beach-dune systems as a tool for their sustainability', *Journal of Coastal Research* SI 56: 1284–8.

Roig-Munar, F.X., Martín-Prieto, J.A., Rodríguez-Perea, A., Pons, G.X., Gelabert, B., and Mir-Gual, M. (2012) 'Risk assessment of beach-dune system erosion: beach management impacts on the Balearic Islands', *Journal of Coastal Research* 28 (6): 1488–99.

Rolling Stone (undated). 'Arctic Monkeys: Biography', *Rolling Stone*. http://www.rollingstone.com/music/artists/arctic-monkeys/biography [accessed 12/07/13].

Rose, C. (1990) 'Toward pragmatic realism in human geography', *Cahiers de Géographie du Québec* 34 (92): 161–79.

Rose, E.P.F. and Willig, D. (2004) 'German military geologists and geographers in World War II', in D.R. Caldwell, J. Ehlen and R.S. Harmon (eds) *Studies in Military Geography and Geology*. Dordrecht: Kluwer Academic Publishers. pp. 199–214.

Rose, G. (1993) *Feminism & Geography: The Limits of Geographical Knowledge*. Cambridge: Polity Press.

Rowlands, M. (2008) *The Philosopher and the Wolf*. London: Granta.

Royal Geographical Society (2010) *Memorandum Submitted by the Royal Geographical Society*. UK Parliament Commons Select Committee: Science and Technology. http://www.publications.parliament.uk/pa/cm200910/cmselect/cmsctech/memo/spendingcuts/uc7602.htm [accessed 24/10/13].

Russo, L., Vakalis, D. and Siettos, C. (2013) 'Simulating the wildfire in Rhodes in 2008 with a cellular automata model', *Chemical Engineering Transactions* 35: 1399–1404.

Said, E. (1979) *Orientalism*. London: Vintage.

Sapozhnikov, V. and Foufoula-Georgiou, E. (1996) 'Self-affinity in braided rivers', *Water Resources Research* 32 (5): 1429–39.

Sandberg, L. and Tollefsen, A. (2010) 'Talking about fear of violence in public space: female and male narratives about threatening situations in Umeå, Sweden', *Social & Cultural Geography* 11 (1): 1–15.

Sander-Staudt, M. (2011) 'Care ethics', in J. Fieser and B. Dowden (eds) *Internet Encyclopedia of Philosophy*. http://www.iep.utm.edu/care-eth/#H2 [accessed 23/10/13].

Saussure, F. de (1916) *Course in General Linguistics* (trans. W. Baskin, 1974). London: Fontana/Collins.

Sayer, A. (1992) *Method in Social Science: A Realist Approach* (2nd edition). Abingdon: Routledge.

Schaefer, F.K. (1953) 'Exceptionalism in Geography: a methodological examination', *Annals of the Association of American Geographers* 43 (3): 226–49.

Scheidegger, A.E. (1968) 'Horton's law of stream numbers', *Water Resources Research* 4 (3): 655–8.

Schlacher, T.A. and Lucrezi, S. (2010) 'Compression of home ranges in ghost crabs on sandy beaches impacted by vehicle traffic', *Marine Biology* 157: 2467–74.

Schlick, M. (1925–1936) 'Meaning and verification, from Philosophical papers, volume II', reproduced in O. Hanfling (ed.) (1981) *Essential Readings in Logical Positivism*. Oxford: Blackwell. pp. 32–43.

Schoemaker Holmes, J. (2006) 'Bare bodies, beaches and boundaries: abjected outsiders and rearticulation at the nude beach', *Sexuality and Culture* 10 (4): 29–53.

Scholz, C.H. (1991) 'Earthquakes and faulting: self-organized critical phenomena with a characteristic dimension', in T. Riste and D. Sherrington (eds) *Spontaneous Formation of Space-Time Structures and Criticality*. Dordrecht: Kluwer Academic Publishers. pp. 41–56.

Schumm, S.A. (1979) 'Thresholds in geomorphology', *Transactions of the Institute of British Geographers* 4: 485–515.

Scream and Shout (2012) will.i.am feature Britney Spears. Santa Monica, CA: Interscope. [no catalogue number: digital download]

Scruton, R. (1995) *A Short History of Modern Philosophy: From Descartes to Wittgenstein* (2nd revised edition). Abingdon: Routledge.

Sharp, J.P., Routledge, P., Philo, C. and Paddison, R. (eds) (2000) *Entanglements of Power: Geographies of Domination/Resistance*. London: Routledge.

Shearer, C. (2012) 'The social construction of Alaska native vulnerability to climate change', *Race, Gender & Class* 19 (1–2): 61–79.

Sheppard, E. (2001) 'Quantitative geography: representations, practices and possibilities', *Environment & Planning D: Society and Space* 19: 535–54.

Shope, J.H. (2006) '"You can't cross a river without getting wet." A feminist standpoint on the dilemmas of cross-cultural research', *Qualitative Inquiry* 12 (1): 163–84.

Simandan, D. (2012) 'Commentary: the logical status of applied geographical reasoning', *The Geographical Journal* 178 (1): 9–12.

Simonsen, K. (2013) 'In quest of a new humanism: embodiment, experience and phenomenology as critical geography', *Progress in Human Geography* 37 (1): 10–26.

Ski Dubai Penguins (2012) *The Snow Penguins Are in Town!* http://www.skidubaipenguins.com/ [accessed 14/08/13].

Smith, D. and Protevi, J. (2013) 'Gilles Deleuze', in E.N. Zalta (ed.) *The Stanford Encyclopedia of Philosophy* (Spring 2013 edition). http://plato.stanford.edu/archives/spr2013/entries/deleuze/ [accessed 11/06/14].

Smith, D.M. (1997) 'Geography and ethics: a moral turn?' *Progress in Human Geography* 21 (4): 583–90.

Smith, D.M. (1999) 'Geography and ethics: how far should we go?' *Progress in Human Geography* 23 (1): 119–25.

Smith, D.M. (2000) *Moral Geographies: Ethics in a World of Difference*. Edinburgh: Edinburgh University Press.

Smith, D.M. (2001) 'Geography and ethics: progress, or more of the same?', *Progress in Human Geography* 25 (2): 261–8.

Smith, D.M. (2007) 'Moral aspects of place', *Planning Theory* 6 (1): 7–15.

Smith, M., Davidson, J. and Henderson, V.L. (2012) 'Spiders, Sartre and "magical geographies": the emotional transformation of space'. *Transactions of the Institute of British Geographers* NS 37: 60–74.

Smith, N. (1979) 'Geography, science and post-positivist modes of explanation', *Progress in Human Geography* 3 (3): 356–83.

Smith, N. (1984) *Uneven Development: Nature, Capital and the Production of Space*. Oxford: Basil Blackwell. Reissued (2010). London: Verso.

Smith, S. (2009) 'Everyday morality: where radical geography meets normative theory' *Antipode* 41 (1): 206–9.

Soja, E. (1989) *Postmodern Geographies: The Reassertion of Space in Critical Social Theory*. London: Verso.

Song, W., Weicheng, F., Binghong, W. and Jianjun, Z. (2001) 'Self-organized criticality of forest fire in China', *Ecological Modelling* 145 (1): 61–8.

Spiegelberg, H. (1994) *The Phenomenological Movement: An Historical Introduction* (3rd edition). London: Kluwer Academic Publishers.

Spellerberg, I.F. and Sawyer, J.W.D. (1999) *An Introduction to Applied Biogeography*. Cambridge: Cambridge University Press.

Sperber, D. (1979) 'Claude Lévi-Strauss', in J. Sturrock (ed.) *Structuralism and Since: From Lévi Strauss to Derrida*. Oxford: Oxford University Press. pp. 19–51.

Stepinski, T.F., Collier, M.L., McGovern, P.J. and Clifford, S.M. (2004) 'Martian geomorphology from fractal analysis of drainage networks', *Journal of Geophysical Research: Planets* 109 (E2) doi: 10.1029/2003JE002098.

Strahler, A.N. (1950) 'Equilibrium theory of erosional slopes, approached by frequency distribution analysis', *American Journal of Science* 248: 673–96, 800–14.

Strahler, A.N. (1952) 'Dynamic basis of geomorphology', *Geological Society of America Bulletin* 63: 1117–42.

Strohmayer, U. (2007) 'Classics in human geography revisited: Dear, M. 1988: The post-modern challenge: reconstructing human geography. Transactions of the Institute of British Geographers NS 13, 262–74: Commentary 2', *Progress in Human Geography* 31 (5): 678–80.

Sturrock, J. (ed.) (1979) *Structuralism and Since: From Lévi Strauss to Derrida.* Oxford: Oxford University Press.

Sun, J. and Southworth, J. (2013) 'Remote sensing-based fractal analysis and scale dependence associated with forest fragmentation in an Amazon tri-national frontier', *Remote Sensing* 5: 454–72.

Tadaki, M., Salmond, J., Le Heron, R. and Brierley, G. (2012) 'Nature, culture, and the work of physical geography', *Transactions of the Institute of British Geographers* NS 37: 547–62.

Tareke, G. (2009) *The Ethiopian Revolution: War in the Horn of Africa.* New Haven, CT: Yale University Press.

The Matrix (1999) A. Wachowski and L. Wachowski (as the Wachowski Brothers). California: Warner Bros. [Film].

The Playmania/Ski Dubai (undated) http://www.theplaymania.com/skidubai/welcome [accessed 22/05/14].

Theodoridis, N. (2010) 'The big fire of Rhodes', in Ministerial Conference on the Protection of Forests in Europe, *Assessment of Forest Fire Risks and Innovative Strategies for Prevention: 4–6 May, Rhodes, Greece. Workshop Report.* Oslo: Forest Europe. p39. http://www.foresteurope.org/documentos/FOREST_EUROPE_Forest_Fires_Report.pdf. Also slides online at http://www.foresteurope.org/docs/other_meetings/2010/forest_risk/16_ThebigfireofRhodes.pdf. [accessed 01/01/14].

The Wizard of Oz. (1939) V. Fleming, California: Metro-Goldwyn-Mayer. [Film].

This is Love (2012) will.i.am featuring Eva Simons. Santa Monica, CA: Interscope. [no catalogue number: digital download] [Film].

Thorn, C.E. (1988) *Introduction to Theoretical Geomorphology.* Amsterdam: Kluwer Academic Publishers.

Thorne, C.R. (1982) 'Processes and mechanisms of river bank erosion', in R.D. Hey, J.C. Bathurst and C.R. Thorne (eds) *Gravel-Bed Rivers.* Chichester: Wiley. pp. 227–72.

Thorne, C.R., Hey, R.D. and Newson, M.D. (eds) (1997) *Applied Fluvial Geomorphology for River Engineering and Management.* Chichester: John Wiley.

Thornes, J.B. (2009) 'Time: change and stability in environmental systems', in N. Clifford, S. Holloway, S.P. Rice and G. Valentine (eds) *Key Concepts in Geography* (2nd edition). London: Sage. pp. 119–39.

Thornton, S. (2011) 'Karl Popper', *The Stanford Enclyclopedia of Philosophy* (Winter 2011 edition). http://plato.stanford.edu/archives/win2011/entries/popper/ [accessed 28/12/12].

Thrift, N. (1999) 'The place of complexity', *Theory, Culture & Society* 16 (3): 31–69.

Thrift, N. (2008) *Non-Representational Theory: Space|Politics|Affect.* Abingdon: Routledge.

Toadvine, T. (2009) *Merleau-Ponty's Philosophy of Nature.* Evanston, IL: Northwestern University Press.

Tong, R. and Williams, N. (2011) 'Feminist Ethics', in E.N. Zalta (ed.) *The Stanford Encyclopedia of Philosophy* (Summer 2011 edition). http://plato.stanford.edu/archives/sum2011/entries/feminism-ethics/ [accessed 20/10/13].

Trudeau, D. (2012) 'IRBs as asset for ethics education in Geography', *The Professional Geographer* 64 (1): 25–33.

Trudgill, S. (2003) 'Meaning, knowledge, constructs and fieldwork in physical geography', in S. Trudgill and A. Roy (eds) *Contemporary Meanings in Physical Geography: From What to Why?* London: Arnold. pp. 25–46.

Tschinkel, W. (2012) 'The life cycle and life span of Namibian fairy circles', *PLoS ONE* 7 (6): e3806. doi: 10.1371/journal.pone.0038056.

Tuan, Y.-F. (1971) 'Geography, phenomenology, and the study of human nature', *Canadian Geographer* 15 (3): 181–92.

Tuan, Y.-F. (1974) *Topophilia: A Study of Environmental Perception, Attitudes and Values.* London: Prentice-Hall International, Inc.

Tuan, Y.-F. (1977) *Space and Place.* Minneapolis, MN: University of Minnesota Press.

Tuan, Y.-F. (1986) *The Good Life.* Madison, WI: University of Wisconsin Press.

Tuan, Y.-F. (1989) *Morality and Imagination: Paradoxes of Progress.* Madison, WI: University of Wisconsin Press.

Tuan, Y.-F. (1993) *Passing Strange and Wonderful: Aesthetics, Nature and Culture.* Washington DC: Island Press.

Turcotte, D.L. (2007) 'Self-organized complexity in geomorphology: observations and models', *Geomorphology* 91: 302–10.

Trudgill, S. (2012) 'Do theories tell us what to see? The 19th-century observations of Darwin, Ramsey and Bonney on glacial features', *Progress in Physical Geography* 36 (4): 558–66.

Ubel, T. (2012) 'Vienna Circle', in E.N. Zalta (ed.) *The Stanford Encyclopedia of Philosophy* (Summer 2012 edition). http://plato.stanford.edu/archives/sum2012/entries/vienna-circle/ [accessed 24/08/12].

Unwin, T. (1992) *The Place of Geography.* Harlow: Longman Scientific and Technical.

Unwin, T. and Rose, J. (2004) 'Regions, Area Studies and the place of meaning', in H.A. Matthews. and D.T. Herbert (eds) *Unifying Geography: Common Heritage, Shared Future.* London: Routledge. pp. 171–88.

Urban, M. and Rhoads, B. (2003) 'Conceptions of nature: implications for an integrated geography', in S. Trudgill and A. Roy (eds) *Contemporary Meanings in Physical Geography: From What to Why?* London: Arnold. pp. 211–31.

Urry, J. (2003) *Global Complexity.* Cambridge: Polity.

Valentine, G. (1989) 'The geography of women's fear', *Area* 21: 385–90.

Valentine, G. (1990) 'Women's fear and the design of public space', *Built Environment* 16: 288–303.

Valentine, G. (2001) 'Whatever happened to the social? Reflections on the "cultural turn" in British human geography', *Norsk Geografisk Tidsskrift* 55: 166–72.

Van de Wiel, M.J. and Coulthard, T.J. (2010) 'Self-organized criticality in river basins: challenging sedimentary records of environmental change', *Geology* 38 (1): 87–90.

Vannini, P. and Taggart, J. (2013) 'Doing islandness: a non-representational approach to an island's sense of place', *Cultural Geographies* 20 (2): 225–42.

Vardy, P. and Grosch, P. (1999) *The Puzzle of Ethics* (2nd edition). London: Fount Paperbacks.

Viles, H. (2005) 'A divided discipline?' in N. Castree, A. Rogers, and D. Sherman (eds) *Questioning Geography*. Oxford: Blackwell. pp. 26–38.

Waitt, G. and Cook, L. (2007) 'Leaving nothing but ripples on the water: performing ecotourism natures', *Social & Cultural Geography* 8 (4): 535–50.

Waitt, G. and Warren, A. (2008) '"Talking shit over a brew after a good session with your mates": surfing, space and masculinity', *Australian Geographer* 39 (3): 353–65.

Walker, P.A. (2006) 'Political ecology: where is the policy?' *Progress in Human Geography* 30 (3): 382–95.

Werner, B.T. and Fink, T.M. (1993) 'Beach cusps as self-organized patterns', *Science* 260: 968–71.

Whalley, B. (1987) 'Book Review: Physical Geography: Its Nature and Methods, Roy Haines-Young and James Petch. London: Harper & Row, 1986', *Annals of the Association of American Geographers* 77 (4): 654–84.

Whitehead, H., Rendell, L., Osborne, R.W. and Würsig, B. (2004) 'Culture and conservation of non-humans with reference to whales and dolphins: review and new directions', *Biological Conservation* 120 (3): 427–37.

Wilson, G.A. (2012) 'Climbers' narratives of mountain spaces above 8000 metres: a social constructivist perspective', *Area* 44 (1): 29–36.

Wood, N. (2012) 'Playing with "Scottishness": musical performance, non-representational thinking and the "doings" of national identity', *Cultural Geographies* 19 (2): 195–215.

Woodroffe, C.D. (2007) 'The natural resilience of coastal systems: primary concepts', in L. McFadden, E. Penning-Rowsell and R.J. Nicholls (eds) *Managing Coastal Vulnerability*. Elsevier: Amsterdam. pp. 45–60.

Woodruff-Smith, D. (2008) 'Phenomenology', in E.N. Zalta (ed.) *The Stanford Encyclopedia of Philosophy* (Spring 2013 edition). http://plato.stanford.edu/archives/spr2013/entries/phenomenology/ [accessed 08/04/13].

World Bank Development Indicators (2012) http://data.worldbank.org/data-catalog/world-development-indicators/wdi-2012 [accessed 06/10/13].

Wylie, J. (2005) 'A single day's walking: narrating self and landscape on the South West Coast Path', *Transactions of the Institution of British Geographers* NS 30: 234–47.

Wylie, J. (2007) *Landscape*. Abingdon: Routledge.

Wyly, E. (2009) 'Strategic positivism', *The Professional Geographer* 61 (3): 310–22.

Yacobi, H. (2008) 'Architecture, orientalism, and identity: the politics of the Israeli-built environment', *Israel Studies* 13 (1): 94–118.

Yeung, H.W. (1997) 'Critical realism and realist research in human geography: a method or a philosophy in search of a method?', *Progress in Human Geography* 21 (1): 51–74.

Young, F.W. (2012) '"I Hē Koe?" Placing Rapa Nui', *The Contemporary Pacific* 24 (1): 1–30.

Zhang, H. and Li, Z. (2012) 'Fractality and self-similarity in the structure of road networks', *Annals of the Association of American Geographers* 102 (2): 350–65.

Index

Note: Page numbers in **bold** indicate an extensive coverage of the topic. Page numbers in *italic* refer to descriptions in the glossary.

CPSIA information can be obtained
at www.ICGtesting.com
Printed in the USA
JSHW010010060722
27594JS00003B/24